The Practice of Eating

The Practice of Eating

Alan Warde

polity

Copyright © Alan Warde 2016

The right of Alan Warde to be identified as Author of this Work has been asserted in accordance with the UK Copyright, Designs and Patents Act 1988.

First published in 2016 by Polity Press

Polity Press
65 Bridge Street
Cambridge CB2 1UR, UK

Polity Press
350 Main Street
Malden, MA 02148, USA

All rights reserved. Except for the quotation of short passages for the purpose of criticism and review, no part of this publication may be reproduced, stored in a retrieval system, or transmitted, in any form or by any means, electronic, mechanical, photocopying, recording or otherwise, without the prior permission of the publisher.

ISBN-13: 978-0-7456-9170-1
ISBN-13: 978-0-7456-9171-8(pb)

A catalogue record for this book is available from the British Library.

Library of Congress Cataloging-in-Publication Data
Warde, Alan.
The practice of eating / Alan Warde.
 pages cm
Includes bibliographical references and index.
ISBN 978-0-7456-9170-1 (hardback) – ISBN 978-0-7456-9171-8 (pbk.) 1. Food habits–Social aspects. 2. Food consumption–Sicial aspects. I. Title.
GN407.W36 2015
394.1′2–dc23

2015019447

Typeset in 10.5 on 12 pt Sabon
by Toppan Best-set Premedia Limited
Printed and bound in Great Britain by CPI Group (UK) Ltd, London

The publisher has used its best endeavours to ensure that the URLs for external websites referred to in this book are correct and active at the time of going to press. However, the publisher has no responsibility for the websites and can make no guarantee that a site will remain live or that the content is or will remain appropriate.

Every effort has been made to trace all copyright holders, but if any have been inadvertently overlooked the publisher will be pleased to include any necessary credits in any subsequent reprint or edition.

For further information on Polity, visit our website:
politybooks.com

Contents

Acknowledgements	vi
1 Introduction	1
2 Towards a Sociological Theory of Eating	12
3 Elements of a Theory of Practice	32
4 Elementary Forms of Eating	52
5 Organizing Eating	80
6 Habituation	100
7 Repetition and the Foundations of Competence	122
8 Conclusions: Practice Theory and Eating Out	149
Notes	167
References	176
Index	190

Acknowledgements

The material for this book was compiled over more than a decade and I have incurred many personal and intellectual debts along the way. The research upon which it is based has been supported materially by the University of Manchester through periods of sabbatical leave, and by the Economic and Social Research Council. A substantial part of the work was conducted at the Helsinki Collegium for Advanced Studies, University of Helsinki, where I had the privilege to spend two years from 2010 as the Jane and Aatos Erkko Visiting Professor in Studies on Contemporary Society as a guest of the Erkko Foundation. To these sponsors of my work I record my gratitude. At the University of Manchester I have worked with very many stimulating and helpful colleagues: through the Centre for Research on Innovation and Competition, the Sustainable Consumption Institute and in the Department of Sociology in the School of Social Sciences, I have been able to discuss many of my ideas in a congenial atmosphere with teachers, research staff and research students. They are too many to name. Friends and colleagues who made a particular contribution to this book as a result of having worked alongside me as co-researchers on projects about food and eating include Lydia Martens, Dale Southerton, Isabelle Darmon, Luke Yates, Cecilia Díaz-Méndez, Mark Harvey, Andrew McMeekin, Modesto Gayo-Cal, Corinne Wales, Tony Bennett, Mike Savage, Elizabeth Silva, David Wright, Unni Kjaernes, Lotte Holm, Mark Tomlinson, Svetlana Kirichenko, Mette Ranta, Wendy Olsen and Shu-Li Cheng. Sincere thanks to all of them. I owe an even greater debt to four people who read the whole of the draft typescript of the book, Jukka

Gronow, Anne Murcott, Sue Scott and Dale Southerton. I am profoundly grateful to them. While I have not been able to incorporate all their insightful comments and suggestions, the book would be immeasurably poorer were it not for their generous and kind efforts. I also benefited from the advice of three readers for Polity Press and from the efficient and patient management of the process of publication by Elliott Karstadt.

Alan Warde
Manchester, April 2015

Some of the chapters in this book have been revised in small or large part for publication here. The author and publishers would like to thank the following publishers for permission to reprint:

Oxford University Press for extracts (4 paragraphs) from Ch. 12, 'Sociology, Consumption, and Habit' from Alistair Ulph and Dale Southerton (eds) (2014), *Sustainable Consumption: Multi-Disciplinary Perspectives in Honour of Professor Sir Partha Dasgupta*, pp. 277–98; and extract (three paragraphs) from Ch. 19, 'Eating' in Frank Trentmann (ed.) (2012), *Oxford Handbook of the History of Consumption*, pp. 376–95. Reprinted with permission.

Sage Publications for 'Consumption and the Theory of Practice' (2005), *Journal of Consumer Culture* 5(2): 131–54, and 'After Taste: Culture, Consumption and Theories of Practice' (2014), *Journal of Consumer Culture* 14(3): 279–303.

Routledge (Taylor and Francis Group) for 'What Sort of a Practice is Eating?', in Elizabeth Shove and Nicola Spurling (eds) (2013), *Sustainable Practices: Social Theory and Climate Change*, pp. 17–30.

1

Introduction

Eating as a Topic of Interest

Public interest in food has increased markedly since the 1980s and scholarly regard has expanded commensurately. Food is a political issue, a matter of leisure and recreation, a topic of health, a resource for media industries, as well as a primary necessity of daily life. Crises in the food system have spurred political parties and social movements to action. A proliferation of food programmes and journalism – on television, in the press and latterly on the internet – has made food and eating a growth area of popular attention and conversation (Rousseau 2012). This reflects new priorities regarding the body and body management, as states, particularly those responsible for funding health care, become more concerned with what people eat. Consequently, food has come under more intense scrutiny from social research. Some aspects of the food system have always attracted scholarly research, and the most prolific contributors remain agriculture, pharmacology, medicine, nutrition, home economics, macro-economics and psychology. However, public preoccupations have made more space for socio-cultural disciplines like anthropology, cultural studies, social geography and sociology to fill major gaps in understanding, not least with respect to failures of policy intervention.

The changing social and economic circumstances occasioned by the post-war boom in the West had the effect of making food relatively cheaper, and older problems of poverty-induced hunger and malnutrition receded. Agribusiness, sustained economic growth, multinational corporations and ever greater international trade transformed the economic foundations of western diets. Abundant, accessible and relatively cheap foodstuffs, sourced globally, presented most people with the possibility of eating in much more varied ways than had been possible for preceding generations. By the end of the twentieth century, food systems had experienced some of the most profound effects of globalization (Inglis and Gimlin 2010). Of course, this did not result in immediate or radical changes in diet or culinary practices for individuals, but there were significant shifts over a few decades at aggregate level, sufficient for serious scholars to diagnose 'a culinary revolution' (Panayi 2008).

Increasing variety, and intensified commentary upon and exploitation of that variety, provided a powerful thrust for examining eating as a type of cultural consumption. Social research moved from an almost exclusive focus on processes of production, especially the circulation of commodities in the market sphere, to activities associated with consumption – recreation, aesthetics and the conduct of everyday life. Acknowledging consumption permitted eating to be treated partly autonomously of questions of the availability of foodstuffs; the presumption of a symbiotic relationship between supply and demand was severed by abandoning the assumption that eating be treated primarily as instrumental to physiological reproduction. However, that research emerged in a period increasingly obsessed by concepts of 'culture' and 'the consumer'. The so-called 'cultural turn' provided a backdrop and impetus to emergent sociological approaches to food consumption. The legitimation of the study of consumption meant that eating could become a bona fide topic of social research.

The Objectives of the Book

A prodigious amount of empirical research on food and eating is now available, to which socio-cultural disciplines have made a significant contribution. The proliferation of handbooks and encyclopediae present the current state of knowledge on a wide range of discrete topics but their integration and synthesis is proving elusive. The task of pulling the accumulated evidence together is becoming ever more demanding. This is, no doubt, partly the result of the multidisciplinary nature of the study of food. Disciplines have their own particular scientific agendas and tend to be committed to incommensurable theories, which have been formulated over time in relation to particular substantive interests. Their key concepts serve to bracket out those forces, processes and facts considered of no theoretical interest, thus militating against theoretical synthesis. Since theoretical synthesis is more likely to be feasible within a disciplinary tradition, I try to reconstruct and extend sociological approaches, and do so by drawing specifically upon practice-theoretical approaches to consumption.

Eating is a form of consumption. Research on consumption is now vast, having expanded rapidly during the last two decades. Radical new departures in multidisciplinary studies of consumption coincided with 'the cultural turn' in the humanities and social sciences in the 1970s. Rather than viewing consumption as an instrumental and practical activity, it came to be seen as a means of communication with others, signalling self-identity through cultivation of distinct 'lifestyles'. Consumption was recognized as an enjoyable and often constructive process, a process of creative appropriation of goods and services which served commendable personal and sociable ends. Reversing also the prevailing condescension towards popular culture and popular practices expressed by critics of mass culture, the cultural turn demonstrated the meaningfulness of consumption. Consumption was shown to play a role in identity formation and aesthetic expression in everyday life.

It is frustrating that progress in the sociology of consumption was slow to filter into research on food. For consumption research offers many promising avenues for food scholars. One is an opportunity to interrogate the activity of eating more rigorously. How exactly should eating be conceptualized? Of course, most people, for most purposes, leave puzzling about its definition to sociologists and proceed happily several times a day to engage in an activity that comes as second nature. However, what is entailed in consumption of food is not simply a given. It might be thought of as a purely physiological process. Arguably, the interpretive social sciences have paid too little attention to the embodied dimension of physical reproduction entailed in eating. However, it would make little sociological sense to restrict attention solely to processes of bodily incorporation of foodstuffs. All peoples surround the physiological process with conventions about what counts as food, and when, where and with whom eating should occur. Even the comportment of the body is subject to social discipline through manners and etiquette. For sociological purposes, a broader framework of concepts is required to position eating and render it explicable. One task of the book is to make clearer what is at stake in defining eating as an activity and to propose a set of concepts to frame it as a moment of *consumption*.

By emphasizing communication, agency and engagement, exponents of the cultural turn, while charting the meaningfulness of these activities and items for self-identity, demonstrated how and why people made consumption into personal and social priorities. However, as I have argued elsewhere, cultural analysis had several weaknesses, both in terms of its focus of attention and its theory of action (Warde 2014). Its proclivities included, first, a focus on the display for others of symbols of identity, obscuring the fact that most consumption is ordinary or inconspicuous (Gronow and Warde 2001). Second, to emphasize culture was to downplay social structure (Abbott 2001), eclipsing distinctive features of the social realm, of social interdependence and social interaction, and of status and class. Third, the cultural turn found little place for objects and technologies as material forces. In addition, however, cultural analysis of consumption contained a deeper set of theoretical weaknesses embedded in its general theory of action. Despite its internal diversity, primary recourse was to a voluntaristic theory of action, upholding models of an active, expressive, choosing consumer, motivated by concerns for personal identity and a fashioned lifestyle. The model of an active and reflexive actor predominated, implying that conscious and intentional decisions steer consumption behaviour and explain its sense and direction. In key respects, its model is similar to the sovereign consumer of neo-classical economics, for it effectively shares in the dominant and basic template of consumption which presents the process as one where the individual engages in very many discrete events, characterized by personal deliberation preceding personal, independent decisions made with a view to the satisfaction of preferences. One feature of this book is to explore how far we can advance without the use of such a concept of choice.

Another of my objectives is to demonstrate the benefit to the sociology of food and eating of greater engagement with theories of practice. Theories of practice offer remedies for both the substantive and explanatory deficiencies of cultural analysis. They are not themselves specifically sociological theories. Many different disciplines are currently attempting to apply them to their conceptual and empirical concerns. Yet, even if they belong to no discipline, practice theories have considerable affinity with sociological understandings of everyday life. They are, however, very diverse; Schatzki (2001: 2-3) noted that three diverse currents of thought, post-functionalist, post-structuralist and post-humanist, all found the practice approach attractive. Nicolini (2012) effectively captures their very considerable range. Consequently, even enumerating their common features is controversial. However, against the model of the sovereign consumer, they tend to emphasize routine over actions, flow and sequence over discrete acts, dispositions over decisions and practical consciousness over deliberation. And, in reaction to cultural analysis, emphasis is placed upon doing over thinking, the material over the symbolic, and embodied practical competence over expressive virtuosity in the fashioned presentation of self. The degree to which these features are pronounced bequeaths weaker and stronger variants (Warde 2014: 285–6).

This book avoids purely theoretical arguments and concentrates instead on demonstrating the relevance of the theory to a substantive domain where it matters. Nevertheless, I retain an ambition to indicate how analysis of a particular, complex practice – eating – might enhance the theory of practice, solve some of its puzzles and develop it in ways relevant to the analysis of other practices. One moot point is whether extant theories of practice have the conceptual machinery adequate for distinguishing between different types of practice. It remains debatable whether all practices have the same basic structure and set of characteristics. Given that, on any definition, the social world hosts a great many practices, reflection on the sources of variation is limited. In the absence of an agreed comprehensive typology, I seek to show that there is something special and specific about eating which demands adaptation and development of the theory. I coin the concept of a compound practice, observe different degrees of coordination and regulation of practices, argue that Practices may be conceptualized as entities, and extend the theory to account for the sharing of practices and also how their rudiments, essentials and nuances are imparted to other, and potential future, agents.[1]

The book oscillates back and forth between the abstractions of theories of practice and substantive analysis of aspects of eating. The aspiration is not only to show that the concepts of practice theory can be applied to eating but also to shed substantive new light on eating. The primary objective is to address explanatory problems and puzzles, and to account for the actuality of how contemporary eating is carried out. Success would entail the identification of some novel and improved accounts of contemporary structure, trends and meaning. I attempt this in relation to the learning of new tastes, the role of handbooks and manuals, the compatibility of diverse performances with integrated Practices, the competing role of cultural intermediaries and their effects on the coordination and regulation of eating, the role of controversy in popular judgements and justifications of behaviour. The evidence I use is, however, little more than a demonstration of the relevance of categories or concepts to the description of unsystematically selected episodes and some illustration of theoretical points. Evidence about contemporary experiences of eating is presented briefly, cursorily and with minimal background, using examples drawn selectively and sparsely from previous research.

The case for theories of practice includes contesting standard modes of social scientific explanation. In line with a long running argument in the sociology of consumption against the concept of choice, practice theories offer a strong alternative by seeking a platform at the meso-level. Rejecting methodological individualisms, emphasis is placed on repetition and on aspects of everyday life which make it impossible to give a satisfactory account of an activity like eating without recognizing its collective and unreflective elements. Standard explanatory models fail to capture the practical, collective, sequential, repetitive and automatic aspects of consumption (Warde and Southerton 2012). First and foremost, standard models presume the defining characteristic of consumption to be purchase, with the manner of appropriation of goods and services within the practices of everyday life at best a subsidiary feature. However, if one considers use as well as purchase, matters are complicated considerably. If consumption is appropriation for the sake of a practice (Warde 2005), it becomes an integral part of everyday life because tools and materials are constitutive of the power to act. Then, consumption is the use of things for the purpose of mundane conduct. Second, the extensive evidence of the social patterning of purchase suggests that 'decisions' are not purely personal. In part, they are practical responses to the affordances and constraints of a shared social environment. People conform to the norms of groups to which they are attached. Social groups differ in their views of what is valuable and desirable; tastes are distinguishing. Equally important, to the extent that different groups participate unequally in different activities, their requirements for goods and services will vary. Third, choices are not independent of one another; decisions are sequential and cumulative, with past performances precluding some options and leaving gaps for new ones. Fourth, many items are acquired repetitiously, with some items routinely depleted and replaced. Repeat transactions are sometimes explained in terms of economy of physical and mental effort and of reassurance afforded in situations of uncertainty. Fifth and finally, the role of deliberation is easily exaggerated. While very expensive purchases or strategic consideration of ethical commitments may entail protracted reflection and consideration of a range of options, a great many items of ordinary consumption are acquired and consumed mindlessly, as for example groceries, fuel, electricity and water. Moreover, given the prevalence of collective and state services, not to mention the unequal social division of labour of shopping, much of what is appropriated is vicarious; the final consumer has no need of deliberation if someone else does the provisioning.

Hence, in this account I pursue a strong programme for the application of theories of practice. I am aware that I do not, for lack of space if no other reason, demonstrate how a theory of practice can be readily applied to many empirical issues or show explicitly how it might be superior to all other approaches. Nevertheless, I hope to indicate its potential, using brief examples, by showing that it constitutes a basis for a theoretical synthesis which encompasses neglected aspects of the activity of eating. I proceed to explore the conjecture that the concept of practice captures eating particularly well. It might then be of use in several ways. First, it brings issues of food into the sociological mainstream with the possibility of contributing to sociological theory. Second, it develops theories of practice in a sociological context. Third, it informs policy making in relation to behaviour change. Fourth, it gives some new and distinctive answers to puzzles about why people eat what they do. Behind these concerns lies also a fundamental theoretical issue about the boundaries of practices and their interrelationships. In an earlier attempt to demonstrate the value of practice theories for studying consumption (Warde 2005), it had been my intention to illustrate the argument using evidence about eating, but it proved too difficult, apparently because of its complexity. Instead, I used the example of motoring – the activity of driving cars – which I subsequently came to view as a more regularized and regulated activity. One purpose here is to demonstrate how theories of practice can be applied to highly complex but weakly regulated activities.

The Structure of the Book

The book falls roughly into two parts. The early part (chapters 2–4) clears the ground for a practice-theoretic account of eating. It reviews research on eating, introduces theories of practice and constructs eating as a scientific object. The second part (chapters 5–7) develops key concepts for the analysis of eating as a practice. It identifies some of the means by which eating is organized and coordinated in order to explain how myriad individual performances are generated. The recursive relationship between performance and practice, which is common to all versions of the theory, is applied to account for repetition and innovation, reproduction and change. A key challenge is to demonstrate that the repetitious and the routine, and also the dynamic, aspects of alimentary life can be fairly represented within the confines of a practice-theoretical analysis.

Chapter 2 reviews the development of socio-cultural studies of food. It considers the role of research in different disciplines in framing understandings of food *consumption*, noting that much more is known about production and provisioning. It argues that rather little attention has been paid to developing theories about eating. After discussing the role of theories in the interpretive social sciences, it finds obstacles in the multidisciplinary formation of studies of food and in excessive attention paid to trying to solve food crises. It also observes that the powerful cultural turn in the humanities and social sciences directed research towards particular fields, with the consequence that other important aspects were neglected. With a view to theoretical innovation, some older traditions of research are explored for their continuing relevance. In the final section, some new themes emerging since 2000 are briefly identified, leading to the suggestion that theories of practice are worthy of careful examination as they may have the potential to provide a distinctive and broad basis for a better understanding of eating.

The third chapter introduces the reader to theories of practice and elaborates on the key concepts relevant to the later arguments about eating. Theories of practice were rediscovered in the 1970s and were developed to deal with particular puzzles in social theory. Attention is paid to the sociological theories of Bourdieu and Giddens in this, the first phase of the modern evolution of the concept of practice. The doyen of the second phase is Schatzki who developed an ontological version of practice theory which has had considerable influence on studies of consumption. Exegesis focuses on his analytic distinctions between practice and performance, dispersed and integrated practices, and the nexus of understanding, procedure and engagement which constitutes practices. Emphasis is put upon the collective nature of practices and the organization that lies behind them. The result is a general impression of the emphases of explanations based in theories of practice and hints at their relevance for analysing eating.

The fourth chapter begins by discussing the value of constructing eating as a scientific object. Eating is positioned as a form of final consumption, therefore inviting a focus on the activities occurring after the many steps involved in production, procurement and preparation of food. But defining eating is not straightforward. A simple dictionary definition of the verb to eat is 'to take into the body by mouth as food' (Chambers 1972). Sociology has never found such a definition adequate; if not entirely deficient, it is surely very narrow because it lacks reference to the social aspects of eating. Episodes of eating typically involve other people, require suitable social settings, as well as often have special connections to whomsoever prepared the food. I review some of the ways that prominent and powerful sociological accounts have attempted to conceptualize the social element. I argue that none is sufficiently comprehensive and all could benefit from further systematization.

The chapter therefore reviews concepts designed to capture the social, culinary and bodily dimensions of eating – the elementary forms, or principal components, of food consumption. I conclude that an inclusive and yet analytically parsimonious definition of the scope of the study of eating would approach consumption as episodic events, menu selection and physiological and sensory processes of bodily incorporation. Each is dealt with in turn, discussing some of the analytic benefits and puzzles associated with their application. Basic features of the concepts and their mutual connections are developed with passing reference to other literature. The aim is to make clear what exactly it is about eating that requires explanation. It is maintained that all performances of eating involve the permutation of the three interrelated elements, and that the associated concepts constitute a sparse and effective analytic framework for describing patterns of behaviour. The final section summarizes the position and presents material from a research interview which illustrates how the concepts capture an everyday account of the organization of eating.

The second part of the book aims to develop a series of concepts, with relevance beyond eating, for the theoretical understanding of practice. Three sets of processes – the organization of practices, the nature of habituation and the capacity for competent performances in changing situations – are dealt with in successive chapters. These processes are illustrated mostly from secondary studies in the field of food consumption – the growth of media coverage of cooking and eating, reactions to the obesity crisis, acquiring a taste for exotic foods and the enthusiasm of 'foodies'.

Beginning from the debate about 'gastro-anomie', the supposed contemporary condition where people are uncertain about the rules governing taste in food, chapter 5 discusses current advice about what to eat. Contradictory recommendations indicate the inherent complexity of the practice of eating. The delivery of competent performances requires orchestration of the elementary forms, a not inconsiderable difficulty. The problem is one of adjusting conduct appropriately to different social settings and meal occasions. At least four integrative practices claim authority in the governance of how to eat, witnessed by texts giving advice about nutrition, cookery, manners and taste. Analysis of instructional and promotional texts shows how cultural intermediaries and professional associations construct, legitimize and contest standards and procedures. It is argued that eating is not a simple integrative practice but a compound of component practices. The consequence is that eating tends to be weakly coordinated and weakly regulated, leaving much discretion to individuals.

While intermediation plays a part in the institutionalization of the practice of eating, it does not account in itself for how performances are enacted. Chapter 6 seeks to assimilate the critique of voluntaristic and decision-making models of human action into a practice-theoretic analysis of eating. In the light of evidence from neuro-science, experimental psychology, behavioural economics and cultural sociology, the orthodox 'portfolio' model of action is shown to have significant weaknesses. Wansick's *Mindless Eating* (2006) is used as an entertaining example of how little attention people pay to the activity most of the time. The implication is that much eating behaviour is habitual rather than a matter of deliberation and choice. Various approaches to the analysis of habit and habituation are examined. Concepts of habit require that environment and context play a substantial role in explaining performances. Some accounts of the interdependence of habit and environment are examined and relevant attributes of environments isolated. The theoretical points are illustrated by a case study of obesity, its possible causes and potential remedies. The general long-term failure of weight-loss diets is highlighted, a failure attributed to several features of the reproduction of practices – embodied habits, temporal routines and the norms circulating within social networks – which are germane to explaining practical competence in everyday life.

Chapter 7 wrestles with the concept of repetition and its many modalities which are fundamental to a sociological analysis of practices. The aim is to explain how performances are fluently staged in a manner consistent with their being shared socially. It examines the basic anatomy of performances and asks how people come to approximate their conduct to the injunctions of practices such that their behaviour exhibits recognizable similarities. This involves a discussion of the concepts of dispositions and practical sense, rescued from Bourdieu. Concepts of custom, convention and especially routine are employed to underpin an account of the conditions for the reproduction of practices. The question of how the procedures necessary for competent performances are learned and how then they are triggered by social environments is examined. This deploys a conception of culture as external to the individual. The chapter continues by asking how people learn new tastes in the light of one standard criticism of practice theories – that they cannot explain change. Explanation of the spread of tastes for 'foreign' cuisine in Britain is taken as a case study, revealing the importance of cultural intermediation. Finally, the issue of 'agency' is addressed, assessing how far the theoretical argument for habituation, routine and convention can be pushed.

The book concludes with a summary of the argument and a discussion of some of its implications. It offers a synoptic account of the key themes and theorems of practice theories to indicate the distinctive emphases brought by their approach to sociological analysis. It reconsiders issues of shared understandings, practical competence, personal and collective routines, conventions, cultural intermediation and institutions. The consequences specifically for an analysis of eating are then summarized, using an extended illustrative example of eating out.

2

Towards a Sociological Theory of Eating

Disciplines, Food and Eating

Opportunities for new departures in research always depend upon the current state of established disciplines. Any historical account of the development of the social scientific understanding of eating must first acknowledge that the vast majority of work on the topic derives from the perspective of nutrition, of the qualities and quantities of foodstuffs that are beneficial to human health. For practical and policy purposes, the problem has been viewed primarily as one of getting individuals to behave in their own best interests in accordance with scientifically determined dietary guidelines. On topics of consumption, economics and psychology, often represented via the disciplines of marketing and consumer behaviour, have proved hegemonic. They are the disciplines most often credited with having knowledge suitable to ensuring the application of the physiological and biological knowledge of nutrition to well-being. Mostly, they have been united in addressing consumption and the consumer in terms of the individual. Also, other perspectives on eating probably shape the popular understanding more than do socio-cultural sciences. Eating is a topic upon which professional food writers have probably had more impact than academic scholars, and for them theory building and the application of theory is not a priority. Medical sciences and marketing are also influential but do not aspire to a theory of food *consumption*.

In the development of the social science of food, an overwhelming degree of attention was paid to its production. Earlier sociological approaches to food were primarily concerned with agricultural production and the types of communities formed in rural areas. Subsequently, many other primarily economic aspects of food production were explored (Murcott 2013). The story of huge food corporations, science, industrial farming techniques, global exploitation of land and people and massive distribution capacities on a global scale is gradually being told. The consequences for health, environment, animals and labour forces are increasingly well appreciated (Pritchard 2013). Theoretically, a generation of research was consolidated around 'agri-food studies', beginning in the 1980s, as the tools of political economy were deployed to analyse food systems. Theoretical sophistication has produced a set of useful concepts to trace food from farm to fork. Carolan (2012) distinguishes two broad approaches within agri-food theory. 'Regime' theories emphasize the political conditions in which food production takes place and explore epochal shifts in the global system. Commodity systems approaches, of which there are several versions, make particularly good use of the metaphor of a chain of processes, which connect different actors through economic exchanges. As Carolan (2012: 61) comments, 'it is now commonsense when studying food never just to look at food *itself* but also at the actors, institutions, and rules and regulations that connect farm-gate and kitchen table'.

The contribution of the political economy of food is impressive and valuable. It has some fine and nuanced accounts of how and why the food that feeds the world comes to be available in markets and supermarkets. Yet it tells mostly of what is grown, made and sold, and on what economic terms, without saying much about how, or in what circumstances, those products are eaten. While, as Carolan (2012: 60) notes, agri-food approaches attribute little power to the sovereign consumer, they nevertheless pay scant attention to the site of consumption or relations of consumption. So, while no sensible theory of consumption would deny that the foodstuffs available and ease of access to them matters enormously to what people eat, what is provided is only part of the story. This book starts at the point where the political economists typically leave off. It is specifically concerned with puzzles associated with processes of consumption. It brackets production, distribution and exchange, making no pretence of giving a comprehensive account of the food system. It says nothing about farming or fork making, nor anything about supermarkets or allotments, except in so far as these might illuminate relations of consumption. It is not that I think these unimportant: if I wanted to give a comprehensive explanation of what people eat, I would certainly not neglect to study seed manufacturers, chemical companies and logistics firms.

Scholars working from political economy and commodity chain perspectives began to call for better understanding of processes of consumption and more effective theoretical analysis of the connections between production and consumption from the 1990s onwards (e.g. Fine and Leopold 1993; Fine, Heasman and Wright 1996; Goodman 2002; Goodman and DuPuis 2002; Guthman 2002). How best to specify the connection between the two domains of production and consumption remains contested theoretically and ideologically. One of the more promising avenues is through analysis of provisioning. The manner in which goods and services are delivered manifestly affects how they are received or consumed. In relation to eating, the domestic mode of provision is particularly important, but market, communal and state modes all play a part (Warde 1992). They affect the way in which people access food. Family obligations, economic contracts, reciprocity and citizenship rights generate different relations of consumption with systematically different consequences for the experience of eating. Provisioning approaches complement the literature in the sociology of consumption about the acquisition of items to be consumed.[1] However, most empirical studies of acquisition have focused on the practices of shopping, budgeting and cooking, which are treated primarily as instrumentally oriented processes of production. The issue of the fairness of the terms upon which labour is allocated in delivering services is often the focus. Yet from the point of view of consumption, the more important question is how the fruits of that labour are received. When children are taught to say 'thank you', they are being educated in the social relations of consumption. When guests invited to dinner bring gifts, follow the lead of the host in the orchestration of the meal, and confer compliments on the cook, they are engaging specifically in relations of consumption. In order to put the moment of consumption at the heart of my analysis of eating, I will address provisioning and acquisition only tangentially.

Guthman and DuPuis (2006) noted the growth of investigations of consumption under the label of 'food studies'. Food studies have been cultivated explicitly in the United States under the auspices of the Association for the Study of Food and Society (ASFS). A scion of the cultural turn, it comprises work from disciplines at the intersection of the humanities and the social sciences. It is multi- rather than interdisciplinary, and shows no signs of reaching, or indeed even of seeking, theoretical or conceptual synthesis. Proponents of food studies now express a good deal of confidence and optimism, not to say self-congratulation, which contrasts with a rather humble and despondent attitude no more than a decade ago. Then, Belasco (2002: 6), seeking to explain the lowly academic status of studies of food, observed that social scientists usually study food not for its own sake but in response to other research agendas. It occurs at the intersites of other intellectual programmes. Behaviour around food consumption is typically explored because it gives insight into phenomena like mental categories, family formation, social distinction, personal identity, material culture or body management. Arguably, none of these streams of investigation have taken eating as the focus or object of attention in its own right, but rather, as Belasco claimed, they deploy food consumption as *illustration* of other processes which are perhaps typically seen by sociologists as more legitimate or scientifically central. The successive treatment of these topics has bequeathed reliable knowledge and insight about several relevant aspects of the activity of eating. However, if 'food studies' have become the focus of scholarship on food consumption, then one would have to point to their very considerable heterogeneity – of discipline, approach and topic – and hence a lack of unified theory or even aspiration towards theory. Published material draws unevenly on a range of theoretical resources to which there seems to be limited commitment, with food studies having shown less theoretical ambition than in the better developed sociology of consumption.

Nevertheless, recent research gathered together under the label of food studies has made notable contribution to knowledge about aspects of food consumption. Although identifying trends in the absence of a systematic review is difficult, food studies (as exemplified by the journal *Food Culture and Society*) exhibits a strong focus on some central topics. One is the cultural aspects of the obesity 'epidemic', including issues of body management and image, consumption of fast food, with children – and school meals – a point of concentration. Another is migration and migrant labour, and in association, ethnicity and identity. Considerable attention has been paid to aesthetic aspects of cuisines, with reference to eating out, ethical issues of food consumption and mobilization through social movements. In this, there are parallels with cultural studies of consumption more generally, with attention heavily focused on the effects of globalization and the formation of personal identities.

The amount of research on eating within the socio-cultural sciences, when compared with other disciplines, is slight, although the overall volume is now very considerable. Anthropology, sociology, geography, history and cultural studies have all made attempts to explain changing patterns of food consumption. They often remain as interested in production as consumption, and perhaps indeed they should. Important shifts have occurred in the better established area of agri-food studies where the new political economy of agriculture has supported a variety of approaches.[2] Eating, however, has rarely been targeted as an object of research. The relevant chapter in Murcott, Belasco and Jackson's *Handbook of Food Research* (2013) is entitled, tellingly, the sociology of 'food consumption'. Even after years of attention paid to consumption more generally within the social sciences, research on food remains centred on products, production and provision. However, articles on food consumption and eating are becoming more common in generalist and mainstream journals of the social science disciplines. A shift is signalled by special issues of *Sociological Research Online* (2011), *Sociological Review* (2012), the *Journal of Sociology* (2010) and *Environment and Planning A* (2010), although, not coincidentally, they focus on crises, risks and the politics of food.[3]

The social science of food, then, is a multidisciplinary venture which operates in the interstices of the big battalions of research in agriculture and nutrition. The social or human, as opposed to the biological and physiological, aspects of these topics in the past were typically addressed through political economy and (social) psychology respectively. The sociological contribution is minimal by comparison but is nevertheless expanding apace.

The Pursuit of Theory

Social scientists do not agree about what theories should be expected to do. Abend (2008) identified seven distinct regular usages of the term in the social sciences, ranging from statistical associations between variables to *Weltanchauungen*. In his view, there can be no final solution to the question 'what "theory" really means [because that] is not the kind of thing one can *find out* or *establish*'; hence he advocates a principle of ontological and epistemological pluralism. Theories derive their importance partly from being central to the creation of professional scientific communities. They embody, for a school of thought or a discipline, the aspiration to articulate general principles of explanation. They act, as Bourdieu would say, as the *illusio* of scientific practice, an often unspoken belief in the value of a joint activity which generates and reinforces personal investment and collective commitment to progress within scientific fields. Thus theory is often presented as a means to sum general, valid and reliable knowledge obtained from prior investigations and explanations, thereby identifying the conditions necessary to give a coherent account of existing observations about a phenomenon.

I propose a naive and all-purpose definition of theory. A theory is a set of propositions (discursive or algebraic) which, if one wants to explain why or how situations (occurrences – processes or events – or states of affairs) (must have) come to be the way they are, will alert you to what to look out for (relevant and important entities – whose properties and propensities will probably be described) and how those entities stand in relation to one another. Such a view permits many different types of theory and different types of explanation. Components of theory include taxonomy (classification and definition of properties of entities), propositions about connections between the phenomena under surveillance and between those phenomena and others beyond, and propositions about the genesis or development of those phenomena. Resultant theories may take the form of description, specification of configurations, or formalized models (of entities and forces). Explanations may come as narrative, analytic and causal.

The prevalence of different and competing views and explanations is to some degree a function of disciplinary preferences and traditions, which in turn are partly related to the nature of the phenomena that they seek to understand. One role of theory is to provide a counterbalance to what would otherwise be an endless series of unconnected descriptive case studies; for example, sociology without theory is dull and hard to use. Another is to make explicit and render consistent assumptions about the connections (causes, co-emergence, mechanisms, elective affinities, contingent or necessary co-presence) between the phenomena observed, which can then serve as the foundations of the analysis and interpretation by means of narrative exposition or analytic explanation. A third role is to subtend causal models which predict behaviour or outcomes.

Sociological or socio-cultural theories are most often conjectures with analytic aspiration. They offer a framework of concepts, mechanisms and associations to capture social interdependence and the logic of multiple situations. They are conjectural (logically consistent, integrated core propositions, connecting concepts, referring to a real world), a lens to aid practical understanding of complex empirical reality. At present, formalization is barely on the agenda for sociology. Whereas models based upon atomistic individual action lend themselves to a-contextual generalization, which may be subjected to formalization in accordance with axioms of rational action, socio-cultural explanation more typical of history, sociology, cultural anthropology and cultural psychology considers the effects of interdependence and context to be the primary object of analysis, in respect of which formalization has proved intractable. Sociology, for instance, rarely generates formal models with discrete predictions for behaviour, although its probabilistic generalizations are no worse than those of any other discipline. At higher levels of abstraction, its meta-theories have often proved impossible to apply in empirical analysis and fail to rule out anything much. There are then few accepted rules for selecting between theories on grounds of truth content.

Above all, theories are instruments of selective attention. A principal effect of any theory is to emphasize some features of the world at the expense of others. They necessarily bracket off most parts of complex reality to give a parsimonious account of how something works. Some disciplines seek more parsimonious or reductive theories than others.[4]

Sociology is especially concerned with interaction in the social settings or situations in which action occurs. Since situations are multiple, varied and fluid, it finds simple causal models with predictive capability extremely difficult to formulate. Historically, sociology, more than other disciplines, has emphasized interdependence, collective conditions and the membership of social groups, and the normative bases of personal conduct. Thus it has been more interested than others in aggregate patterns of behaviour and less in processes of individual decision making and, by association, mental processes. In addition, it has emphasized the social nature of behaviour, the way in which egos adjust to alters, the manner in which people subscribe to shared views of what is right and wrong to do, and how that is a function of the binding conventions and supporting institutional processes of the societies into which they are born or to which they migrate. Arguably, most forms of sociology bracket off few features of complex situations.

Obstacles to a Theory of Eating

Among the reasons why advances in sociological theories of eating have been limited, three are particularly trenchant. First, eating has been looked at as a series of practical problems, as a terrain of crises. Second, the topic has been dealt with in multidisciplinary contexts where theoretical synthesis has low priority. Third, consumption remains subordinated to concern about production.

One explanation for limited theoretical ambition in any arena of activity is the urgency of dealing with practical difficulties. For almost all human beings, eating more than once daily is an unremitting practical objective. In many societies, its achievement has proved extremely taxing. The reasons why getting one's next meal might be precarious vary enormously over human history, not just because the problems facing hunter-gatherer societies differed from those of settled agriculture. Seasonal availability and annual variation, with years of plenty and years of dearth, were always expected. Interruptions of supply through natural disasters, wars, profiteering and ineffective political management have often resulted in populations, or sections of populations, having insufficient access to food. Such eventualities have strongly affected social relations, witness the impact of food riots, migration consequent upon famine and colonial expansion. In capitalist societies, obtaining enough food has often occupied most hours of a labourer's day and a large proportion of a household's financial resources. Unsurprisingly, then, early social scientific investigations of food consumption focused primarily on whether people got enough, or enough of the right kinds of, food to remain healthy. Tied to policy issues of poverty and inequality, the social circumstances of malnutrition were a primary focus of study from the later nineteenth century. Thereafter, the task was revised in order to try to understand and overcome the social and economic obstacles to the implementation of the recommendations deriving from twentieth-century research in medicine and nutrition.

On the face of it, many of these problems have been eliminated in societies with highly developed capitalist economies and mature consumer cultures. In rich societies like the United Kingdom and the United States, no one starves to death.[5] The proportion of the average household budget devoted to food is very small (little more than 10 per cent). Regional, seasonal and annual variation in food supply has long been minimized. Food supply has probably never been more secure than in Europe and America during the last 50 years, notwithstanding recent inflation of food prices on the world market. Yet food and eating remain sources of considerable popular and institutional anxiety. The apparent problems differ from those of the past. Anxieties are voiced by experts and pundits, circulate in the media, arouse controversy, and become part (though often a rather vague part) of popular understanding. Modulating anxiety has come to be a primary mission of the social sciences.

These anxieties may be put into five categories – physical, social and moral, symbolic, economic, and ethico-political. Arguably, much of the research about eating in the social sciences in the last 20 years can be located within those parameters. The first concerns hazards associated with modern industrial foodstuffs, including their de-natured properties. Fears about foodstuffs and raw materials attributed to the system of industrial manufacture of food – additives, chemical fertilizers, hygiene and safety, new breeding techniques and the nutritional properties of partially or wholly pre-prepared items – fuel anxiety about what should be avoided. The nature, perceptions and evaluations of risk are widely investigated, and the malign effects of profit seeking in the industrial food chain are frequently invoked (e.g. Nestle 2006). Second, there are worries about the de-structuring of meal arrangements. The meal, central to sociological accounts of eating, has been thought to be under assault since the 1960s from the individualizing potential of convenience foods and the informalization of manners and personal relationships. Symbolized by the – not new – panic about the decline of the family meal, the question has become how to eat, raising practical and moral issues associated with the maintenance of valued social relationships. A third anxiety reflects uncertainty about the ideal structure and content of the diet. It envisages a crisis of meaning arising from escalating and potentially unmanageable choice among wide varieties of available foods. Once there is no compulsion to eat from a single, established, nationally validated or traditional menu, then the practical and aesthetic rationale for selection becomes, it is argued, highly troubling. The question of what it is best to eat has become an obsession. Fourth, particular versions of the perennial economic issue of the monetary value of food have surfaced. Popular anxieties probably focus less than in the past on fraud or malfeasance of commercial actors, and rather more on manipulation by means of sophisticated selling techniques, the excessive power of retailers and value for money. Finally, food, like many other consumer items, has become a complex political matter. People mobilize as consumers and citizens around issues of animal welfare, environmental degradation, international trade and the consequences of global transportation of food, fair trade, food quality, and much more. Such concerns make shopping a difficult, contentious and quasi-political practice, as well as raising questions about behaviour change.

How these anxieties should be explained, and how seriously they should be taken, are subject to considerable scholarly controversy which, it would be fair to say, has produced empirical studies of real value, making many aspects of eating more visible, transparent and comprehensible. However, such studies, if they address matters of theory at all, typically adopt very divergent theoretical starting points and give little weight to theory building or theoretical synthesis. Nevertheless, even if crises are a poor source of theory, they have returned eating to the centre of attention; as Poulain (2012) put it, issues of health risks, animal welfare and poverty (and global inequality) have reinstated food as a prominent 'social question'.

Approaching social research with a view to solving perceived practical social problems has an effect upon the form in which knowledge is organized and consolidated. Typically it encourages inter- or multidisciplinary inquiry. For policy makers and funders of research, disciplines often seem to complicate matters unnecessarily. In the face of a pressing practical problem requiring a solution, the niceties of the theoretical assumptions which disciplinary specialists uphold are at best a diversion, at worst an irresponsibility. Interdisciplinary research, in the current political climate, is therefore widely promoted. It is not new; interdisciplinarity as a form and goal of scholarly organization has been around consciously since at least the 1920s. The research institute is the classic form of interdisciplinary organization, while the university department and the professional association have been the key organizational forms of the discipline. These two modes of organization of intellectual inquiry have developed side by side, coexisting together for at least a hundred years. Jacobs and Frickel (2009), using sources on the formation and organization of academic disciplines and research organizations within the universities, studies of journals and citations across disciplinary boundaries, and studies of the intellectual impact of explicitly interdisciplinary scholarship, concluded that there is no evidence for the general superiority of one mode over the other. However, disciplines probably have greater investment in theory. Disciplines find their integrity in the accumulation of knowledge related to recurrent intellectual puzzles entailed in the specific types of explanation to which they have been committed over time, even while they exhibit internal disagreement. It is therefore unlikely that theoretical syntheses would emerge either from investigations of practical issues like food security, obesity and snacking, or from a multidisciplinary, humanistic programme of research like that of food studies.

A third obstacle, though not itself a source of regret, has been the relative strength of analyses of food production. The political economy of food has had considerable success in charting how multinational corporations, in agricultural, manufacturing, pharmaceutical and retail sectors and in interaction with states and international bodies, have operated to transform the world's food system. Implications for risk, opportunities for profit and costs in terms of exploitation and insecurity are recognized. The contributions of sociologies of rural life, agriculture and domestic work have also been equally valuable.

However, in most cases powerful accounts of production have not encouraged advances in the analysis of consumption. Indeed, the sociology of consumption developed largely in reaction to economistic explanations, by which I mean the presumption that consumption is subordinate to, and may be explained in terms of, production, the stereotypical example being the Marxist base and superstructure theorem. Subsequent developments suggest that the understanding of consumption required a sharp break with production-led accounts, allowing space for recognition of the autonomous features of the moment of consumption. It remains difficult to agree on a definition of consumption, partly because of the meanings associated with two separate roots of the term in English. One, emerging from Latin, has a negative connotation – to destroy, to waste, to use up. The second emerged with the description of market relationships by political economy in the eighteenth century, which distinguished consumer from producer and, analogously, consumption from production. This second meaning signalled interest in the changing value of items exchanged, rather than the purposes to which goods and services might be put. From a sociological perspective, the dimension of use is crucial, and elsewhere I have defined consumption as 'a process whereby agents engage in appropriation and appreciation, whether for utilitarian, expressive or contemplative purposes, of goods, services, performances, information or ambience, whether purchased or not, over which the agent has some discretion' (Warde 2005: 137). In this definition, appropriation involves practical activities entailing the use of goods and services for personal and social purposes while appreciation covers the myriad of processes giving meaning to provision and use. These processes are closely intertwined with a third – acquisition – which involves exchange through market or other mechanisms to supply the means for personal and household provisioning. However, in this book I largely bracket off processes of acquisition and with them other aspects of the long chain from agricultural production to the point of exchange in the retail outlet. This is not because it is irrelevant – far from it. What is eaten is necessarily a product of production processes – of domestic and paid labour, fabrication and manufacture, capital investment and advanced distribution networks, corporate activity involved in modern industrial food manufacture and distribution, of hunger, famine and food insecurity. These processes determine what is available to be eaten. However, not only is this a vast topic to which a section of a short book could not do justice, but it is also one which is already well served. Moreover, too often these matters have swamped attempts to understand how consumption is organized. Here I seek to deal instead with the social processes surrounding final consumption, with activities beyond the point at which commodities are exchanged or labour applied in the preparation of food. Matters of production do enter the story because, when selecting what to eat and when passing judgement on dinner, the final consumer distinguishes good food from bad in terms of origins, qualities and provenance. The blandishments of the commercial communications industry and radical social movements circulate information about production which affects popular appreciation of food during the consumption moment. Nevertheless, accounts starting from production tend to focus on the functional aspects of foodstuffs and barely get to matters of meals, manners, pleasure and the symbolic aspects of eating. Bracketing off production allows a distinct and more detailed focus on eating.

Mining Older Traditions and Recent Research for Alternative Framings

Theoretical inquiries in the field of eating have been disappointing. Effective challenge to currently dominant approaches to a subject is often mounted by returning to earlier formulations based on different theoretical assumptions. Abbott (2001), for example, offered a neat and thought-provoking account of the uneven progress of the social sciences in terms of oscillation between different poles of central theoretical antinomies, like structure and action, choice and constraint, conflict and consensus, and so on. It should therefore be fruitful to look back to some themes and concerns that were diminished, if not snuffed out, by the onrush of the cultural tide in the 1980s. I therefore begin by reprising earlier work to excavate framings for theoretical revision. The aim is to retain and incorporate the valuable ideas which emerged during the cultural turn while developing new concepts to overcome some of the main associated problems. The objective is to reframe the most valuable elements of a sociological understanding of eating within a more comprehensive and synthetic sociological theory.

Existing sociological textbooks on food and eating when surveying the field (e.g. Mennell, Murcott and van Otterloo 1992; Atkins and Bowler 2001; Belasco 2008; McIntosh 1996) refer to few relevant alternative theoretical currents. While sociology is awash with competing theories, the simple classification of Mennell et al. (1992), who distinguished between functionalism, structuralism and developmentalism, is frequently reiterated. Other theoretical framings do exist, although they are often implicit and left in the background. It is notable that theoretical differences are better described in French sociology; Jean-Pierre Poulain (2002a), for example, reviewed contributions grounded in symbolic interactionism. Poulain (2002a: 190) also helpfully mapped approaches to eating along two dimensions. The first contrasts universalist with developmental explanations. Universalism tries to account for the role of food anywhere and everywhere, an approach which is more common in anthropology, though other disciplines offer accounts which describe the function that eating plays in human societies. Of the most widely celebrated theorists, Lévi-Strauss and Douglas tend to the pole of invariance. By contrast, Elias, Harris, Mennell and Goody focus on historical processes generating variation. Poulain's second dimension concerns the degree to which the autonomy of the social is posited, with Bourdieu and Grignon exemplifying sociological accounts of consumption, by contrast with a greater focus on individuals, for example Fischler.

Eating is prototypically a process of consumption. However, it has never been a very popular topic of study among the interpretive social sciences or sociology. The copious research in nutrition sciences is generally disparaged, a tendency reinforced by the focus of the cultural turn on meaning and its social construction, rather than corporeality and physiological processes. Recent trends in the sociology of the body, along with the centrality of the crisis of obesity which sociologists have felt obliged to address, are beginning to reconsider the issue, although mostly not in the dominant positivist manner of nutrition science.

The expansion of social scientific research in the last third of the twentieth century introduced a new set of themes and theoretical considerations. Economists were, and remain, especially interested in the effects of industrialization or affluence on patterns of spending, with corroboration of Engel's law being the primary focus. Changing allocation of household expenditure on food provides useful evidence about aggregate eating patterns. Political economy, if somewhat hampered by the economistic assumptions of neo-Marxism, generated work which had valuable residual effects on the understanding of consumption, with the Regulation School (Aglietta 1979 [1976]) at one pole, and Mintz's (1985) *Sweetness and Power* at the other. Mintz's examination of the integral connection between production and consumption in the history of the spread of sugar remains a beacon of synthetic analysis.

Historical materialist accounts were supplemented by studies like Mennell's *All Manners of Food* (1985), an application of Elias's theory of the civilizing process which contrasted eating habits in Britain and France since the Middle Ages. Sociologists also examined closely the social arrangement of the meal as an institution (building often on the insight of Simmel 1994 [1910]) for the drawing of the boundaries of sociability and, increasingly, as a means of social differentiation. For example, Bourdieu (1984 [1979]) documented graphically the role of eating in symbolizing social hierarchy in Paris and Lille. These were major pioneering sociological works from within the developmentalist paradigms. At the same time, structuralist anthropology and semiotics created new understandings and approaches to the symbolic significance of eating; the culinary triangle and a semiotic deconstruction of steak and chips were noteworthy contributions (Barthes 1973 [1957]; Lévi-Strauss 1965). Anthropologists also found food habits and rituals in modern societies important sources of cultural meaning and diversity which revealed patterns of social organization (e.g. Douglas 1984).

After the mid-1980s, few studies exhibited the equivalent level of originality or innovation. The political economy of the agro-food industry, agri-food studies, continued to make the most progress, using concepts of food system, the commodity food chain or food regimes (Carolan 2012; Pritchard 2013). Little was said explicitly about the stage of eating. Nevertheless, a burgeoning literature on food reported an increasing number of empirical studies about different aspects of food consumption and eating. Mintz (2013), having described decade-by-decade development of food research up to the 1980s, noted that the profusion of studies thereafter became increasingly difficult to catalogue and classify. Normal science seemed neither to clarify and consolidate existing positions nor to create conceptual integration and new syntheses. However, specifically with a view to sociological accounts of eating, a roughly sequential series of approaches with distinct conceptual foundations can be seen to have contributed to the development of a socio-cultural understanding of food consumption. Each has been guided by different theoretical attachments and has typically had different empirical foci.

Structuralist analysis of symbols, symbolic systems and discourses was carried out in the conviction that food served to reveal social categories and mental structures of groups and individuals. Structuralism proved a valuable methodological tool of cultural analysis, but as a general theory has long passed out of fashion. The methodological apparatus continues to prove useful in pointing to basic structural oppositions expressed in texts and images, the analysis of which shows how symbolic forms impart meaning to foods and meals. While structural anthropology and structuralist theory disputed the universality of such oppositions, their identification and interpretation within specific cultural contexts served to locate dominant understandings and controversies. Structuralism was exclusively a form of cultural analysis, conducted at the level of meaning and language. Its principal application was in anthropology but it found a use in cultural analysis more generally. Classic contributions to the study of food came from Lévi-Strauss (1965, 1969), Barthes (1973 1957]) and Douglas (1972).

A second building block, owing no debt to the cultural turn, arose from concerns with the division of labour, especially the division of labour within the household. Inspired by feminism in a period when the Marxist labour theory of value was much debated, one object of study was the provisioning and preparation of meals. Some theories of consumption made very positive use of the concept of 'provisioning' to indicate the conjunction of commercial provision and domestic use, with unpaid labour as a crucial intermediating process. For sociologists of food, the social and affective relationships built up within households around meals were of greatest interest because they revealed and reproduced gender inequality while simultaneously nurturing positive affective relationships as women provided nourishment for their families (Charles and Kerr 1988; Murcott 1983). The much revered family meal symbolized love and care, a solidarity emanating from eating together just as it shaped social divisions (DeVault 1991). However, the main features of this solid body of research were drawn into the sociologies of work and gender division, rather than consumption (though see Glucksmann 2014). Evidence of a gendered pattern of provisioning and the idealization of the family meal have been found many times in different contexts (Brannen, O'Connell and Mooney 2013; Kaufmann 2010 [2005]; Sobal, Bove and Rauschenbach 2002), though changed patterns of female engagement in the labour market in the West have prompted some significant changes in domestic divisions of labour.

A third body of work examined the connection between social hierarchy and patterns of food consumption. Although from different theoretical starting points, Mennell (1985), Goody (1982) and Bourdieu (1977 [1972], 1984 [1979]) all showed an association between class structure and cultural taste: foods consumed and the manner in which meals are organized reflect social position; and more elaborate cuisines develop in contexts with particular types of social hierarchies. Such analyses bridged material resources and cultural competence. For Pierre Bourdieu, in addition, judgements about taste actively reproduced the system of unequal social relations because what and how people ate was one mechanism for the accumulation of 'cultural capital'. Bourdieu showed that food preferences are coded in such a way that they convey messages about social worth. Yet while the products consumed by different classes vary, even greater difference is signified by the way people organize eating – 'ways of treating food, of serving, presenting and offering it' (1984: 193). Subsequent research in different countries continued to show the relevance of social class to food expenditure on different items (Darmon and Drenowski 2008; Grignon 1993; Régnier, Lhuissier and Gojard 2006; Tomlinson and Warde 1993). Convincing qualitative studies of differentiation in the manner of food provisioning and delivery were fewer in number but still succeeded in demonstrating class effects (Darmon 2009). The general principles illustrated in relation to class divisions were also applied to other forms of social differentiation, of gender, ethnicity and generation (Caplan et al. 1997; Charles and Kerr 1988; Diner 2001; O'Doherty and Holm 1999).

The fourth major repository of materials bequeathed to the field of food and eating comes directly from cultural analysis. It is hard to exaggerate the importance of the cultural turn for social scientific work in the areas of consumption and eating, for it had effects across all the humanities and the social sciences. 'The cultural turn' generally redirected scholarly attention in the interpretive social sciences – by which I refer primarily to sociology, anthropology and geography – away from issues of economic production and material life towards communication, symbolic meaning and lifestyle. It exposed the social sciences to a wide array of philosophical and theoretical impulses from the humanities, and specifically emphasized the importance for social organization of cultural processes and systems of signification and communication. This comprised the body of work known as food studies (Ashley et al. 2004). While it is widely agreed that the component ideas were very diverse, cultural analysis and explanations in terms of cultural processes became de rigueur (Kaufman 2004).

Programmes of social research (as opposed to moralistic commentary) on consumption had gathered momentum in the context of the cultural turn in the 1980s. The dominant line of investigation concerned the profound cultural consequences of globalization and especially whether the consumerist culture of the United States would be diffused everywhere. Appadurai (1990, 1996) characterized globalization as a multi-dimensional phenomenon comprising five types of 'flows': of people, money, messages, ideas and commands. Some of the most prominent features of globalization could be observed in the field of food. Due attention was subsequently directed towards the mobility of goods, people and ideas. This brought into focus processes of commodification and aestheticization, and their consequences for self-identity, cuisine and textual (and visual) representations of eating (see Warde 2012). Increasingly revolving around the concept of identity, the association between nation, ethnic group and food choice was examined for the ways in which eating expressed and represented personal and group belonging.

The cultural turn offered special opportunities to anthropology, both because of the centrality of the concept of culture itself, and also because of a long tradition of concern for the analysis of the role of food in everyday social relations (see Mintz and Du Bois 2002). Accordingly, much of the best recent work on food consumption has come from anthropologists who have managed to combine ethnographic research with a sound historical perspective to deliver impressive studies of changing patterns of eating (e.g. Counihan 2004; Goody 1982; Mintz 1985; Sutton 2001; Wilk 2006). Historians also made major contributions, including particularly critical evaluation of a tendency to overestimate the distinctiveness of globalization in the late twentieth century (e.g. Nuetzenadel and Trentmann 2008). In addition, the new academic domain of cultural studies, with its special expertise in the analysis of changing forms of mass communication, drew attention to the proliferation of media content dealing with food (Ashley et al. 2004; Rousseau 2012).

As a result, by the end of the twentieth century, the foci of the study of eating came to be personal and ethnic identity, nation building and national identity, food scares, eating out, consumer movements and migration, all wrapped up more or less in the problematic of globalization and consumer culture. These topics have dominated recent contributions to the understanding of how people eat and what they eat. As a result, attention shifted away from famine, food riots, Engel's law, poverty, credit and debt, etiquette, meals and class differences. However, there are increasing signs that the tide is turning and that the hegemony of cultural analysis is eroding.

Developments After the Cultural Turn

While the achievements of the cultural turn for the analysis of consumption are increasingly subjected to scrutiny and criticism, it must be reiterated that those achievements were very considerable and included laying the ground for the expansion of scholarly and social scientific research on food and eating. Nevertheless, the influence of the cultural turn has begun to diminish (Warde 2014). Cultural analysis tended to ignore practical and routine activity in favour of the more expressive and conspicuous aspects of lifestyle. A celebration of agency and reflexivity obscured the importance of embodied procedures and habits. Being a partial repudiation of the ethos and procedures of science, it discouraged scholars in socio-cultural fields from engaging with the materialist concerns of nutrition, chemistry and psychology and their experimental and statistical methods and findings. In short, the material and instrumental aspects of life were downplayed, a tendency for which recent investigations have begun to compensate.

One important development, mostly arising from studies in anthropology, was the emergence of a rich vein of research developed on the topic of material culture. Daniel Miller (e.g. 1987, 1998, 2010) has been one of the most creative and prolific exponents with fascinating studies of the experience of the use of goods, their role in making and maintaining social relationships and their personal, practical and political significance. The idea of exploring consumption through goods and other material objects has spread rapidly. Increasingly, food studies show off the product biography to good advantage, excelling in capturing the fact that foodstuffs have material, biological, economic, social and symbolic aspects, and that a complex material sub-structure lies behind the many products available in the supermarket (e.g. Dixon 2002; Harvey, Quilley and Beynon 2002). From another direction, science and technology studies (STS), it has been shown how objects, tools and instruments come to prescribe ways to approach particular tasks and activities. The industrial refrigeration system (Freidberg 2009), the domestic freezer (Shove and Southerton 2000) and the food processor (Truninger 2011) provide examples of how machines alter procedures, performances and possibilities with respect to domestic food provisioning.

Another fresh departure thematizes embodiment. Traditionally within sociology, basic biological aspects of the ingesting of food were avoided because they resonated with essentialist views of nature and the natural.[6] When socio-cultural analysis approached the body much of the focus was on its integrity, its management or its gender. This despite food being deemed a particularly significant form of consumption because, it is said, bodily incorporation of substances is prone to arouse emotions of apprehension, fear and disgust (Cervellon and Dubé 2005; Douglas 1966; Falk 1994; Rozin and Fallon 1987). More prosaically, the publicity given to the 'obesity epidemic' has spawned work on cultural understandings associated with body shape, but also a mountain of research and speculation about the causes of, and means to restrict, weight gain (Guthman 2011; Ogden 2013; Poulain 2009). Attention is now also being accorded to the role of the senses in the experience of eating, part of a move to redirect attention from mental towards bodily processes, or rather their cooperation (Sutton 2010; Wilhite 2014). In addition, impressive research about bodily competence in a range of other activities requiring skilful physical coordination holds promise for future investigation of the physiological and procedural aspects of eating (Ingold 2000; Lyon and Back 2012; Sudnow 1978; Wacquant 2004, 2014).

Although the sociological tradition of research on food was eclipsed and partly retarded by the cultural turn, its accounts of the specifically social aspects of food consumption were defended and developed. However, investigations were narrow in focus and proved relatively ineffective at making a theoretical contribution to the interdisciplinary mix, as emphasis shifted from social relations and resources to media communication and culinary cultures. It nevertheless generated valuable evidence about specific topics. Lotte Holm (2013), in a synoptic review of sociological research on food consumption, described an ongoing systematic series of studies; knowledge is being consolidated, through the making of comparisons across time and space, about meal patterns, commensality and the family meal, social differentiation of behaviour by gender, ethnicity and class, and on the formation of dispositions and preferences. The last of those topics, essentially about the formation of taste, explores the changing role of *habitus*, manners and rules of hospitality in determining patterns of consumption. Holm indicated the contribution of sociology to uncovering the origins of taste preferences, social organization, the importance of social context for explaining behaviour, the role of food in social solidarity and the maintenance of social relationships. In doing so, the sociological understanding of eating has drawn extensively upon steady accumulation of knowledge about consumption more generally (see Sassatelli 2007).

Notably, Holm situated her review of meal patterns and temporal rhythms in a practice-theoretical framework. She frames her account of recent research and the specific and distinctive contribution of sociology in terms of consumption as a practice – largely in order to distinguish the sociological approach from those of economics and psychology. (Implicitly, she also distances herself from nutrition science with its field-specific enquiries into the nutritional content of the diet.) Sociology dissects the context of eating, and perhaps thereby explains why people do not act according to the advice extracted from the natural sciences: Holm remarks that, while epidemiology may sensibly explain the sub-optimal diet of the poor as resulting from lack of money, knowledge or convenience of access, it remains an open question whether and why the poor *like* 'unhealthy' food, a question typically asked only by sociology.

In 2001, Schatzki, Knorr Cetina and von Savigny announced 'The Practice Turn in Contemporary Theory'. Since then, theories of practice have been canvassed as a viable alternative to cultural analysis. Practice theory is not strongly aligned with a single discipline and is gradually being incorporated into many disciplines – business studies, organization studies, linguistics, cultural geography, media studies, as well as sociology. Formulated in direct opposition to the presuppositions of orthodox neo-classical economics and much experimental psychology, in particular rejecting their models of individual action, practice theories are being used as a framework to distance analysis from individualism and calculative rationality. They also simultaneously contest key principles of some of the main forms of cultural analysis. Theories of practice are becoming recognized for their potential to unite approaches of the interpretive social sciences, and to bring the social back in. In focusing attention on norms and conventions, on bodies and embodiment, on material objects, on everyday conduct, and on the institutional settings of action, they point up some core sociological concerns. They promise potentially a more thorough and distinctive sociological analysis of food and eating in contrast to the assumptions and axioms of other disciplinary approaches. The next chapter attends in more detail to theories of practice.

3

Elements of a Theory of Practice

Introduction: Elements of Theories of Practice

In this chapter, I selectively review recent developments in theories of practice in order to introduce a series of interrelated concepts which might aid the analysis of eating. Since theories of practice are, by common consent, diverse, this entails some examination of their variety and their mutual compatibility. Existing theories exhibit family resemblance; all give precedence to practical activity as the means by which people secure their passages through the world thereby emphasizing doing over thinking, practical competence over strategic reasoning, mutual intelligibility over personal motivation, and body over mind. Consequently, they also contest individualist explanations.

Concepts of practice and *praxis* have a long history in the social sciences (see Nicolini 2012). However, they were revived and revised in the 1970s to address some fundamental puzzles in social theory by, among others, Pierre Bourdieu and Anthony Giddens. Renewed attention, a couple of decades later, saw the rhetorical announcement in 2001 of 'the practice turn' in contemporary social theory (Schatzki, Knorr Cetina and von Savigny 2001). Reformulation concentrated the focus, by proclaiming practices to be the most fundamental unit of social analysis, and added some new concepts. A substantial amount of empirical work was subsequently generated, though without doing much to enhance theoretical coherence. Even so, Omar Lizardo was able to proclaim triumphantly in 2010 that 'It can be said without much danger of exaggeration that practices now play as central a role in sociological thinking as values and normative patterns did during the functionalist period' (Lizardo 2010: 714). In this chapter, I will introduce some of the key concepts of theories of practice by way of a sketchy history of ideas. I will then review some of the problems that seem to arise when applying them in substantive sociological analysis. Some of the difficulties are directly relevant to my project of giving a practice-theoretical account of eating, and they will be dealt with in greater detail in subsequent chapters.

Rediscovering *Praxis* in the 1970s

In a widely cited article about trends in theory in anthropology, published in 1984, Sherry Ortner observed that 'a new key symbol of theoretical orientation is emerging, which may be labelled "practice" (or "action" or "*praxis*")' (1984: 127). She described its emergence from the intersection of theoretical schools in anthropology formed in the 1960s and interdisciplinary Marxism and political economy in the 1970s. The principal authors credited with the development were two sociologists, Pierre Bourdieu and Anthony Giddens, the anthropologist Marshall Sahlins, and Michel Foucault. A primary common objective was to account for action in a manner complementary to the study of systems and structures. Ortner observed an emergent response from this conjuncture: 'For the past several years, there has been a growing interest in analysis focused through one or another of a bundle of interrelated terms: practice, praxis, action, interaction, activity, experience, performance. A second, and closely related, bundle of terms focuses on the doer of all that doing: agent, actor, person, self, individual, subject' (1984: 144).

Though never severed, the two bundles of terms distinguished by Ortner turned out to underpin rather different orientations towards social analysis; understanding 'doers' does not necessarily encompass the analysis of 'doing', and vice versa. This might be seen by comparing the theoretical trajectories of Bourdieu and Giddens. Both provided widely celebrated versions of the new practice theory in the 1970s, elaborating frameworks of concepts to capture the interplay of structure and agency, subject and object. Bourdieu's account, when specifically a theorization of practice, was more thoroughly grounded in an empirical investigation of the Kabyle and established largely through its analysis (Bourdieu 1977 [1972]). Giddens's version was generated from the resources of classical and modern social theory and was thus more an exercise in philosophical anthropology.

Giddens made no bones about wanting a theory of action. The explicit primary task of *Central Problems in Social Theory* (1979: 2) was to remedy 'the lack of a theory of action in the social sciences'. Structuration theory, formalized in *The Constitution of Society* (1984), which sought through the concept of duality of structure to present a balanced and symmetrical account of the sway of structure and action, had as a primary objective the recovery of agency from the battering it had received from the sociological tradition. According to Giddens, the domain of study of the social sciences

> is neither the experience of the individual actor, nor the existence of any form of social totality, but social practices ordered across space and time. Human social activities...are recursive. That is to say, they are not brought into being by social actors but continually recreated by them via the very means whereby they express themselves as actors. (Giddens 1984: 2)

Social practices are thus made a principal object of analysis of social sciences and the recursiveness of activity provides the mechanism for their reproduction. This is the basis of his theory of structuration:

> I regard social practices, together with practical consciousness, as crucial mediating moments between two traditionally established dualisms in social theory. One...is the dualism of the individual and society, or subject and object; the other is the dualism of conscious/ unconscious modes of cognition.... [T]he theory of structuration substitutes the central notion of the duality of structure. By the duality of structure, I mean the essential recursiveness of social life, as constituted in social practices: structure is both medium and outcome of the reproduction of practices. Structure enters simultaneously into the constitution of agent and social practices, and 'exists' in the generating moments of this constitution. (Giddens 1984: 4–5)

This passage seems to allocate to practices a meso-level role, as the link constituting both subjects and structures. Thus Giddens located the concept of social practices as a vital mediation, systems being defined as 'reproduced relations between actors or collectivities, organized as regular social practices' (1984: 25). However, Giddens barely elaborated his notion of social practices, as an inspection of the passages identified in the index of *The Constitution of Society* readily reveals. Practice was never defined, neither were practices with specific content discussed, and nor, apparently, were practices envisaged as a topic for empirical study. Instead, he emphasized routines and routinization, and the role of practical consciousness. Subsequently, however, 'reflexively monitored social conduct' compromised the importance of the concepts of routine and of practical consciousness in *Modernity and Self-Identity: Self and Society in the Late Modern Age* (1991), and in the more controversial *Transformation of Intimacy* (1992), which emphasized lifestyles, risk, individualization and the role of individual reflexivity in conducting 'pure' relationships, with a recitation of the individualization thesis. This later work makes a few references to practical consciousness, and to practices only in the context of a definition of lifestyle. Giddens appeared to lay aside the arguments of *The Constitution of Society* (1984) when discussing lifestyles (1991: 80–7) where attention to reflexivity caused him to veer in the direction of voluntaristic analysis of individual action: 'Lifestyles are routinised practices, the routines incorporated into habits of dress, eating, modes of acting and favourite milieux for encountering others; but the routines followed are reflexively open to change in the light of the mobile nature of self-identity' (1991: 81). In such an account the core terms in the second bundle – actor, person, self and individual subjectivity – break free from firm anchorage in a concept of practice. As the cultural turn unfolded, Giddens's account became not easily distinguishable from the individualization thesis and the view of consumption as communication in pursuit of self-identity.

While Giddens made comparatively little reference explicitly to the concept, practice was absolutely central to the early work of Pierre Bourdieu. Not coincidentally did he put the term in the title of two of his major, primarily theoretical texts (1977 [1972], 1990 [1980]). His understanding of practice emphasized the components in Ortner's first bundle of concepts (*praxis*, activity, experience), although his resolution of the sociological puzzle about structure and agency explicitly preferred the concept of agency to that of action.

Bourdieu worked extensively on the concept of practice in the first half of his career, resulting in significant theoretical formalization in *Outline of a Theory of Practice* and *Logic of Practice*. Those two books laid out the principal concepts of his theory – *habitus*, structures, embodiment, *doxa*, symbolic capital, domination and practices, but not at this stage field. Practice was the ground for the erection of a framework of concepts emphasizing practical sense over scholastic reason and habituated practical competence over deliberative decision making. Bourdieu never subsequently disclaimed his attachment to the version of the theory of practice developed in those works. Yet, apart from constant reiteration of the epistemological position, which contrasts practical sense with scholastic reason, he allowed most other aspects of the theory of practice to fade into the background. Its place was taken by the concept of field, the primary analytic tool for his major empirical studies in the 1980s and 1990s, and by a more extensive, and increasingly overburdened, use of *habitus*.

Central to his venture, his most controversial concept, *habitus*, was the lynchpin of structure and agency. As Crossley put it well, for Bourdieu *habitus* is a concept designed to obtain

> a conception of human action or practice which can account for its regularity, coherence and order without ignoring its strategic nature.... An agent's *habitus* is an active residue or sediment of past experiences which functions within their present, shaping their perception, thought and action and thereby shaping social practice in a regular way. It consists in dispositions, schemas, forms of know-how and competence, all of which function below the threshold of consciousness. (Crossley 2001: 93)

So, '[d]ispositions, schema, know-how and competence', which constitute a combination of minimal mental properties and processes with an embodied facility to carry out appropriate practical procedures, effectively bear the burden of explanation of regularized activity. People act in a competent, regular and coherent fashion, without requiring conscious direction of their activity. This is not the pure repetition associated with a behaviourist notion of habit, for practice involves '*intentionless invention* of regulated improvisation' (Bourdieu 1977 [1972]: 79), which is sufficient to sustain the capacity to act effectively without deliberation. In addition, people act in ways similar to others with similar life experience, for individuals are powerfully constrained, though not determined (as some critics charge), by the social circumstances and circles in which they live: 'the *habitus*, the product of history, produces individual and collective practices, and hence history, in accordance with the schemas engendered by history' (Bourdieu 1977 [1972]: 82).

Thus *habitus* is a collective property, Bourdieu's generic contention being that social position, which allocates differential resources, entails similarity in the experiences of people in similar locations or with similar trajectories. This, a sociological platitude, accounts for the probability, but never the certainty, that socio-demographic characteristics will be correlated with different patterns of action. In Bourdieu's words:

> One of the fundamental effects of the orchestration of *habitus* is the production of a commonsense world endowed with the *objectivity* secured by consensus on the meaning (*sens*) of practices and the world, in other words the harmonization of agents' experiences and the continuous reinforcement that each of them receives from the expression, individual or collective,...improvised or programmed,...of similar or identical experiences. (Bourdieu 1977 [1972]: 80)

In such a manner (1977 [1972]: 83), *habitus* will provide 'the unifying principle of practices in different domains'. What is learned from common experience is sedimented into capacities for action in the future and, according to Bourdieu, although much more controversially, this results in a high degree of not just collective but also individual coherence.

In these early pioneering works of modern practice theory, there seems to be an inchoate notion of practices as entities which might be attributed the function of organizing both individual and collective experience. Practices give to common sense an impression of an objective and shared world because they harmonize individual with collective understandings. However, in subsequent empirical work, the anatomy of practices was not the focus of attention. Giddens conducted no empirical work himself, and followers enamoured with structuration theory were much more likely to take up concepts of agency, reflexivity and self-identity, concepts fitted to 'the cultural turn', rather than the notion of practice. As his work developed, Bourdieu tended to conflate practice with *habitus*. For example, in *Distinction*, the concept of practice is barely used for analytic purposes, and it is *habitus*, unifying class *habitus*, which, along with the distribution of capitals, drives the account of discrimination through taste in France. Subsequently, field became a central organizing concept and, while fields were designated and named after the practices around which they had formed, practices, as entities with their own logics or organizing principles, were subsumed by the 'game' which structured competition for capitals within the field. This led to the frequently advanced criticism that Bourdieu cannot grasp the internal goods associated with a practice because the logic of rivalrous fields overrides the integrity or autonomy of their constituent practices (Sayer 2005).

From *Praxis* to Practices

The edited volume by Schatzki, Knorr Cetina and von Savigny, entitled *The Practice Turn in Contemporary Theory* (2001), conveniently marks the arrival of a second phase of the modern theory of practice. The work of Theodore Schatzki constitutes the most thorough and sustained analysis of social practices of the second period. Three substantial volumes (1996, 2002 and 2009) develop various aspects of a theory which puts practices at the core of social order and personal conduct. Practices are presented as the primary entities of the social world, society itself being 'the *field of practices*' (2001: 2).

Practice as a Unit of Analysis

Schatzki's treatise *Social Practices* (1996) laid new philosophical foundations for an explicit general theory of practices. Schatzki located practice theories in the space between the two dominant approaches to social ontology: holism and individualism. As Schatzki noted, contemporary currents of social thought have challenged both the notions of social totality and of the unity and integrity of the individual, sometimes in the name of post-modernism, sometimes as a resolution of the structure-agency dilemma, and sometimes specifically in terms of practice theory. Schatzki sought to develop the later, in Wittgensteinian vein, theory of practice by incorporating elements from contemporary social thought which rejects the idea that society is a functional or organismic whole, integrated by evolutionary processes or overarching principles. However, Schatzki is equally concerned to avoid collapsing into an approach giving ontological primacy to individuals when conceptualizing the nature of social existence. Individualism, in its primary form of utilitarianism, has been expressed in the twentieth century through

> game theory, neoclassical economics, methodological individualism (e.g. Karl Popper), symbolic interactionism, and most versions of ethnomethodology... All give theoretical pride of place to the actions, strategies, mental states, and rationality of individuals, the cooperation, negotiations and agreements reached among individuals, the rules, norms, and threats governing people's behavior, and the unintentional consequences of behavior that often extend beyond actors' purview. (Schatzki 1996: 6)

In such a view of the social world, there is nothing beyond individuals and their relations or interactions. Individualism is however problematic, partly because of the existence of institutions which are hard to comprehend simply in terms of individuals and their conduct, and partly because the individual is, as has been argued in post-structuralist theory, inherently socially constituted, with the identity of the subject being precarious and unstable.

The alternative to the common choice between these two dominant ontologies which Schatzki sought to develop is practice theory, which he associates in his earlier work principally with Bourdieu, Giddens, Lyotard and Taylor. These authors, despite their differences, share 'the idea that practices are the site where understanding is structured and intelligibility articulated' (Schatzki 1996: 12). For Schatzki (1996: 16), social organization, or sociality, can be premised exclusively neither upon normative regulation nor upon rational individual cooperation because these are impossible without, in addition, mutual understanding and intelligibility of objects and actions. Schatzki continues, 'By virtue of the understandings and intelligibilities they carry, practices are where the realms of sociality and individual mentality/ activity are at once organized and linked. Both social order and individuality, in other words, result from practices' (1996: 13).

It was Schatzki who, most insistently, proclaimed practices to be the fundamental unit of social analysis. He identified two central notions of practice: practice as a linked or organized nexus of elements; and practice as performance. The first notion is of

> practice as a temporally unfolding and spatially dispersed nexus of doings and sayings. Examples are cooking practices, voting practices, industrial practices, recreational practices, and correctional practices. To say that the doings and sayings forming a practice constitute a nexus is to say that they are linked in certain ways. Three major avenues of linkage are involved: (1) through understandings, for example, of what to say and do; (2) through explicit rules, principles, precepts and instructions; and (3) through what I will call "teleoaffective" structures embracing ends, projects, tasks, purposes, beliefs, emotions and moods. (Schatzki 1996: 89)

Important to note here is that practices consist of both doing and sayings, suggesting that analysis must be concerned with both practical activity and some of its forms of representation. Moreover, we are given a helpful, if ultimately restrictive, depiction of the components which form a 'nexus', the means through which doings and sayings hang together and can be said to be linked such that they may form farming practices or recreational practices. In this trio, understanding entails that an actor understands what doings and sayings are appropriate to a given practice and would, when observing someone else, recognize that s/he was engaged in that specific practice. This condition of mutual intelligibility is fundamental to the sense that people share in practices. The second component refers to explicit injunctions associated with competence, though even highly competent practitioners may be unable to enunciate such rules, implying that tacit knowledge is typically involved. Third, 'teleo-affective' structures, a rather cumbersome concept, represent the purposive element of practices, the ends towards which engagement in the practice is oriented. The discussion of the teleo-affective structures conveys the sociologically useful idea that action is purposive even when it is not explicitly formulated in terms of explicitly chosen and intended goals. The idea of this nexus needs some reformulation to give a better understanding of how it may be coordinated in order to connect practices with performances.

The second sense, practice as performance, refers to the carrying out of practices, the performing of the doings and sayings which 'actualizes and sustains practices in the sense of nexuses' (Schatzki 1996: 90). The reproduction of the nexus requires some level of enactment. A performance presupposes a practice. But it is in performance that individuals carry that practice forward, expressing, affirming, reproducing and transforming it. Some version of this idea of recursive process, which links individual acts to the manifold of a collective practice, circumventing the opposition between structure and agency, is both common and vital to any practice theory. An essentially Giddensian notion is thus retained.

Schatzki indicates the broad scope of the concept of practice and its potential application when drawing a distinction between dispersed practices and integrative practices. 'Dispersed practices' (1996: 91–2) appear in many sectors of social life, examples being describing, following rules, explaining and imagining. Their performance primarily requires understanding; an explanation, for instance, entails understanding how to carry out an appropriate act of 'explaining', an ability to identify explaining when doing it oneself or when someone else does it and an ability to prompt or respond to an explanation.[1] This is about 'knowing how to' do something, a capacity which presupposes a shared and collective practice involving performance in appropriate contexts founded upon mastery of common understandings, which are the grounds for a particular act being recognizable as explaining.

'Integrative practices' are 'the more complex practices found in and constitutive of particular domains of social life' (Schatzki 1996: 98). These are ones which Schatzki says are generally of more interest to sociologists. Examples offered include farming practices, cooking practices and business practices. These involve, sometimes in specialized forms, dispersed practices, which are part of the components of saying and doing which allow the understanding of, say, cooking practice, along with the ability to follow the rules governing the practice and some acquiescence in its particular 'teleo-affective structure'.

An integrative practice is concrete and substantial in the sense that it is not constituted solely, or even primarily, by shared understandings. Integrative practices are necessarily complex because each performance presupposes competence in at least several others. They also involve technical expertise and dedicated equipment, features which help fix shared procedures. That complexity, however, raises questions about what exactly to identify and isolate as the phenomenon which constitutes the practice to be examined, and *inter alia* what might be its boundaries.

The importance of these questions might be appreciated by asking 'What might be included in a list of integrative practices and what not?'. Schatzki (1996) does not address this question directly but suggests a number of criteria to be taken into account. First, people have, and share, words denoting the activity and permitting its identification. Second, performances are mutually intelligible among people who are exposed to the same activity as part of the same culture. Members of a culture will recognize what is being done without need for explanation. Third, this recognition occurs because practices (or performances?) are social, by virtue of exhibiting 'coexistence with indefinitely many other people' (Schatzki 1996: 105); i.e. similar performances are mounted by unknown actors in distant locations. Fourth, performances can be read as correct, acceptable or innovative (1996: 101–2). That a performance can be judged correct or incorrect is a crucial feature of the inherently normative character of practices; performances are both normal, in the empirical sense of being regularly repeated (by 'indefinitely many other people'), and 'proper', in that they are subject to judgement in terms of their acceptability. Schatzki also says, fifthly, that a performance 'expresses components of that practice's organization' (1996: 104). This could mean either that every performance is implicitly mindful of the linkage between the three elements of the nexus, or that there are some forms of arrangement or architecture of integrative practices which are external to it. Finally, some essential attributes exist which are not simply in the minds of individuals: 'the organization of an integrative practice is out there in performances themselves not in the minds of actors' (1996: 105). This is a key function or feature of a practice's teleo-affective structure. A practice is thus more than the sum of the doings and sayings involved in the performances of individuals. In all, these characteristics suggest that an integrative practice has some integrity due to its 'organization'; it exists 'for itself'. The examples advanced are ones where the practices have a history or evolution and, importantly, can be transmitted, through teaching and learning, from person to person, such that novices come to share understanding, and sometimes facility or capacity, in a historically generated collective accomplishment.

What does it mean, for Schatzki, to say that a practice is 'organized'? In the first instance, organization refers to the circulation and reproducibility of a 'nexus of doing and sayings', comprising understanding, rules and a teleo-affective structure, which can be observed as fitting together when observed in competent performances. Individual performers, who hold or weave the elements of the nexus together, exemplify its organization. However, probably something beyond the particular performances, something supra-individual, is intimated. Perhaps, that 'nexus of doing and sayings' might be considered an entity possessing emergent properties and with collective and institutionalized arrangements existing for its ongoing coordination. Schatzki himself seems ultimately reluctant to accord practices an ontological existence beyond the sum of their performances. In his later work, he explicitly prefers accounts which veer towards the individualist or action-centric pole of practice-theoretic accounts: 'The most viable sort of societist ontology, in other words, is the one closest to individualism' (2003: 188). On this point there is controversy.

Performances and Practices

Theories of practice divide over what importance to accord to processes of collective generation, organization and regulation of performances (and therefore what explanation to offer). All are committed to practices being mutually intelligible, such that it is possible to recognize that a sequence of actions is an instance of, say, eating or cooking. This, almost by definition, entails that some estimation can be made regarding the correctness, appropriateness or acceptability of a particular performance. Practices must have standards.

To admit of standards portends a likelihood of the existence of agents responsible for the formulation of those standards and probably agencies taxed with inducing compliance with those standards. Standards of performance are a lynchpin in the case for seeing Practices as entities. They are a key part of what is shared, as Schatzki correctly intuits in his discussion of teleo-affective structures. The standard is not a motivation or reason for doing something – it doesn't matter if no explicit and discrete objective can be identified – but it is a key parameter or threshold in relation to which practitioners may gauge the adequacy of their performance. Standards are neither reasons for participation in the practice nor drivers of behaviour, although they may be critical when an actor monitors the effectiveness of her habits or perceives that another procedure needs to be implemented. Nevertheless, they are the primary reason for saying that practices are irreparably normative in character.

Standards of performance are mostly implicitly understood but are often explicitly articulated, not by actors in the course of performances so much as in commentary upon practice. While practice theories emphasize doing over thinking and *praxis* over theory, it would be imprudent to neglect the influence of vast amounts of the accumulated commentary that surrounds most practices, and probably all integrative practices. When subject to commentary, verbal or documented, the normal and the normative are unavoidably elided (see Rouse 2006). What people usually do is readily translated into a sense that this is what ought to happen. Understanding of activity can only be approached in the light of knowledge of performances, and recognizing it to be an instance of a Practice can only be achieved by judging it to have been adequately carried out. What is inevitably bequeathed by commentary is an awareness of standards associated with a Practice; it bestows the capacity to make some judgement about when a performance has met a minimum standard of effectiveness to pass as an instance of the practice.

It is not easy to explain how someone recognizes and judges another actor's (and by extension their own) performance to be an instance of practice and adequate to its standards. Complex practices are complex precisely because of their internal variety. Rarely, if ever, is there simply one way to carry out a Practice, or one sole manner of performance that will be acceptable. Yet such capacity for recognition is presumed by any practice theory which asserts that practices are units of analysis. A performance effectively conforms to a template of some kind in order that it can be confirmed to be an instance of the Practice. Fortunately, this presumption finds full collaboration in observations of the conduct of everyday life; people recognize what they and others are doing in terms and concepts of the type identified by practice theory, and they perceive opportunities in the same terms. That, in other words, is the sense in which there is mutual understanding and that people 'know' what they are doing.

How standards are formulated and how they are disseminated within groups of practitioners bears upon the contentious question of whether a practice should be considered as some kind of emergent entity.[2] In the process of diffusion of the appeal of theories of practice after 2000, two powerful articles of Andreas Reckwitz (2002a, 2002b) proved influential. Both suggested that theories of practice offered fresh potential by way of breaking the dominance of cultural theories in the previous decades. His importance lay in placing practice theory in relatively close relation to established orthodox perspectives of the cultural turn. His critique of cultural theories for having a singular focus on meaning (2002b) and their exclusion of the material aspects of life (2002a) furnished a distinctive approach to practice theory. He also distanced himself from the main proponents of late twentieth-century practice theory when suggesting that greater systematization would be valuable. While drawing upon the work of Schatzki, Reckwitz reformulated the key elements of a practice, which for sociological purposes indicated additional objects requiring empirical investigation, and he restated the distinction between practice (*praxis*) and Practices (*Praktiken*):

> Practice (*Praxis*) in the singular represents merely an emphatic term to describe the whole of human action (in contrast to 'theory' and mere thinking). 'Practices' in the sense of the theory of social practices, however, is something else. A 'practice' (*Praktik*) is a routinised type of behaviour which consists of several elements, interconnected to one another: forms of bodily activities, forms of mental activities, 'things' and their use, a background knowledge in the form of understanding, know-how, states of emotion and motivational knowledge. (Reckwitz 2002b: 249)

His distinction between *Praktik* and performance was especially emphatic. (I will usually use the term Practices, with a capital 'P', to refer to the former concept.) As Reckwitz put it:

> a practice represents a pattern which can be filled out by a multitude of single and often unique actions reproducing the practice...The single individual – as a bodily and mental agent – then acts as the 'carrier' (*Trager*) of a practice – and, in fact, of many different practices which need not be coordinated with one another. Thus, she or he is not only a carrier of patterns of bodily behaviour, but also of certain routinized ways of understanding, knowing how and desiring. These conventionalized 'mental' activities of understanding, knowing how and desiring are necessary elements and qualities of a practice in which the single individual participates, not qualities of the individual. (Reckwitz 2002b: 249–50)

The notion of individuals as carriers of practices suggests the possibility of considering Practices as entities, which has implications for analysis of the organization or coordination of practices.

Practice theory could be less shy of explicitly grasping the notion of Practice as an entity. A major reason for reticence is fear of collective concepts that reify, in an unwarranted manner, interpersonal relations, connections and engagements.[3] Although giving a convincing account of the ontological and epistemological status of Practices is challenging, the notion is instructive for the sociology of consumption and thus of eating. Three issues pertain. How should Practices be characterized in terms of elements, arrangements, and so on? How are they established, delimited, reproduced and organized? And how do they inflect performances?

It is essential to take care not to anthropomorphize Practices. Practices do not themselves do anything; qua entities they do not give performances. However, individuals, groupings of people and organizations display serious commitment to the proper conduct of such Practices – both their own proper conduct and that of others who participate. These agents act not only as exemplars and innovators, but also as guardians and enforcers of conduct fitting to practices to which they feel obligation and in which they engage in an orderly and regularized manner.

This suggests ways in which a practice might be an entity which is 'coordinated'. In this regard, it goes beyond the form of organization described by Schatzki in terms of a 'nexus of doing and sayings', comprising understanding, rules and teleo-affective structures which can be observed as fitting together only when observed in competent performances.[4] Coordination may be purposively fashioned by interested parties. It is a common feature of the existence of a Practice that coordination is a collectively established, and internally contested, process. Individuals and organizations assume responsibility for defining standards of performance and recommending techniques for meeting those criteria. For example, integrative practices are sometimes coordinated by formal organizations. Associations like professions, governing bodies of sports, statutory regulatory state agencies, not to mention educational institutions, may play central roles in coordination. They then attempt to regulate performances – prescribe rules, prohibit or discourage particular forms of behaviour, teach acceptable conduct, present prizes for excellence, and so on. While not all integrative practices are so constituted or steered, formal and often authoritative agents are an essential component of the ordering and coordination of many practices. Exactly what it is that is 'out there' is critical to explaining how (some) practices are coordinated as shared, collective modus operandi.

Sometimes, as with most dispersed practices, coordination is no more than an informal, unformulated nexus based upon shared understandings. In other cases of integrative practices, we find artefacts, texts, organizations and public events which anchor the Practice, providing it with substance. One means by which performances may be adjusted or improved is through attempts at describing and recording, for public circulation, accounts of how to do something, how to do it better and how to do it well. I have in mind things like rule books, teach-yourself primers, instruction manuals for improving performances, guidebooks, and so on. Practice manuals are good evidence for the existence of a Practice; simple acts are neither likely to be thought of as practices nor to have manuals devoted to them.[5] Formalization of tacit knowledge is a continuous process in literate cultures and one which probably accelerated sharply in the twentieth century (e.g. Taylorism, self-help and guidebooks, instruction manuals, formal education and vocational training).[6] Codification and formalization of a Practice is thus normal, even routine. Since teaching institutions, professional bodies and voluntary associations operate to prescribe, instruct and transmit the procedures constituting practices in which they have a stake, they have the effect of codifying proper procedure, or 'good practice'. However, and critically, this neither entails that actual performances will become uniform in the face of their recommendations, nor that they will meet standards of correctness. While performances are necessary for the reproduction and development of a practice, they are not enacted in the same way on each occasion; they exhibit individual distinctiveness and perhaps innovative aspects, and, because they are context dependent, they are always adjusted to particular situations. Performances are best seen as continual improvisations within more or less precise or fuzzy parameters which permit confirmation that each displays sufficient similarity to be recognizable as an example of that particular Practice. Codification of a practice may thus have relatively little direct or conscious effect on actual performances, and reference to manuals in the process of making decisions or planning courses of action should be anticipated only in rare and exceptional circumstances. Nevertheless, the components of the Practice 'out there' are significant in their own right. The state of development is evidence of the social process whereby nondescript activities are constructed and developed to become integrative Practices.

Applications

Since the announcement of the practice turn at the beginning of the new millennium, the concept of practice has circulated widely. Scholars from different disciplines and sub-disciplines discovered, identified and sought to promote the use of practice-theoretic tools. Practice theory has been presented as a 'new paradigm' or lens in media studies (Couldry 2004), in management learning and organizational behaviour (Gherardi 2009; Nicolini 2012), in linguistics (Pennycook 2010), in economic geography (Jones and Murphy 2011), in planning (Binder 2012) and in consumption studies (Warde 2005). These contributions have sometimes taken the form of a manifesto for practice-theoretic approaches, although most do little more than restate some of the concepts developed in the earlier phases. Reckwitz's pleasing and elegant formulations were widely quoted, particularly by those who had been closely engaged with, whether for or against, the cultural turn. Others emerging out of the linguistic turn were more likely to fix on concepts from science and technology studies (e.g. Gherardi 2009). Yet others owed debts to the very influential work of Lave and Wenger (Lave 1988; Lave and Wenger 1991; Wenger 1998) whose concept of 'communities of practice', conceived as the result of successful social and collective learning with particular relevance for business organizations, has been extensively disseminated and redeployed.

Postill (2010), in his contribution to a volume of essays entitled *Theorising Media and Practice*, identified a third phase in the development of contemporary practice theory in terms of its inspiration for dedicated empirical studies. Themes arising from the first two phases of theoretical development were employed to address problems of description, interpretation and explanation of social processes and behaviour in particular substantive domains. This process can be observed not only in organization studies, management learning, socio-linguistics, media studies, economic geography and the sociology of consumption, but also in sustainable consumption (Shove, Pantzar and Watson 2012; Shove and Spurling 2013), marketing (Schau, Muniz and Arnould 2009), and gender studies (Poggio 2006). Some of the associated research has taken food consumption as an object of analysis in areas such as, for instance, food preparation (Halkier 2009), waste (Evans 2014), kitchen equipment (Truninger 2011) and temporal routines (Cheng et al. 2007).

While practice theory has begun to be used to address activities around food, it has not been applied specifically to understand eating. In ordinary language, the term 'eating' has multiple referents, both physiological procedures and cultural phenomena of daily living. Studies of food have typically paid little attention to the former, to matters like ingestion, chewing, swallowing and digesting. They have also demonstrated rather uneven interest in the social, economic and political aspects of the latter. One task, therefore, for an approach premised on practices as units of analysis is to specify parsimoniously the relevant component elements of the complex of activities involved. I will attempt to do that in detail in chapter 4 by examining eating for its potential to be represented as a scientific object.

Unsurprisingly, as theories of practice become more widely used in empirical studies, some difficulties of application have emerged. One concerns the specification of the links between performances and Practices. A second revolves around decisions about where to draw the boundaries between discrete Practices and, thereupon, how to picture the relationship between them.

First, it is difficult to be entirely clear exactly *how* performances draw upon *Praktiken*, the coordinated entities that constitute integrative practices. It seems to me that there cannot be a practice which does not have some forms of collectivized integument associated with its performances. In the absence of some vehicle for transmission, it would be hard to see how one can talk of, or explain, a practice being shared. This may be nothing more than collective memory of how, and perhaps why, some ritual should be performed. It will often be an informal consensus about proper behaviour characteristic of groups of people involved in continual face-to-face interaction. These are some of the bases of the 'out-thereness' that Schatzki called teleo-affective structures and which indicate standards to which acceptable performances should aspire. However, in other instances, it may take forms that are scholastic, conveyed by means of books, instruction manuals, and so on.[7] They are constructions, normally derived, abstracted or inferred from observation of everyday performances and then typically reconstructed in a systematic manner, which, always from a particular point of view, contribute to the regularization of performance and recommendations of best practice. An example might be recipe books which codify performances in cookery by introducing into the public domain not only explicit guidance about techniques, but also implicit recommendations about what to eat.

Second, strong versions of the theory of practice propose that practices are the basic units of all explanation. This requires a protocol for deciding how to bound practices. Sometimes this is unproblematic. Almost any non-trivial, relatively self-contained activity can be treated analytically as a practice. Many empirical case studies to date have taken relatively autonomous integrative Practices as the subject of analysis. Cookery seems to be an unambiguous example. Irrespective of the way in which a person learned to cook, understandings, procedures and standards are mutually recognizable in terms authorized by cookery books and enacted in meal preparation. Cooking is an autonomous practice, codified, with common standards and rules and clearly distinct from shopping, laying the table or eating. To be able to cook is a complex and diverse accomplishment but understood by scholar and layperson alike as a set of instrumental procedures for transforming foodstuffs into items for final consumption. Like every other practice, cookery is interdependent with others. Practices higher up and lower down the food chain condition what foodstuffs are available for preparation and what concoctions might be welcomed by diners. No practice operates in isolation. However, some are much less self-contained than others and they pose an analytic problem.

Arguably, the status of eating is more complicated, problematic because the elements contributing to performances are not per se objectivated in the form of a single, self-contained integrative Practice. There is no one-to-one correspondence between performances and a constructed or evolved Practice; there is no equivalent to the cookery book, no volumes with the title teach-yourself-to-eat. Eating appears to be unusual in this regard, although not unique, because the elements of performances do not constitute unequivocally the content of a single, discrete, identifiable, autonomous, integrative practice. Instructions about procedure or enunciations of standards governing excellent performance derive mostly from other Practices. Several formalized Practices subtend performances of eating. Advice and recommendations about how and what to eat arise from formulations with origins in nutrition science, cookery, etiquette, the food industries and the culture industries. These are domains where different professional, amateur and commercial organizations operate, each with its own logic and its own procedures and standards of practice. Typically, they make mutually inconsistent recommendations. They draw on different conventions of worth. They compete with one another for authority. It is therefore difficult to firmly fix the boundary of eating and thus to account for its relationship with other practices. If eating is not a self-contained, autonomous practice with firm boundaries but, instead, has porous edges and is subject to overlapping jurisdictions, then some means are required to specify its relationship to, and its degree of dependence upon, those other Practices. I will argue that the existence of these adjacent, complementary but also invasive integrative practices, which affect mundane behaviour, call for an additional concept, namely the 'compound' practice, to properly characterize eating.

Conclusion

A foundational insight of the sociological versions of practice theories, made most explicit in Schatzki and Reckwitz, is that social explanations which attempt to derive individual behaviour from social systems, or social systems from individual behaviour, are doomed to failure. Neither holism nor individualism is satisfactory. The alternative is to seek entities or mechanisms which can generate observed effects at both individual and societal levels. Theories of practice begin from the assumption that practices play that role; practices are the fundamental units of social existence and hence the core concept of social analysis. Practices precede individuals; and practices, because they adumbrate standards, determine the basic parameters of mutually intelligible acceptable behaviour. This is achieved by virtue of the co-constitutive interrelationship between Practices and performances.[8] Individuals then are the creatures of their accumulated performances (and perhaps some of their anticipated performances) in a vast range of Practices (Warde 2005), which allows considerable potential not only for individuality but also for variation in the extent to which the experiences of each are coherent or fragmentary.

Social institutions are the emergent consequence of the multiple performances of activities which, in order that they may be intelligible to persons for whom they are relevant, objectivate the principles or logic of the Practice which inform performances. If some awareness of the principles or logic of the Practice was not available, then no observer could recognize a performance as specific to the Practice. Practices have institutional form and are not imaginary reifications; institutionalization takes the forms of organizations, binding injunctions (laws, contracts) and regulative intervention, as well as conventions and rituals which exercise agency irreducible to the behaviour of individuals. However, their role is not one wherein individuals consult their principles or rules when evaluating the situation in which they find themselves. Practice theories precisely reject that view. Individuals mostly do not give shape to their performances in the light of having given conscious consideration to the welter of forces operating extraneously or externally. Rather, their performances are intricately poised in a web of potentiality conducive to appropriate courses of conduct afforded by interconnection with other entities in their environment. In this manner, theories of practice provide an alternative to what Whitford (2002) called the portfolio model of action.[9] The trappings of practices are not background considerations from which actors deduce what is appropriate, calculate risks, and so on. Later chapters (5–7) attempt to unpack in greater detail the recursive relationship between Practices and performances and the means through which both are learned, coordinated, implemented and reproduced.

4

Elementary Forms of Eating

Constructing Eating as a Scientific Object

If, theoretically, practices are the fundamental unit of scientific analysis, a first step in an investigation is to determine the sort of practice that eating is. How should eating be defined and delimited so that it becomes amenable to scrutiny? Previously, eating has been treated as a topic rather than an analytic concept. A well-known lay term, its features are taken as given. The basic dictionary definition of the verb 'to eat' is 'to take into the body by mouth as food' (Chambers 1972).[1] All social scientific approaches accept that the 'taking into the body' of substances which are identified as 'food' are two basic aspects of eating. The interpretive social sciences observe, in addition, that both processes always occur in a social and cultural context. They insist that the social foundations and social consequences of these processes are essential to their understanding. Thus is the basic definition insufficient for the purposes of sociological explanation, and concepts are required to capture a more complex conception of the activity. By contrast with the political economy of food production, which has successfully established concepts of the commodity chain and the food system as organizing principles of inquiry, the sociology of eating lacks a satisfactory central scientific object to direct its investigations.

The notion of a scientific object arises from a tradition in the philosophy of social science which finds the foundations of science in its manner of concept formulation. It finds unsatisfactory a simple correspondence model, which says that concepts refer directly to real objects in the world. It also rejects social constructionism, the view that concepts are simply parts of a system of concepts which is ultimately arbitrary in relation to the properties in the world to which they refer (i.e. they could be completely otherwise if scientific communities had developed in different ways and promoted different ideas). Instead, scientific concepts are seen as refinements of ordinary language terms, which are fashioned, sharpened and developed in order to address particular questions valuable for the purpose of specifically scientific analysis. This may re-conceptualize lay practical problems in such a way that they are more tractable and understandable. It involves juxtaposing old and new, lay and scientific, concepts so as to redefine them in an internally coherent manner, and with reference to specific features of an external empirical world which in some degree constrains the scientific propositions that can be made.

Disciplines formulate their scientific objects in different ways. If eating is, indeed, 'taking into the body by the mouth as food', inquiries will foreground different features. The biologist may focus on how chemical properties of ingredients are transformed in the gut; the economist will ask what foods will people buy at what price; the nutritionist will seek optimal combinations of foods which, when incorporated into the diet, will promote health; while the agronomist may concentrate on isolating chemical compounds which can be introduced into ingredients. Different problems thus entail different scientific objects and specialized explanation.

Sociologists have frequently addressed questions of what counts as food and also the manners prescribed for procedures involved in 'taking into the body by mouth'. Regarding the first issue, they have concentrated mainly on the implications of the basic insight that not everything that is edible is acceptable and that foods have differential symbolic values. On the second, they have examined table manners and bodily comportment in the traditions of Simmel and Elias. However, the main and distinctive preoccupation of sociology has been with a dimension lying outside the basic definition – with the social interdependencies, relationships and interactions required for eating to take place. These have typically been approached via the concept of the meal but whether that is optimal is now in dispute.

This chapter therefore aims to discuss the fundamental component elements of the activity of eating so that its performances can be analysed succinctly. The objective is to isolate a small set of consistent and related concepts which capture its culinary, corporeal and social dimensions. Performances of eating are described with reference to elements within each dimension and their interrelationship. The contention is that variety and competence in performances derive from the permutation of alternative ways to integrate, practically and symbolically, foods, their bodily incorporation and social settings. These common core concepts can be shared across theoretical divides for they identify the fundamental properties of eating. Thereafter, theories may offer different explanations of how and why patterns of behaviour emerge. Subsequent chapters attempt to depict distinctive claims arising from theories of practice. Here I first look at the work of some sociologists and anthropologists who have made relevant theoretical contributions to the analysis of eating as a process of consumption.

Some Sociological Approaches to Eating

Eating was not a central strategic topic for the instigators of contemporary practice theory. Nevertheless, both Sahlins and Bourdieu used food and eating as illustration when engaging in theoretical debate. Sahlins (1976), an anthropologist writing at the beginning of the period when interest in *praxis* was developing, engaged in the ongoing Marxist debates about the primacy of production. He was principally concerned to examine the relationship between material production and symbolic communication. His pages on food were largely devoted to arguing that processes of economic production are always culturally inflected. He illustrated the argument by examining the symbolic attributions of different foodstuffs, recounting different taboos about eating animals. All societies, he notes, have hierarchical classifications of what is edible. The definition of what is edible is culturally variable and in some respects arbitrary, a matter jointly of nutritional properties and aesthetic judgement. In the contemporary West, the hierarchy runs from cattle, to pigs, to horses, to dogs; it is much more acceptable to eat cows than dogs, an ordering which Sahlins attributed to degrees of closeness to humans. Sahlins also noted the different status of meat and innards, and the uproar in the United States when in the economic downturn associated with the crisis of oil prices in 1973, the government suggested that the poor should eat offal. Sahlins captures well the potential of food to arouse disgust. Normal behaviour cannot be explained simply in terms of the use-value or function of foodstuffs because there is always a symbolic supplement – culture being a system of signs – which cannot be explained by material necessity. There is no reason to show a preference for steak over kidneys and tongue from the point of view of the amelioration of hunger or human survival. The implication was that food was analysed more for its part in a symbolic classificatory system than in relation to practical matters of bodily reproduction and sensations of taste.

Bourdieu wrote surprisingly little about food and eating. Food appears in detail in only two major works, *Outline of a Theory of Practice* (1977 [1972]) and *Distinction: A Social Critique of the Judgement of Taste* (1984 [1979]).[2] *OTP* was based on an ethnographic study of Kabylia conducted during the Algerian War in the late 1950s. The interpretation was largely in terms of the relationship between everyday practices of a traditional rural society and the beliefs and symbolic representations through which they were understood and justified. The analysis proposed the existence of structured homologies or parallels across the series of symbolic categories that were employed to give meaning to the organization of daily, annual and lifelong temporal durations. Despite the presentation and conscientious formulation of most of the key concepts of his version of practice theory, in *Outline of a Theory of Practice* Bourdieu analysed food, in the typical manner of structuralist anthropology, for its symbolic meaning. The techniques of cooking played a significant part in the symbolic universe of the Kabyle. Different foods appeared, or the same foods were cooked differently, in different ritual circumstances and at different times of the year. Bourdieu interpreted the meaning of habitual practices in terms of the mimetic representation of key conjunctures of human life – of procreation, of marriage and ploughing, of death and resurrection. Crucially, different foods, or ways of cooking, could be read as indicators of the fundamental categories of existence and practical ways of understanding the natural and social universe of the Kabyle. Bourdieu thereby offered a very detailed and incisive decoding of the cultural categories of the Kabyle, reinforcing and illustrating many of the points that anthropologists have typically made concerning how the preparation and consumption of food symbolize social processes and social relationships.

In his other, and principal, contribution to the understanding of food and eating, Bourdieu elaborated the same fundamental insight in relation to modern France. The story of *Distinction* is one of the social alchemy involved in the powerful successfully and repeatedly establishing that what they like is objectively best (that is to say, aesthetically the most valuable), and then obtaining regard or respect from others for their good taste. On the basis of that good taste, they achieve other forms of reward and privilege; they convert the recognition and acceptance of their good taste, their 'cultural capital', into other types of resources or 'capitals' – economic (money, jobs), social (connections to other people who might subsequently offer them favours or support, for example in marriage) or symbolic (recognition, high status and prestige). Thus for Bourdieu the possession of good taste is a weapon in social struggles. Taste is constituted through judgements concerning the aesthetic qualities of particular items and activities. Much judgement is tacit, recorded in and expressed through people's possessions, learning experiences, comportment and accumulated cultural competence.

Bourdieu used food habits as one key example of these processes, identifying class differences to show that food preferences are coded to convey messages about social worth. Differences in meal content are also associated with body shape and movement. Tastes find their expression in bodies; taste, Bourdieu observed (1984 [1979]: 190), is 'a class culture turned into nature, that is, embodied', and 'the body is the most indisputable materialization of class taste' – a point that he supports with photographs of men from different social classes and discussion of how aesthetic standards vary between classes. Moreover, this is a realm of judgement which is at least as much about morality as it is about beauty, for 'legitimate use of the body is spontaneously perceived as an index of moral uprightness' (1984 [1979]: 193) – an observation which resonates strongly in the context of reactions in the West today to increasing obesity in the population.

If there is significant differentiation in the products consumed by different classes, even greater difference is signified by the way people organize eating – 'ways of treating food, of serving, presenting and offering it' (1984 [1979]: 193). Bourdieu compared working class and bourgeois meals, contrasting their features. The themes of the working-class meal include an appearance of abundance, a preference to serve with a ladle to avoid much measuring or exact division, different size portions for men and women with second helpings for adult males, putting everything on the table at once to save labour, and using the same plates for different courses, all of which features symbolize freedom, liberty and a relaxed relationship to eating (1984 [1979]: 195). By contrast, the bourgeois household 'is concerned to eat with all due form' (1984 [1979[: 196). Form includes restraint, observing proper sequences especially through separate courses, taking modest amounts of food and cultivated table manners. In comparison with the working class, Bourdieu saw oppositions between the deferred and the immediate, the difficult and the easy, form and substance. The bourgeois modality is 'the expression of a habitus of order, restraint and propriety' (1984 [1979]: 196).[3]

For Bourdieu, *habitus* is a central concept, referring to the ingrained perspectives, experiences and predispositions which one person shares with others in a similar social position. Acting from within the generative schema of a *habitus* results in behaving almost automatically, in an unreflective way that seems like second nature. In *Distinction*, most attention is paid to the characteristics of class *habitus*, though it is shown also that dispositions vary by gender. Food was just one domain among many where tastes confirmed social position, and *Distinction* goes on to show that the divisions in the field of eating find parallels (or 'homologies') in every other realm. Thus Bourdieu did not pay attention to eating as a practice per se, but rather used aspects of food use and the symbolic codification of foods to exemplify everyday life and everyday social divisions. He indicated beyond doubt that in modern societies what is eaten, how it is eaten and how it is prepared are a means of expression of social distinctions. However, that insight was deployed less as a way to develop or illuminate theories of practice, and more as a contribution to cultural sociology and social stratification. Thus neither Bourdieu nor Sahlins provide a systematic conceptual apparatus for the analysis of eating which explicitly or intentionally exploits the potential of theories of practice in this domain.

Two proposals for a more direct and general organizing principle of analysis have been proposed within sociology. The first, arising initially from the work of Lévi-Strauss, concerns *gustemes*. Ilmonen (2011: ch. 7) defined *gustemes* as 'rule-like principles governing food choices, though they are not followed slavishly in every situation. The most significant examples are the distinctions between *everyday and festive* food and *breakfast, lunch and dinner* (Douglas 1984: 15; Goode, Theophano and Curtis 1984: 211)'. Ilmonen makes partially effective use of the notion in trying to establish the nature of the 'cultural frame of reference' which, he postulates, lies behind food choice. One response might be 'how do we know that these are the most significant of *gustemes* and how could we tell if new and equally important ones had emerged?' Arguably, for instance, location is equally significant in the twenty-first century. Also, cultural frames of reference change with the passage of time. Another limitation of this formulation is that it focuses entirely on mental constructs that order our map of culinary possibilities. Lévi-Strauss is famous for saying that 'food is good to think with', but food may be equally good to eat. A focus for analysis which addresses, in addition, the material and the bodily processes associated with ingestion is needed.[4]

Neither is the latter requirement for understanding the corporeal aspects of eating ever likely to be provided by the second alternative organizing principle – the meal. Sociology has always considered the social organization of eating occasions to be of utmost importance.

The mainstays of the theoretical heritage – Simmel, Elias and Douglas – emphasized the fundamental role and the formal aspects of the organization of eating together. This has resulted in the meal having become the most central of all sociological topics (Wood 1994). This has greatly enhanced our understanding of the social role of eating, and the breaking down of the meal into its component parts – matters of timing, format, content, and social organization – has generated many vital insights. The meal gives us an appreciation of the importance of the social situations and social relations which structure what is still the most central institutional form of eating occasion. However, more can be said about eating than most sociological accounts of meals have cared to consider. Not only do they ignore entirely the alimentary and physiological aspects of ingestion, but they also rarely consider its relation to other matters like sourcing, preparation or inter-subjective justification of taste.

Sahlins, Bourdieu, Ilmonen and Douglas have explored different dimensions of the process of eating. Sahlins's concern is how cultures determine what shall pass as food. Bourdieu is more interested in how different groups of people get access to acceptable foods, while also paying attention to how people take food into the body through the mouth. Both Ilmonen and Douglas focus on the role of the social occasion in determining choice of foods. Taken together these four accounts go some way to mapping out what needs to be explained by a general theory of eating. They identify different dimensions of the activity and point to associations between them. All help to build a general or comprehensive account which would then, it seems to me, require the development of a set of concepts that could capture the interrelationships between the food which is consumed, bodily incorporation and social occasion. These constitute three dimensions for examination by any general theory of eating. I will therefore review selectively concepts which have been used to populate these dimensions with a view to formulating a coherent set of concepts to account for how people eat. In doing so, I bear in mind that for theories of practice this is a matter of uncovering the basic elements of performances.

Elementary Concepts

Any general sociological theory of eating needs to explain the relationship between foods consumed, bodily processes and social arrangements. These are the basic elements which a sociological explanation of performances of eating must address. I review some of the available subsidiary concepts that have been used to describe eating and consider their meanings and their merits. The general purpose of honing concepts in this manner is to improve description, understanding and explanation of phenomena of interest. The objective is to make it possible to speak clearly, fluently, precisely and unambiguously about the process of eating.

The ultimate proof of the superiority of one set of concepts over another is its capacity to give better and broader descriptions and explanations. However, at the point of initial construction and framing of concepts, it is only possible to demonstrate that some 'raw' data can be fitted into the categories by illustrating that the categories can reveal accurately some distinctive aspects of eating. To that end, I draw on material from several empirical inquiries in which I have been involved. Contingently, therefore, illustrations are primarily drawn from studies of Britain, but most of the processes and mechanisms discussed have no such narrow geographical limits. In this chapter, a study of cultural consumption in the United Kingdom, the Cultural Capital and Social Exclusion (CCSE) project, provides occasional evidence.[5]

Events and Occasions

The interpretive social sciences have been particularly concerned with and are adept at dealing with the many social functions and meanings of eating, and especially of eating together. Anthropology has pored over the cultural variability of the rules of commensality, as well as the ritual features of meal organization and their role in differential allocation of food. Sociology has also typically introduced the social elements of eating via the concept of the meal, with attention especially focused on meal patterns and family meals.

Sociologists are attracted to the meal partly because of the routine, regular and collective observance of mealtimes. Meal patterns constitute a very strong example of collective behaviour. Evidence from time-use studies reveals population-wide patterns of sequence and scheduling (Saint Pol 2006; Kjaernes 2001; Southerton, Díaz-Méndez and Warde 2012). From another angle, meals are also occasions which constitute a sequence of meaningful and regular punctuations in daily life (Zerubavel 1981). Societal routines, which revolve around the regular sequencing of daily practices such as work, recreation and sleep, give eating a specific place in daily schedules.

Family meals have been important for their focus on intimacy and bonding, on the one hand, and on power and exploitation on the other. They also provide a model of the coincidence of food content and social setting. The proper family meal was defined in terms of the coincidence of the appropriate occupant of the provider role, the companions, the setting and the structured content of the main course (Charles and Kerr 1988; Murcott 1983). This model of the family meal allowed sociologists to commandeer a popularly identified crisis tendency, the de-structuration of meals. Sometimes this is presented as a matter of threat to commensality, as in France, and sometimes of moral decline, as in Britain. The empirical trends are much contested. However, to have this model serve as the general template for the occasion of eating has become analytically counterproductive. Snacking, eating alone, eating away from home and eating informally suggest that the family meal presents too specific and narrow a focus. Moreover, 'the meal' is a slippery concept because of its dual reference to content and occasion, both to foods that are ingested and to the encompassing social arrangements of an event involving location, time and companions. It tends to conflate food content and social occasion.

Although the meal has served well to draw attention to the social aspects of eating, analytically it can be broken down into some more basic elements. One move has been to see the meal as only one type of eating event. Not all occasions for eating can now be designated as meals. Mary Douglas (1972; Douglas and Nicod 1974) recognized this when proposing that the *event* rather than the meal be adopted as the generic unit of analysis. In her terms, the meal had a socially structured form and should be distinguished from unstructured episodes (Douglas and Nicod 1974).[6] This allowed her subsequently to isolate the structural features of the ways foods are combined for social and symbolic effect. It does indeed seem best not to presume other contexts for ingestion as degraded or imperfect forms of the family dinner and instead to isolate the specificity of different types of eating episode. The concept of event has been effectively exploited as a methodological procedure, rather than as theoretical proposition, when survey respondents are asked what they ate during a day without presupposing the following of a conventional sequence of named episodes (see Kjaernes 2001). However, this move poses some challenges for sociological analysis, not least because sociology is not very well equipped to deal with events. Sociology lacks a language of occasions, as for instance DeLanda's (2006) discussion of unique particulars reveals. Yet eating is episodic, and it proceeds as a series of performances of delimited events or occasions which make sense partly because they have time-space coordinates.

A primary source of regularity is the framing of events via classificatory schema which unite places and times. Eating events can be defined by their temporal and spatial characteristics, by timing and location, for example:

- Lunch – out
- Brunch – café
- Monday dinner – home
- Snack – street
- Christmas dinner – family home

Potentially, a wide range of types of occasion (for these are the basic modalities of recognizable social occasions) derives from the cross-classification of timing and location.

Timing is most frequently symbolized and discussed through the name of the event. The terms for meals in Britain, for instance, are many: breakfast, second breakfast, elevenses, dinner, lunch, afternoon tea, high tea, evening meal, formal dinner, supper, midnight feast. The class system of industrial Britain determined that the working class ate 'dinner' in the middle of the day and 'tea' in the early evening after work, typically around 5 pm or 6 pm. Dinner was the major meal, but tea, while secondary, usually involved hot cooked food. The middle class, by contrast, had lunch in the middle of the day and a more substantial family dinner in the evening, somewhat later than 6 pm. Thus both the terminology referring to meals, which recognized the range of appropriate occasions, and the practical organization of the daily round of eating varied. Different groups used different terms, ones which register different rhythms, sequences and formats, rather than identifying specific food content. Thus are elements orchestrated into structured eating regimes. So while the understanding that occasions are the component parts of eating regimes is widely shared, their types and forms are differentially combined.

Also, sequence matters. One could not have breakfast after having had dinner, nor dessert before appetizer. Although the exact hour at which a given named meal occurs varies from country to country and over time historically, sequencing (and periods of time between meals) is fairly rigid. Relevant timings inhere not merely in the daily round but extend across the week, the year or even a lifetime, including Christmas dinner, marriage breakfast, funeral wake, and so on. How rigidly the sequence is superimposed upon calendar or clock time is variable. The much-admired article by Rotenberg (1981), describing the five-meal daily pattern typical of Vienna in the later nineteenth century, exemplifies the normative force of socially binding and shared sequencing of eating events. Regimes, however, vary seasonally as well as locally, with peasants in early modern Europe, for example, taking three meals in summer but only two in winter. Very strongly shared communal patterning of eating events is probably no longer in evidence anywhere in Europe, but some countries are more collectively routinized than others. For example, a significantly greater proportion of the population of Spain eat lunch and dinner at the same hour than is the case in Britain (Southerton, Díaz-Méndez and Warde 2012). Nevertheless, there remains a recognizable hierarchy of eating events, rather as Douglas described it, with more important events having more elaborate formats and more prestigious foods.

Second, location has become increasingly important as part of the definition of eating events. Key basic contemporary spatial coordinates distinguish eating at home and eating away from home. Implicitly, it was long assumed that the family meal would always occur in the same domestic setting, the domicile of the elementary (nuclear, or perhaps extended through co-residence) family. In actual fact, the same kin members may eat together in different homes and, important now, they may eat together in a café or restaurant.[7] Once a preserve of the rich, the growing popularity of eating out as a recreational activity in western societies is one of the most significant developments affecting the practice of eating, arguably a change as consequential as the globalization of food supply and the emergence of supermarket chains (Warde and Martens 2000). Its implications are not yet thoroughly documented, but it has major consequences for culinary knowledge, domestic cookery and domestic organization, diffusion of new tastes, and definitions of commensality and companionship.

A third and vital feature of the event concerns who is present. The hierarchical dimension of events is profoundly marked and reinforced by expectations of types of companion. The temporal regime alone does not determine the nature of a specific performance. Formats and content tend to vary systematically, depending on whether a person eats alone, eats with members of the elementary family (and whether the nuclear household includes children), eats with extended kin or close friends or eats with colleagues and acquaintances.[8] The rules for such events vary, with meals becoming more elaborate in the context of honoured guests or occasional visits by close relatives; for example, a study of feasts in 2010 showed that the most elaborate celebratory family dinners were ones where adult siblings were present.[9] Historical and anthropological research shows that eating events are arranged in accordance with conventions regarding appropriate companions. This may mean: regulating gender relations, determining when or whether men and women should eat together; marking of generational relationships, as when in Britain nannies used to give upper-class children meals in the nursery, rather than have them eat with parents; or an obligation to feed strangers, which obtains in some societies but would be unthinkable in others. Companionship, classified in terms of categories of social affinity, remains of critical significance. Discernible social differentiation occurs on all three dimensions – timing, location and company. It matters greatly, now as before, with whom a person eats. Getting the appropriate people together, at the proper time for a particular type of meal is precisely the practical skill of arranging an event.

Alice Julier's *Eating Together: Food, Friendship and Inequality* (2013), a study of domestic hospitality in the United States, captures well the nuances and the importance of commensality. It concentrates more on hosting than being a guest, but, since most hosts are also at other times guests within the same social circle, their manner of provisioning reveals understandings of the procedures and standards expected within the group. Looking at different events for entertaining non-kin, ranging from the dinner party to pot-lucks, she demonstrates that class, ethnic and gender composition impacts upon how eating together is arranged and managed. When the event is controlled and orchestrated by a host couple, the pattern of interaction and the type of social capital developed are different from that generated at an event organized jointly by several members of a community or voluntary association. In almost every case, the exception being competitive males among the professional middle class cooking for dinner parties, sociability and conviviality takes precedence over the aesthetic quality of the menu. In this regard, women are more sensitive to, and take more responsibility for, acts of care for visitors. Making sure that guests are comfortable, ensuring that they will be in congenial company and achieving an appropriately convivial atmosphere is very much the domain of hostesses. This requires, in addition, however, ensuring that food is appropriate to the gathered company, for the type of food served mediates social interactions and facilitates relationships. So while the aesthetic quality of food expected varies markedly across social circles, all seek to make the food fit the social situation.

Specific social and cultural meaning is attached to the performance of eating occasions from the permutation and juxtaposition of time, place and company. Occasions are neither equivalent nor randomly ordered. They provide a basis of social routine. When, where and with whom an event takes place will reveal some of the considerations which, usually tacitly, subtend its character. For example, the presence or absence of children at an event affects formality, tempo, duration and content (Cheng et al. 2007; Yates and Warde forthcoming). While there are no simple or rigid rules of correspondence between type of event and food consumed, there are shared understandings which restrict the range of foods which might be eaten at different types of occasion. To detect the form and substance of such patterns in contemporary situations is one of the most difficult of empirical tasks.

Food, Menus and Dishes

Eating occasions demand food. But food is a multifaceted phenomenon and the term has many referents. The foods that people eat pass through many stages. Foodstuffs have to be grown, exchanged and prepared. That, however, is a story of production, not of final consumption. Thereafter, individuals consume a very small proportion of all imaginable preparations. How they select among the innumerable options is an intriguing question. It has long been recognized that groups and populations define only some edible items as food. From among acceptable foodstuffs, daily selection is an intricate matter. The most common explanation of what is selected is personal choice, but that leaves much unexplained. Events appear to attract specific foods and restrict choice. For example, eating leftovers for dinner is frequently explained by the absence of a significant companion. Thus a CCSE interviewee used his partner being away from home the previous day as a matter-of-fact piece of background information to explain the content of an improvised dinner which consisted of 'quorn, vegetarian meat, like minced up with mangetout, carrots and a tomato base, cumin'. Whether food is eaten with due decorum around a table or casually while working at the computer – with all that that does for bodily comportment and the rhythm of incorporation – shapes what is eaten. How, then, should we conceptualize the process of selection?

No event or occasion, even the most ritualized and symbolically significant, automatically or predictively prescribes exactly what shall be eaten.[10] Yet neither content nor sequence of foodstuffs is arbitrary. So while a satisfactory account requires some explication of both the content of foods consumed and their ordering, observed patterns have proved very difficult to specify in terms of underlying rules or principles.

Douglas (1972) made one of the most impressive attempts to link food with occasions by positing correspondence between parallel hierarchical ranking of food preparations and events. For Douglas, more elaborate meals, which might mean more luxurious foodstuffs or more courses, are typically served on more important occasions. Thus Christmas dinner is more significant, in both culinary and social terms, than a weekday meal, and it prescribes in the United Kingdom several courses, typically a main dish of luxurious meat, several vegetables and multiple trimmings. Less elevated, ordinary events have fewer courses, dishes with fewer ingredients and require much less preparation and expense. The number of courses and the structure of the foodstuffs served at each sitting are the key indicators of symbolic order in the British system of eating events. Her somewhat eccentric abstract notation to capture the 'marked' aspects of a meal has occasionally been redeployed to effectively re-describe food combinations (Julier 2013; Marshall 2005).[11] Perhaps, however, the more abstract concepts of staples, centrepieces and trimmings, which Douglas also employs, allow greater historical coverage and flexibility. However, both are somewhat culturally inert regarding the substantive culinary properties of what is served. A more precise and elegant conception specifically for the purpose of analysing the food content of eating events would be welcome.

Cultural analysis shows that foodstuffs are highly symbolic. The association of red meat with masculinity is a much-used example (Fiddes 1991; Lupton 1996). Roland Barthes (1973 [1957]), master in the semiotic analysis of popular images, decoded representations of comestibles, like steak and chips, and wine and milk, to reveal the patriotic, national and social meanings beneath. The manner of presentation of food is perhaps even more significant. Knowing what to eat, and especially what to serve to others to eat, is a matter of considerable delicacy, the rules of which are subject to spatio-temporal and socio-demographic variation. Lay vocabularies make sense of these issues with terms like 'food', 'dish', 'course', 'menu' and 'meal', none of which are ideal for analytic purposes. The sociology of food and eating has adopted technical concepts such as food content and meal format to capture two separate sources of symbolic effects. It matters how foodstuffs are combined together and how they are sequenced as portions of food. Whether soup comes first or last, whether one eats cheese before dessert or not, whether all foodstuffs appear at the same instant or whether they are serially presented, are defining features of culinary and dining regimes.

'Menu' is not used as a technical concept in social science but has some promise as a term to capture food content and meal format. The menu is most obviously a device of the catering industry which announces all the items available for consumption, usually structured in terms of a series of courses or types of dish. In ordinary parlance, it is used only rarely with reference to domestic events, and then probably for more formal occasions. However, from the individual diner's point of view, the total consumption at any event might be re-described in terms of a personal menu. A personal menu (experienced, observed or written) could be considered as a recording of food content and the order of proceedings at any given event. Even a mundane dinner has structure and content which could be represented as a menu analogous to that of the restaurant.

In a restaurant, the menu is a catalogue of the 'dishes' potentially available, usually grouped as a proposed sequence of courses.[12] A dish involves the assembly of foodstuffs into a portion presented for consumption. Reference to the dish usefully reminds us that processes of production and provisioning, or preparation and combination, are prerequisites to the moment of consumption. By dishes, I of course mean not items of crockery but edible portions of prepared foodstuffs, culinary preparations symbolically recognizable in a given cultural context. The prepared dish thus links provision, by whatever route, to consumption. Dishes may comprise a single item or a combination of items.[13] Configurations of dishes underpin menus. Dishes listed may be compulsory, or the diner might be invited to make a selection. The list of dishes may propose them in series, as in a three-course meal, or simultaneously, as with a smorgasbord or thali. Menus name foodstuffs and their combinations, and categorize them in terms of the sequence in which they should be addressed. While recognizing the specificity of the commercial context, the menu and its dishes provide a conceptual template for both form and content of food consumption.

In the contemporary West, discussions of what to eat or serve increasingly revolve around the names of dishes. What we swallow is mostly the substance of specific dishes – boiled beef and carrots, lemon cheesecake. Cooks typically (though not always) prepare dishes, and restaurants (always) put dishes on their menus. Much of the proliferating output of professional food writers focuses on dishes, which are the stock-in-trade of television programmes, cookery books, recipe books, restaurant columns, and so on. Dishes are basic products of cooking, used to describe the food put on plates in front of the diner.[14] The world knows many dishes and a significant proportion have been codified in recipe books, which have been a principal vehicle for the classification of dishes. Names are differentially recognizable; Burnett (1989: 312) for example reported a survey in 1976 showing that less than half of Britons recognized foreign dishes such as chilli con carne and moussaka, although the proportion was significantly greater than twenty years earlier. Dishes have symbolic overtones, and may evoke repulsion, excitement or gratification. Giving to children their favourite dish or to adults 'comfort food' symbolizes social relationships of intimacy and belonging, in which cases delivery of nourishment seems a minor consideration. Dishes also display a categorical character. For example, recipes are compiled to fashion a sense of regional, ethnic and national belonging; Appadurai (1988) argued that nationhood in India was promoted among the middle class through construction of a national cuisine transmitted through recipe books. One tendency since the Second World War, according to both Panayi (2008) and Moehring (2008), has been for national culinary identity to be emphasized through the compilation of recipes classified as belonging to different culinary traditions. Thus the conventional selection and combination of dishes is deemed capable of conveying intense symbolic meaning. Dishes also have a hierarchical dimension. Some items carry status and prestige, as with honouring occasions like Thanksgiving in the United States through a conventional menu with turkey as its centrepiece. Other dishes are merely workaday. The vocabulary, syntax and grammar of the world of dishes are socially and culturally complex.

Nevertheless, it is worth recalling Giard's (1998) observation that dishes for domestic consumption, as for instance recorded in personal recipe collections, often do not have names. At home, many unauthorized combinations of courses and dishes occur. Interviewees in the CCSE study[15] were asked what they ate for dinner yesterday, almost all reported only one course, plus a drink of fruit juice, tea or coffee.[16] While the format was basic and common, some reported elaborate compositions, with the single main course having up to half a dozen component dishes. A working-class couple in their thirties had eaten roast turkey, roast potatoes, sweet potato, carrots and other vegetables, while a secondary school teacher had accompanied her beef bourguignon with rosemary potatoes and vegetables. Some were simpler, for example sausage, mash and gravy, chicken pie and chips, sandwiches or macaroni cheese. South Asian interviewees tended to report meals which had more than an average number of components: a driving instructor in his forties, for example, had had frozen fish and chips, chapattis, vegetables and lentils, followed by coffee. Many of the personal menus described were undoubtedly hybrid from the point of view of classificatory systems based on the authenticity or purity of nationally defined cuisines. Among the composite dishes that were described were: Chinese pork, stir-fry vegetables and mashed potato; potato mashed with Stilton cheese, pork steaks, chilli and teriyaki sauce; fish in batter, pasta and vegetables; as well as fish and chips, chapattis, vegetables and lentils. Most reported meals had a structure of meat plus carbohydrate plus vegetables (or conceptualized more abstractly, centre plus staple plus trimmings) including: braising steak, potatoes and carrots; couscous, broccoli, venison burger and steak; roast pork, stuffing, broccoli, cheese, sweetcorn, roast and mashed potatoes.[17] However, several households had culinary traditions deriving from South Asia where it is common to have more than one centrepiece dish; one meal had consisted of chapattis, salad, chutney, fish and a lentil dish, another chicken and meatballs (with mixed vegetables). Such a meal resembles more the older format, 'service a la Française', where many dishes appeared on the table simultaneously, rather than the modern European 'service à la Russe' which proceeds one dish at a time. Such evidence shows that, in contrast to models of the three-course meal – the format in which a restaurant in Britain would typically present dishes for dinner – domestic meals were simpler and less formally structured. It is also indicative of the multicultural character of food selection in the United Kingdom in the twenty-first century and of variation between culinary cultures.

In sum, the implication is that the number of possible permutations of dishes capable of forming a single menu, and therefore even more an annual sequence of menus, is prodigious. For the majority of events, there are many possible acceptable foods. Yet, despite almost infinite freedom of choice in principle, what people eat exhibits detectable patterns. The organization and ordering of dishes is a matter of convention and some indication of loose adherence to culinary traditions or systems. However, identifying an event as a particular type of occasion may provide strong guidelines governing what should not be eaten and what sequence should not be followed. Selection is a disciplined activity, one subject to many restrictions. Limitations of resources, control and imagination, when married to processes of situational entailment which make current preferences contingent upon earlier ones, make it likely that selection is de facto constrained (Warde and Martens 1998). In this light, the trope of the menu as a device for restricting choice, allowing a limited selection from a limited set of dishes, organized in sequence, may prove useful. The distribution and order of dishes divulge the social importance of occasion. Local conventions identify more or less which, if selected, would be fit for purpose.

Until recently, the pleasures and privileges of selection and symbolic expression were probably not a very pressing matter except among the very rich. Necessity supervenes when money is scarce and affordable food seasonal. However, one outcome of the recent aestheticization of eating, inspired especially by the spread of eating out, is that dishes have become more sharply thematized. As a function of globalization and commodification, people have broadened their recognition of the range of dishes and have extended their experience of formerly exotic preparations. Dishes gain higher profiles because they are the stock-in-trade of professional food writers and broadcasters, because recipe books have become much more specialized and because restaurant menus are catalogues of names of dishes which many people read, thereby broadening their recognition of the range of dishes. Selecting dishes is a key part of the practical skill involved in achieving a suitable match between menu and occasion, for many permutations are possible. Variation on the three dimensions of timing, location and companions, singly and in combination, when married to dish and menu selection ineluctably generates social differentiation. The picture becomes even more complex when issues of bodily incorporation are added.

Incorporation

Wilk (2004) observed that the grand metaphor for the analysis of consumption has been the process of eating. He objected that this was problematic since some of the more bodily processes associated with eating, including hunger, chewing and swallowing, digestion and excretion, are not features transposable to other acts of consumption. Thus, he argued, eating will often be a misleading metaphor. By the same token, however, when considering eating itself, such processes should engage the attention of the social scientist. Yet most sociological work brackets off physiological and alimentary processes as topics for other sciences to examine. As Poulain (2012) observed, sociology has been reluctant to study eating because it was not thought by Durkheim to be sufficiently clearly a '*social* fact'. One early and rare exception to this general rule was Marcel Mauss's (1973 [1935]) formulation of the concept of 'techniques of the body'. Issues of embodiment were subsequently addressed in the sociology of health and illness and feminism, with eating disorders having some prominence. But the perceived crises in the food system since the 1990s, particularly in relation to obesity, reversed the tendency in the sociology of food to ignore bodily matters and to focus on physical manifestations in and on the body. More recently, social aspects of sensory experience have come to be appreciated with potential for understanding the rather less visually apparent physiological mechanisms behind experiences of tasting (Davis 2012; Korsmeyer 2005; Sutton 2010).

An integrated account of eating might be expected to synthesize knowledge of the physiological, alimentary and sensory processes associated with it and demonstrate their intersection with the social and aesthetic aspects of events and dishes. Such an amalgamation has yet to be achieved. As criticisms of the cultural turn declared, the material aspects and functions of the body were neglected in cultural analysis (Reckwitz 2002a). Jackson and Scott (2014: 566) note a persistent 'tension between essentialising the natural body and treating the body as a social construction'. Reviewing the emergence of the sociology of the body from studies of health and medicine in the 1980s, they recommend a route for sociology which runs between seeing the body, its functions and its capacities, either purely through the social constructionist lens or as an unalterable natural entity. They commend Crossley's (2001) resolution, which draws together both social interactionist and phenomenological elements to capture subjective aspects of embodiment in the context of a constructive development of Bourdieu's *habitus*. For analytic purposes, one resource for food studies operating in a practice-theoretical mode is some excellent work on how skilled performers learn and refine embodied procedural habits (e.g. Noble and Watkins 2003; Sudnow 1978; Wacquant 2004). An overall reconstruction with particular relevance to eating might also draw on more recent work on the senses which discusses links between the sensory capacities of the body and the interpretative aspects of tasting food, where an emphasis on synaesthesia (the combined effects of the senses) aligns mental and neurophysiological processes (Sutton 2010).

Evidence concerning eating disorders throws into high relief the normal and taken-for-granted role of learned bodily techniques in the process of eating. In cases both of extreme obesity dealt with by surgery and of anorexia nervosa, recovering patients perforce re-learn how to eat. Undergoing a medical operation to introduce a mechanical tie to reduce the volume of the stomach inevitably entails a radical change in eating performance, involving new routines, habits and tastes.[18] The operation requires that eating episodes thereafter have to be frequent, involve small quantities and therefore usually be brief, and also that some bulky and fatty foods become inedible or indigestible. Tensions arise for social participation. Other people eat different foods and take longer over fewer events, compromising both the commensality and the shared culinary grammar which underpin social membership. The temporal rhythms of society run counter to the personal capacities of the reformed stomach, imposing a severe social cost by dealing with extreme obesity in this manner (see also Throsby 2012). The negative social effect is a consequence of the fact that bodies get used to the rhythms associated with the sequential ordering of routine eating events and tend to protest if the intervals between events are too long or too short.

Such effects of disrupted routine occur in a less severe form in more mundane circumstances. Kristensen and Holm (2006) in a qualitative study in Denmark, show that the temporal organization of meals directly affects not only types of food consumed, but even the feeling of being satisfied. Darmon and Warde (forthcoming), examining the adjustments made by partners in cross-national Anglo-French couples, show that eating meals at unfamiliar times of the day is among the most difficult of transitions, with the different lunch arrangements in the two countries causing difficulties in synchronizing appetites for evening meals. The disjuncture between the rhythms of a societal meal pattern and long-established personal embodied habits creates a source of tension.

In another instructive study, Mabel Gracia Arnaiz (2009) examined interventions to rehabilitate women suffering from anorexia in Spain. Again, the cure was seen by all as a matter of the patients literally learning to eat. Techniques varied depending on whether the problem was regarded as a psychological disorder or a nutritional problem. Nutritionists tended mostly to advise very strict dietary regimes; regimented mealtimes, strict meal formats (three-course meals several times a day), and scientifically regulated meal content, with dishes defined strictly by nutritional content and balance. As Gracia Arnaiz points out, partly through the words of her interviewees, such therapies lacked appreciation of the social nature of the initial problem – arguably the disciplined nature of the cure looks little different from the cause – and patients returned to everyday life find it in practice extremely difficult to follow the rules insisted upon in the institutionalized therapeutic context of treatment. '[N]utritional recommendations are based on a fairly inflexible dietary pattern...[and] demand a daily routine which is difficult to carry out' (2009: 195). Recovery from both obesity and anorexia carries with it major difficulties of readjustment to the mundane constraints of provisioning and commensality, revealing, per contra, how embodied aspects of eating performances are normally managed.

To diet has become normal. A desire to be slim – despite the difficulty of achieving that condition – is almost universal in the twenty-first-century West. This is considered relevant to the aesthetics of appearance, good health and moral rectitude; fatness is seen as moral turpitude, a slim body as evidence of self-discipline and self-control (Offer 2006). Dietary regimes are targeted precisely at shaping and regulating the corporeal body. Dominant nutritional discourses about healthy eating merge with strategies for controlling body weight. The general failure of long-term exercises in restraint, like the weight-loss diet, is sociologically most instructive. As Crossley (2004) observed, involuntary weight gain is an indubitable and prominent social fact and is an excellent case study for understanding the interaction between biological and social processes. He proposed that gaining weight 'tends to operate in the blind spots of agency', a condition which ' "creeps on", largely unnoticed, coming as something of a shock to the agent when it is noticed after the intervention of a mediator', but is for social reasons remarkably difficult to reverse (Crossley 2004: 246, 242).

Perhaps less commonly observed, forms of dietary regulation have emerged which deem there to be some special fit between specific food items and the individual body. Professional consultants can pronounce that you have a body which does not deal well with blackberries and halibut. People increasingly frequently announce food allergies, sometimes legitimized by medical diagnosis (FSA 2014). Caterers for events like conferences routinely enquire whether delegates have special diets or allergies. Packaged products indicate on their labels if the factory of origin also processes nuts. It is unclear whether the physiology of the human body has changed, or whether people in the past simply suffered in silence and ignorance. Possibly it is a new phenomenon caused by the properties of manufactured foodstuffs. Another possibility is that bodies are trained to deal with fewer categories of item. Alternatively, it might be just a by-product of stylization, a consequence of a belief that everyone should consciously adopt an individualized dietary regime as a component of a fashioned lifestyle, the impulse to self-discipline or the search for meaningfulness in the face of gastro-anomie.

Furthermore, populations in the West eat more than before. Eating to satiation, or beyond, was a privilege of the rich in many historical periods. The obesity epidemic implies that, for many, capacity before satiation has increased. This is made possible partly by abundance of accessible foodstuffs and its availability to the populations of rich countries, and partly by changing exercise regimes in societies with sedentary jobs and automobiles. These factors are, however, unlikely to comprise a sufficient explanation (Guthman 2011). Being overweight may possibly also be a function of eating more quickly. In most countries, people spend less time eating than they used to (Warde et al. 2007). Since it is documented that bodies take something like twenty minutes to register satiation, a distinct danger exists that eating more quickly will bypass body regulatory mechanisms for eating a sufficiency rather than a surfeit. Eating quickly is probably best explained in terms of other social processes; the same reasons that are advanced for the expansion of convenience foods probably account for reduced time spent eating or preparing meals (Warde 1999).

When Norbert Elias in his account of the civilizing process described the reform of table manners in fifteenth-century Europe, he was simultaneously describing changing bodily techniques, from the prohibition of spitting to learning the use of a fork. The increased range of food items accompanying twentieth-century globalization has occasioned the use of new implements, and therefore the learning of new body movements, to get food from plate to mouth (see Giard 1998). Early twentieth-century British etiquette books made much of the exceptional acceptability of using fingers when eating chicken – a central issue in table manners in Britain when class differences were detected through the handling of food. The spread of restaurants boasting foreign cuisines has created a situation where food items rare in the British household early in the twentieth century now have to be consumed in public. Pasta, the rice dishes in Asian restaurants, and shellfish pose particular manual management problems because they are difficult to eat in a decorous or comfortable fashion. Such matters also raise issues of social distinction: the ability to eat Chinese food with chopsticks – an activity that I can attest is not second nature to Britons – is seen as an indication of cosmopolitan sophistication in some quarters, and may partly explain the class composition of the clients using them in Chinese restaurants.[19] Getting food into the mouth undoubtedly requires dexterous bodily techniques which are unevenly distributed and change over time.

Posture and bearing also affect pleasure and play a role in defining the occasion. One element of manners is proper bodily hexis. Children are still told to sit up straight and not slouch, to pull the chair into the table and to refrain from leaving elbows sticking out. Such instructions, found in etiquette books about the comportment of the body, are not just a matter of manners but also associated with the material nature of the furniture, tools and utensils related to eating. For example, the use of cutlery involves the embodiment of procedures for graceful and effective manipulation of food that will not upset others, make for easy coexistence at table and keep food on one's own plate.

Dealing with food once in the mouth is also a sign of social position and social distinction. Bourdieu (1984 [1979]) observed that French men do not much like eating fish because the danger of swallowing bones requires that the flesh be processed at the front of the mouth with the tongue, a technique less masculine than the gulp from the back of the mouth. His account of good and vulgar taste in the act of eating compels recognition of culturally differentiated ways of undertaking the physical act of eating and that judgement may be passed about the competence of performance.

The texture of popular foodstuffs has also changed. Affluent western populations probably tackle fewer items that are tough, hard, dry and chewy; hard tack, tough cuts of mature animals and brown rice come to mind. Chewing is a physiological act that varies over time. There was a movement in the early twentieth century, inspired by one Horace Fletcher, to chew foods very much more thoroughly than was the norm then or now (Levenstein 1988: 86ff).[20] While a dietary fad, it reminds us that chewing is a technique and procedure of the body.

Much more attention has been paid to the corporeal than the sensory in sociology, with taste more likely to be treated as an aesthetic than as a tactile, gustatory or sensual matter. The senses have proved hard for sociology to analyse (and often they are treated as a matter of cognition rather than as embodied response). It is increasingly apparent that different national and regional cuisines operate with strongly preferred flavour combinations. Fusion foods and molecular gastronomy aside, the bulk of recipes and culinary recommendation suggest that cuisines can be recognized by the dominant flavour combinations. Olive oil-onion-pepper-tomato means Spain, olive oil-lemon-oregano means Greece, onion-lard-paprika means Hungary, and so on (Rozen 1983). A superb article on food pairing, using social network analysis, shows in much greater detail that the flavour compounds shared by groups of ingredients explain why they are conventionally prepared together, with basic preferences varying from continent to continent and region to region (Ahn et al. 2011). The implication is that people become accustomed to particular flavours, their preferences organized by the perceived palatability of different combinations of flavours. That bodies mostly get used to flavours and tastes might be indicated by the contrary example of pregnant women developing cravings for unusual, and sometimes alien, foodstuffs (Murcott 1988). Changed hormonal states are often invoked to explain the temporary attractiveness of foods which in normal circumstances would be avoided, bearing witness to the routinized and conventional everyday classification of what foods are acceptable. Thus there seems to be an aesthetic-affective dimension to food preferences which is located in the body's capacity for sensory appreciation that extends beyond the conscious selection of dishes at particular meals.

There is increasing discussion of the ramifications of the fact that the sensual experience of eating is not just a matter of the tongue recording the flavours of foodstuffs. Davis (2012: 137) uses the practice of contemporary and highly innovative professional chefs to emphasize the complexity of the mundane processes of tasting. He comments on the fact that 'Chefs around the world are beginning to play with tastes by not only manipulating the sweet, sour, salty, bitter and umami tastes detected by the papillae on the tongue, but also by manipulating the taste>memory>emotion reaction invoked by all sensory perception' (2012: 135). As he says, 'one of the characteristics that distinguish the world's great chefs is their desire (and ability) to manipulate complex sensory relationships, to play with cultural connections to food, to wrangle emotions, and mess with memories all during the course of a restaurant meal' (2012: 137). Taste, smell and flavour are often recorded involuntarily, yet they trigger memories and emotions. Davis maintains that the normally supposed causal direction between taste, memory and emotion can be reversed, and he argues that this is increasingly achieved through appeal and reference to spatial and temporal attributes of foodstuffs. Foods subjected to particular techniques of preservation acquire umami characteristics, and foods conveying the unique flavours of terroir bear the distinguishing marks of their geographic origins. Aesthetic appreciation supplements the senses. Experience of taste can be refined and even reversed by doctoring appearance, carefully constructing context, making visual associations with landscape and the like. Davis uses the ingenious and playful presentation of foods from the repertoires of restaurants adopting the techniques and philosophy of molecular gastronomy (using the often cited examples of Noma and El Bulli) to demonstrate the complex and multifaceted recognition of taste through the body. The manner in which chefs like Redzepi and Adria successfully experiment with the presentation and taste of their dishes demonstrates just how many different bodily procedures combine to generate the capacity for taste. In most daily situations, people are not challenged to enter the gymnastics of decoding sensations that this new culinary movement serves up. But the capacity of the human body to do so when, *in extremis*, exposed to the novel and unusual illustrates the complexity of the process in which the cognitive, the conative and the affective dimensions of tasting intertwine in the experience of eating.

Observations from the area of bodily techniques and processes have not, to my knowledge, yet been systematized. There would be value in so doing, for much regularity is attributable to the sensory and bodily features of eating. This is the realm of important non-cognitive and essentially embodied processes, to which Bourdieu drew attention thirty years ago, but which is yet to be capitalized upon. Bodily technique is integrally connected with both occasions and dishes. For example, discomfiture while eating out is reported to arise from settings being too formal and the requirements for bodily composure too strict (Warde and Martens 2000: 121–31).[21] Or, to take other examples, aesthetic appreciation of novel items with an unusual flavour, or the procedural difficulties of wrestling awkward foodstuffs from plate to mouth, often present trying episodes of bodily incorporation.

Elementary Forms and Performances: An Example

To sum up, occasions, menus and techniques of incorporation constitute the three principal analytic dimensions of performances of eating. This parsimonious set of concepts facilitates description of conventional ways to eat. This formulation is intellectually indebted to earlier sociological accounts but also to second-generation theories of practice. Theories of practice emphasize especially the embodied aspects of eating, understated in most sociological accounts, and also their relationship to the instruments (utensils) used in the process. They also cope readily with the singularity or uniqueness of performances. The number of alternative performances that could be obtained by permutation of these three elements and their component parts is astronomical, hence we have to assume that individuals are not engaged in an exercise of mental computation when they resolve the issue of how to eat. Rather, relatively few options appear to make sense and the remainder – vast ranges of other combinations – are practically irrelevant. Most fundamentally, eating is situated within established patterns of social relations and shared understandings which steer the orchestration of timings, settings and companions in a conventionally recognizable and acceptable manner. Identifying ways in which it is determined what it makes sense to do is examined in subsequent chapters.

Theoretically speaking, then, eating *performances* reside in the orchestration of three foundational elements: events – menus – incorporation. Any episode can be re-described in terms of the alignment of available options. Empirical study therefore seeks regularities, of doing and saying, which may be captured by observation, measurement, interview or testimony. The regularities associated with each element, and the regularity with which they are coupled in specific ways, supply the fundamental elements of a description of the anatomy of different regimes of eating.

According to their own reports, people coordinate their performances, through permutation of social event, culinary products and bodily and sensory experience. People readily transmute a potentially enormously problematic series of decisions into mutually intelligible performances. Let me revisit an example from an interview from the CCSE study of cultural consumption in Britain (Bennett et al. 2009: 167). The interviewee (her pseudonym is Teri) was an educated woman in her forties who lived in London with her two children. The interviewer asked her who prepared the last meal at home, to which she replied: 'I can't remember that far back! God! We must have had something, what day was it yesterday, Thursday. Well it would have been me that prepared it for sure. I can't remember what we had.'

The interviewer persisted by enquiring, 'What did the last meal consist of?' She then continued:

> Oh, Jasmine [small daughter] went to Mike's [father living elsewhere], ah ha. I know what happened. We had a leaving lunch at work so I had a very big lunch and Jake [son] had an afternoon off school so he had, he'd made toasted sandwiches, toasties just before I came in, so I made him cheese and biscuits and I had leftovers from the night before which was – ok, the day before we had had sausages, broccoli and potatoes. And Jake was in a bad mood and didn't eat his, which is why I had them last night. (Teri)

There are many things that might be said about this short extract, which occurred in the context of a much longer interview about many different types of cultural activity and cultural taste. One reaction might be that this is a disorganized and rather scatty woman, with a poor memory and no penchant for planning a household food regime. Alternatively, it could be read as a series of highly skilled improvisations in response to contingent and unexpected circumstances, a woman typically 'juggling' (Thompson 1996) labour, time and family responsibilities. However, the process may be more one of responding to circumstances in light of practical sense than making decisions and choices. Things fall into place. Yet the outcomes are not unpalatable; the performance occasions neither regret nor apology. Arguably, while she is not thoroughly in control, her familiarity with the conventions of the Practice ensures an acceptable outcome.

Many of the features of the practice of eating are revealed in even this short quotation. Clearly, what was eaten yesterday was not initially uppermost in Teri's mind. This may in part be because this was a minor event which she had limited responsibility for planning or orchestrating.[22] The means by which she remembers is through recalling the time-space paths of household members, suggesting that this meal was first and foremost a social and familial event. In passing, she refers to all three of the elementary alimentary forms. There are events: a leaving lunch at work; a daughter visiting her father for tea. There are dishes: toasted sandwiches; cheese and biscuits; and sausages, broccoli and potatoes. And there are bodily conditions: 'a very big lunch'; and a bad mood. The story is tied together by the interweaving of the personnel, events and foodstuffs. Notably, sequences are very important. What Teri had for lunch affected her preparation of an evening meal; and an afternoon off school explained Jake's menu. Also, there is an implication throughout that the household does have a normal routine – and indeed Teri subsequently described a weekday pattern. In this household, eating may often be the lynchpin in the sequencing of activities but it is not always, and departure from routine does not inspire remorse.

Conclusion

My contention is that eating can be described by reference to three elementary forms. If this constitutes a scientific object, it is a conception of eating not itself generated by any particular theory. Scholars of different theoretical persuasions might deal with food consumption in these terms. It is a framework for description and data collection without any inherent theoretical loading. It claims no specification of what causes any relationship between the elements. Rather, it presents a scaffold around which an explanation might be built for why different populations orchestrate their performances in different ways. To date, it is rare to find sociological accounts which fully dress the scaffold. Mary Douglas, for example, could be deemed to have focused only on events and menus. The dominant orthodox approach from medical and nutrition sciences concentrates on menus and bodily incorporation. Pierre Bourdieu in *Distinction* did address all three dimensions, but not in great detail.

It remains to be seen in subsequent chapters whether using a theory of practice can give a productive and distinctive explanation of how and why ordinary people orchestrate their performances. The contention is that anyone involved in eating will make a permutation from variants of each element when mounting a performance. People combine elements in diverse ways, and from their reports of behaviour and their justifications for their conduct can be derived an understanding of the relationship between the performances and the Practice. Performances, as Teri's experience suggests, are singular and particular, each being an event unique in space and time. They exhibit considerable variation along their several dimensions. Orchestration through coupling together of the three elements is mostly achieved with little fuss in everyday life. People intuit or understand what goes with what – which dishes are suitable for breakfast, what kinds of foods in combination are most effective for maintaining health, whom it is appropriate to entertain at an elaborate dinner, and so forth (including whether dogs can be served, and how quickly one can get rid of one's guests). This capacity for orchestration is marvelled at by social scientists, treated as evidence of forms of tacit knowledge, or even genetic or evolutionary dispositions. Actors, in the normal course of everyday life, seem to be able to align their performances without conscious deliberation or self-questioning. They may, if confronted in interview, be able to give a partial account of their understanding and behaviour, but orchestration seems to occur as a matter of practical sense, of knowing how to go on, without thinking. The theoretical puzzle is how this is normally achieved. The remainder of the book attempts to throw some light on the matter.

5

Organizing Eating

Disorderly Eating?

The question that has driven more social scientific research projects than any other in the field is: 'Why do people eat what they do?'. Given the range of possible sources for diversity identified in the previous chapter – which even a small number of illustrative instances confirms – this is a difficult question to answer. The range and the variation in the performances of eating in Britain present at first glance a very complex picture and have led to projections and predictions implying increasingly disorderly and disorganized behaviour. It is particularly difficult to answer if one adopts the orthodox notion that this is a matter of the free choice of individuals. That any sort of order might be fashioned from the chaos of available options must then be a source of wonderment. Analyses of consumption have often assumed that such arrays of possibility are a source of uncertainty and anxiety. Ever-expanding options make the act of choosing daunting. Besides the risks associated with the unknown, the conundrum, so nicely expressed by Giddens, that now 'there is no choice but to choose' such that the consumer will be held accountable for her choice, provokes anxiety. In the field of food studies, the most charming and challenging expression of this more generic problem was advanced under the concept of *gastro-anomie* by Claude Fischler (1980).

Gastro-anomie is a crisis of gastronomy, 'the sets of rules, norms, meanings associated with food and acting as constraints upon food habits' (Fischler 1980: 947). Gastro-anomie is a condition where:

> Modern individuals are left without clear socio-cultural cues as to what their choice should be, as to when, how and how much they should eat. Food selection and intake are now increasingly a matter of individual, not social, decisions.... But individuals lack reliable criteria to make sense of these decisions and therefore they experience a growing sense of anxiety. (Fischler 1980: 948)

For Fischler, the lost past was one where food habits were 'shaped by coherent, traditional, matrilocal, culinary patterns' (1980: 949) and, in their absence, reliable collective criteria for making selection decisions are unavailable. This diagnosis has come to serve as a way to understand the hyper-modern predicament in western societies more generally (Ascher 2005). The pivot of Fischler's account is the omnivore's paradox – a biological necessity for eating many different foods, which poses a threat since finding new types may be as physically dangerous as it is aesthetically pleasing. He identifies various pressures, arising from the industrial food system and its state regulation, which destabilize earlier resolutions to the paradox and which make people worry about eating.

In general, the diagnosis makes most sense in a country like France where there is a tradition of gastronomy – a scholarly and formalized, though perpetually contested, compilation of the rules, conventions and possibilities of fine eating. Sociologically, however, there might be objection that the scenario overestimates the extent of individualization and its propensity to generate anxiety. Another possible problem with this formulation is that it pays too much attention to personal knowledge and the mental processing of information, suggesting that the difficulty is one of making quasi-rational decisions about what to eat. A third issue is that it is primarily focused on the content of dishes, rather than other aspects of the elements which stabilize eating patterns. A further objection, explored at some length by Jean-Pierre Poulain (2002a, 2002b), is that the current condition is one of pluralism rather than anomie; a single authoritative and presumably traditional model of how best to eat has given way to several alternative but equivalent modes.

Fischler and Poulain are both partially correct. No wholeheartedly agreed upon authoritative template for the practice of eating is adopted by whole populations. Some people are uncertain about the best way to eat and are prone to worry, silently or explicitly. Others, usually partly mobilized behind a banner or movement, proclaim allegiance to and attempt to stick very rigidly to the tenets of specific dietary regimes – stretching from vegetarianism and veganism, and Slow Food, through commercial weight-control programmes, to following state nutritional guidelines. It is not entirely unreasonable to think of these as responses to an excess of choice and a fear of anomie, but the proportion of the British population expressing allegiance to any one such regime is small. A larger, but less eloquent section of the population inexplicitly operates with the threads, remnants and patchwork patterns of a traditional, familiar, local or national way of organizing eating. As recalling the debates about the difficulty entailed in identifying national cuisines will suggest, the actual pattern on the ground of people in this category is likely to be diverse and differentiated. No encompassing rationale could be captured in a book of rules. The same might also be said about those in conscious pursuit of novelty and diversity.

Recent debates about taste in cultural sociology have revolved around the concept of omnivorousness. Very simply, the contention is that, during most of the twentieth century, elites derived high social status from their command of high culture while the masses were entertained by a popular culture which was considered of little intrinsic aesthetic value. However, as the separation between high and popular cultures began to blur from the 1960s onwards, social distinction increasingly derived from exhibiting tastes for diverse cultural styles. In the contemporary world, to have eclectic tastes is a sign of cultural competence, a mark of cultural capital, and is often further justified and celebrated as an expression of social tolerance and cosmopolitan sympathy. Such a logic can be detected in the domain of food in relation to restaurant preferences, selection of ingredients and dishes, and so on.

So some groups seek to follow powerful, even rigid, exclusive and bounded alimentary regimes which in most cases they have at some time adopted deliberately, although in everyday life their behaviours will have been re-routinized in a way that does not require the rationale for following the diet to be explicitly reaffirmed. However, other significant sections of the population exhibit no clear principles or attachments to an identifiable regime, so could hardly be said to be adherents even of an alternative among a plurality. Whether they are truly dumbfounded or bewildered by choice is highly questionable; lack of explicit scholastic justifications for their practice does not preclude their drawing upon common understandings and a passing awareness of some of the features or precepts of many, not necessarily consistent, specialized systems of dietary recommendations.

Practices and Instruction

Theories of practice diverge with respect to the importance they accord to processes of the collective generation, organization and regulation of performances. All are committed to practices being mutually intelligible, such that it is possible to recognize that a series of actions is an instance of, say, eating or cooking. This entails that the correctness, appropriateness or acceptability of a particular performance can be estimated. Practices have standards beneath which performances should not fall if they are to be considered acceptable by observers. It is worth commenting that when practice-theoretic accounts use terms like 'acceptable', 'competent' or 'correct', it would always be preferable to say 'not unacceptable', 'not incompetent', 'not incorrect', as this would reflect the high degree of tolerance of the varied range of particular performances. Options usually are available. However, the threat of the copy-editor's red pen expunging such infelicities demanded that mostly I shall avoid the double negative.

In order to explain how Practices come to acquire widely acknowledged standards of performance, it helps to analyse them as entities. How multiple and idiosyncratic performances are aggregated into the institutionalized representation of the rules and standards defining acceptable practice is infrequently addressed directly as a sociological problem. The shared templates and normative understanding of acceptable ways of conducting events, constituting for example eating out or entertaining, imply the existence of processes of transmission of common and collective standards governing performances. Many channels exist by means of which awareness may be consolidated and subsequently diffused. Detailed analysis requires an appreciation of the operation of intermediation processes which formalize and publicize Practices. I suggest that shared understanding emanates from processes of *objectivation* which suffice to supply the necessary clues and cues for the restriction of the range of acceptable conduct. Life in public and shared space, material and virtual, utilizes modes of symbolic communication and social coordination to steer performances.

Texts: A Theoretical Interlude

Bookstores and libraries, newsagencies and television archives are bursting with textual material about good and bad alimentary practices. Cultural artefacts pertinent to the domain of eating usually carry implicit or explicit normative injunctions. Perhaps, then, the most obvious first port of call when trying to understand objectivation is the mass of written, and more recently audio-visual, materials offering guidance about normal and appropriate ways of conducting the practice of eating. So, although theories of practice emphasize doing rather than thinking, there is nothing inconsistent about examining written and visual artefacts, so long as they are not confused with what people do. Recipe books, for instance, provide much interesting and relevant evidence about the practice of cooking, but they do not reveal the patterns of performance; they do not tell us what dishes are prepared, by whom and under what circumstances. They do, however, provide vital relevant evidence of three kinds, as do other commensurate eating-related textual sources on the topics of manners, taste and nutrition. First, texts with a partly didactic function constitute prime evidence of the very existence of a Practice. Second, texts supply information about the parameters of ways in which populations imagine it possible to organize activity – indications about how performances might be orchestrated and especially what might constitute acceptable practice. Third, they play a part in the mobilization of personnel who organize and regulate Practices so as to obtain further recruits and maintain their adherence.

As Collins (2010) noted, the modern world is strongly inclined to the codification of knowledge. One result, *inter alia*, is the proliferation of handbooks, manuals and guides which purport to sum up and offer advice on good practice. Such texts contribute to the articulation and clarification of standards, often through commentary on the elements of successful performance. Schatzki claims (1996) that performances of an integrative practice can always be subjected to judgements of correctness and acceptability, implying that standards are publicly recognizable. One source of recognition is precisely a body of textual material explicitly formalizing the objectives or purposes in view in a domain of activity and the ways to go about attaining such goals. Indeed, one way to identify a Practice is to point to formalized specifications of adequate performances.

One common means of formalization, which may facilitate improvement of individual performances in the light of the standards of a Practice, is to describe and record, and release for public circulation, instructions about how to do something, how to do it better and how to do it well. Prototypical are artefacts like rule books, teach-yourself primers, instruction manuals for improving performances, guidebooks, and so on. These are sociologically interesting phenomena. Practice manuals give us robust prima facie evidence of the existence of a Practice. For Practices only exist where performances can attain some standard of excellence and thus, for most individuals, can be improved. Manuals also seem to provide solid evidence of the facticity, and common recognition, of the existence of some underlying foundations for correct or acceptable performances of a complex and widely shared Practice.

This suggests an operational criterion for resolving the vexed question in practice theory about how to distinguish an integrative practice from mere activity. Although on the surface perhaps a trivial hypothesis, I submit that for an activity to pass as an integrative Practice it should be possible, in principle, for a book about the activity to be included in a 'Teach Yourself' series! 'Teach Yourself' books have a number of defining characteristics. First, they usually offer a simple or preliminary account of content or relevant know-how, presented in terms of rules or facts, in a manner suitable for novices.[1] Second, they outline the nature of and the means by which to acquire the competence to deliver performances which would be recognized as adequate when relayed to a competent audience. Third, they also present the activity as a coordinated form of activity, with shared norms of performance. That is to say, they are texts with a format and content which divulge the basic structure of a practice as defined by second-generation theories. Understanding, practical procedures and standards are described.

No doubt an insufficient definition, it might be supplemented by some other characteristics of activities typical of those integrative practices which Schatzki says are of primary interest to sociologists. To pass as an integrative practice, the activity must be one that can be learned, and also one that quite a lot of people would consider worth learning. It will have a knowledge base, comprising at least a set of basic and shared understandings. It will also have a purpose, or set of goals, objectives or anticipated satisfactions, sufficiently adumbrated to produce instructions for attaining successful standards of performance. It will have rules of performance suitable for the purpose of coaching novices. It will make clear what types of performance are deemed competent and distinguish good from bad performances. Thus will there be *enough* to say about it to underpin its codification; integrative practices are sufficiently complex to justify the effort involved in codification and dissemination.

Manifestly, much can be said about eating, yet it does not comfortably meet the above criteria to be described as an integrative practice. Despite many manuals associated with activities surrounding eating, no single coherent genre of writing deals comprehensively and simultaneously with occasion, menus and bodily incorporation. It is almost as if there is *too much* to say about eating. Eating is an especially complex practice. At present, the guidance necessary to determine how best to eat is distributed across a number of different domains of practice, each with its own purposes and priorities which are not easily commensurable. It is for this reason that I have concluded that eating is not an integrative practice (Warde 2013) in Schatzki's sense, but rather a *compound* practice. Eating is formed from the articulation of different practices, including many in the long food-supply chain, the domestic and commercial preparation of meals, and the organization of occasions for the consumption of food. Some adjacent integrative practices are particularly influential in steering aspects of performances of eating. Codified and formalized advice is published in the manuals and handbooks associated with nutrition education, cookery, etiquette and taste. These autonomous practices deal with only some dimensions of the activity of eating, giving priority to their own preoccupations and objectives. Performances of eating are thus subject to, and also a complex corollary of, the intersecting injunctions of several relatively autonomous integrative practices. This multiplies the difficulties faced by individuals when orchestrating their performances and obstructs any definitive collective and comprehensive prescription for the practice of eating.

Restaurant Guides: An Empirical Interlude

Consider the example of a type of literature bearing upon eating and illustrating processes of rationalization and instruction – the restaurant guide. Restaurant guides give advice in a different manner to, say, the technical instructions in cookery books. They offer neither explicit instruction, nor rules to follow. Rather, they make recommendations justified in terms of the qualities of the experience of an eating occasion. The restaurant guide has developed over the last hundred years and has played an important part in the making of markets and the formulation of taste. Guides with a high-profile brand name, like *Michelin* and *Zagat*, offer advice in many different countries. They attend mostly to the high end of the market for eating out, but cover most segments of the catering industry. For instance, Britain has guides to transport cafés, teashops and fish-and-chip restaurants.

Guides function to objectivate a practice. They circulate and express accounts of justifiable norms of market exchange from the customer's point of view. While their ostensible instrumental purpose is to reduce the uncertainties associated with being a consumer (Karpik 2000), they also implicitly prescribe norms of appropriate conduct – including manners, aesthetic judgement and especially tastes. Objectivation of performances – in the form of a normative representation of appropriate, suitable or acceptable ways to engage in the practice of eating out – is thus achieved through the published text. Its recommendations have no mandatory force; they neither determine whether people shall dine out in upmarket restaurants, nor which they will patronize. However, they provide systematized discussion and classification of the elements for the fashioning of competent and distinguished performances. The reader is steered towards establishments with a reputation for excellence, with the grounds for that excellence having been made clear by means of instruction in what a connoisseur might value, increasingly with an eye to trends in cuisines and dishes.

Guides vary. Some are constructed on the basis of professional inspection, like the *Michelin Red Guide*, others through a form of plebiscite, as with *Zagat*. Some guides act explicitly as campaigning instruments, while others are more passive, claiming simply to reflect the current offerings in the marketplace without interfering with them. Some are vehement about their independence, announcing their refusal to take advertisements and insisting that their inspectors remain anonymous and would never accept free meals, while others are less scrupulous. Some guides focus solely on the food, employing technical criteria of cooking skill, while others consider the whole dining-out experience. One general tendency has been for competition to intensify and the method for ranking performance to become almost an end in itself. In this way guides come to define standards of excellence. Some offer a definitive or authoritative ranking of the quality of entries with very little explicit justification of the principles underlying their judgements, while others describe in considerable detail food and ambience. The latter type may have a significant educative effect in relation to taste.

One interesting example is the *Good Food Guide* (*GFG*), the most widely cited consumer guide to fine dining in the United Kingdom. First published in 1951, its content revolves around identifying and listing the 'best' places to eat out in Britain. It has provided information, of different types and levels of detail over the years, about what sorts of food and drink, at what kinds of price, are available. The principle for the inclusion of only a small proportion of the commercial establishments serving food to the public throughout the United Kingdom is their approximation to standards of excellence.

At the outset, the *GFG* was an active, campaigning movement, what Rao (1998) would call a self-appointed consumer watchdog organization. The *GFG* assumed responsibility for challenging current practice and advocating change. This was done through discussion of the qualities that make a good restaurant. It raised issues of what it might be good to eat, and in what circumstances eating in a public context might be rewarding. Referring to itself as a club until the 1980s, it depended upon its members – defined as anyone who bought the *Guide* – to submit reports on restaurants which they had visited. These were then duly compiled into the next year's published *Guide*. Thus it was primarily a consumer guide which revolved around identifying and listing good places to eat out in Britain.

The editor reiterated annually that its readers' reports were the basis of its capacity to have an impact. The *GFG* always had to enunciate, elaborate and operationalize standards for good food. These standards were not, initially, phrased in gourmet or gastronomic terms. The original aim was decidedly modest: merely to find decent food. However, its functions changed later as it became entangled in the co-production of a market niche, moving from cataloguing acceptable places to organizing a contest between restaurants. From the 1980s, it became more engaged with aesthetic issues and conducted discussion and commentary in the discourse of taste. In the last few years, it has reverted simply to describing, cataloguing and ranking selected establishments, now using professional reporters, with commentary and features primarily the reflections of celebrities in the catering trade. Although formally still independent in its judgement, it is increasingly a mode of classified advertisement functional for the upmarket sector of the industry, having abandoned campaigning or intentionally educative functions (Mennell 2003; Warde 2003).

Nevertheless, while ostensibly a guide to shopping, restaurant guides constitute a potential collective learning device about current trends and prevailing standards of cooking and eating. Concentration on the act of market exchange ignores the difference between reading a guide and using it as a means to choose between restaurants. As with recipe books, guides are as much a literary resource as they are a device for making a decision about what to cook or where to eat out. People may read about a restaurant without ever intending, except perhaps in their imagination, to buy dinner there. Those guides which offer detail about the menus of different restaurants, or which have editorial and feature articles about the current state of the restaurant trade, are more than simply a handy gazetteer for a traveller wary of an unsatisfying repast. They are a source of education, a resource for developing critical judgement about the offerings of the catering industry, a way to learn about what is good food, something to talk about with friends and a means of following cultural trends. They offer a literary representation of some of the parameters of the practice of fine dining and contribute to the formation of aesthetic standards and the refinement of judgements of taste.

In sum, guides are intermediaries between the consuming public and producers in niche markets. Their content and their manner of addressing their audiences accompany and enhance the development of the practice of eating out.

Intermediation of a Compound Practice

Many sources of advice are available for the purposes of improving aspects of eating behaviour. They concentrate in texts offering guidance about how to perform Practices adjacent to eating. Texts tend to specialize in only some of the elements of eating and no one genre of literature covers all the relevant ground. Not only does this mean the absence of a comprehensive set of instructions about how to practise eating, but the recommendations of each genre will often appear to be at odds with one another. Good taste and good health are not necessarily immediately compatible.

The field of gastronomy might be expected to be the most promising source of an instruction manual book about how to eat, and it has claimed authority for its judgements about several elements. Its texts – as Ferguson (2004) noted, it is in major part a literary endeavour – pay close attention to dishes, tastes and the social arrangements for convivial meals. Operating in an intensively aesthetic register, gastronomy also insists on a proper orchestration of events and menus. Nevertheless, although obsessive about ingredients, it is generally indifferent to nutrition. Nor has it maintained the interest in aspects of bodily incorporation that were prominent in Brillat-Savarin's tellingly entitled classic treatise on the subject, *The Physiology of Taste* (1994 [1825]). Whatever its potential, gastronomy has had limited impact on popular understandings about how to eat – at least outside of France where, Poulain (2002a) claims, it has peculiar and specific power. The practice and organization of gastronomy has been sparse in North America, Britain and northern Europe. Where found, it was an elite pastime which impacted little on ordinary people or everyday eating behaviour. Relatively cheaper food and the growth of eating out have brought to wider populations the experience of meals with pretensions to fine aesthetic standards. The figure of 'the foodie', a common object of gentle mockery in North America and the United Kingdom, indicates a growing enthusiasm for distinctive ways of eating perceived to be of higher quality and marked by authenticity or tasteful innovation (de Solier 2013; Johnston and Baumann 2010). Foodies dally in a universe of discourse and practice steeped in the language and dispositions of the tradition of gastronomy. Such enthusiasts may use primarily aesthetic standards to guide the overall orchestration of some of their performances. However, as Julier's (2013) evidence suggests, that impetus may be reserved for special occasions and affect only higher echelons of the middle class. Much of everyday eating probably still dances to the beat of another drum. Foodies remain a minority with a limited ability, and no driving motive, to change the behaviour of a wider population. To the extent that gastronomical commitment is an exclusive mode of distinction, diffusing the practice to others may be anathema. On the other hand, campaigning organizations like the Slow Food movement have a political rationale for reforming institutions governing both the production and the consumption of food. Raising the aesthetic expectations of a broad public is a basis for extending the availability of fine victuals. Whether movements of that kind, with a mix of economic, convivial and aesthetic purposes, might have greater impact in the future remains to be seen.

Several other practices have widespread and probably greater influence on the orchestration of eating. They may be seen as somehow more instrumental, more purposeful, better organized, gaining wider media exposure, detaining larger proportions of the population, sponsored by states or facilitated by the wealth and influence of large corporations. For example, lots of resources are applied to promoting good health by means of a nutritious and carefully monitored diet. Much popular discussion is informed by medical and nutrition sciences whose messages are repeated in popular media, medical consultations, government campaigns, proprietary diets, the school curriculum, and so on. They typically deal in a reductive manner with the orchestration of eating performances because they are preoccupied with the links between the chemical properties of foodstuffs and the health and efficiency dimensions of bodily incorporation. Nevertheless, they currently circulate highly influential messages with surveys indicating that western populations are very well aware of dietary recommendations. The injunctions about how to eat healthily are received deferentially but are not followed consistently or assiduously in practice. Reasons for failure to abide by the rules are several. Some people have difficulty in translating the nutrition guidelines into palatable menus. Many others find that the mundane circumstances of everyday life militate against their observance. Countervailing messages from the commercial sector of food manufacturers and retailers may be another reason. Many foods are promoted on grounds other than their nutritional value through a fragmented set of messages emanating from advertising, supermarket shelves, signs in the street, brand images, and so on.

A third major source of advice derives from guides to social etiquette. Complex societies have sets of expectations regarding proper modes for the management of social intercourse which are exemplified in etiquette books. Etiquette books flourished in a period of greater social formality where appropriate conduct could be expressed in terms of rules of good behaviour. One of their main functions in contexts of significant social mobility was to give guidance to people about the different behaviours acceptable among people of higher social rank. Such books include instructions on morals, decency, privacy, rank and social roles under the cover of instructing readers about good manners. Texts on etiquette target only some aspects of eating but in those respects they have continuing influence. Addressed mostly in the context of domestic hospitality, topics include the obligations of guest and host, due deference, gifts and compliments, topics of conversation, body management, use of utensils and when it is permissible to use the fingers. Typically, they say little about what food should be eaten but are concerned with the form of its presentation. Julier (2013), in her study of the hosting of meals in the United States, shows that recommendations in texts changed during the twentieth century as middle-class dinner parties became less formal, ceased to depend on the labour of servants and came to be governed more by ideas of intimate friendship. While few people probably ever read such manuals, they persist in having an effect because they have bequeathed a cultural template for the organization of well-mannered meals. Bourgeois etiquette is now found not only patriarchal but also prissy, inauthentic and overly polite (Kaufmann 2010). Nevertheless, table manners are something that parents are at pains to ensure that their children learn. Many CCSE interviewees in Britain were insistent on the importance of eating dinner at table with their children both to teach manners and to affirm the solidarity of the elementary family unit. As one young woman put it, 'Especially if there's children around, I think it's important that they learn how to interact properly at the dinner table.' Dress codes survive, prescribing smart attire for special occasions and an implicit converse injunction to dress casually on most recreational excursions to eat out. Informalization of meal arrangements is just one aspect of the general informalization of manners in the later twentieth century (Wouters 1986). Note, however, that while rules become less explicit manners remain important and present an even more intricate challenge.

If public instruction about manners is diminishing, the influence of cookery books is in the ascendant. Cookery is a prototypical integrative practice. Hundreds of cookery books are published every year, testimony to the existence of a well-developed Practice and a sizeable body of participants. Cookbooks are both idealized and formalized records of what cooks have done in the past and instrumental texts for consultation, instruction and recommendation about cooking in the present and future. The classification and codification of recipes provides evidence of the existence of a collective, socialized and mutually comprehensible practice of preparing dishes which might be tempting to eat in accordance with conventions current at the time of their publication. Cookbooks all describe how to produce a recognizable dish from a set of ingredients. But they do other things in addition. Some contain not only recipes but also the history of dishes, advice about utensils, suggestions for menus (i.e. sequences of recipes for particular occasions), discussion of the provenance of the dishes in a geographical region or culinary tradition, nutritional advice and more. It is possible to learn from cookbooks which foods and dishes might be good to eat. However, cookery books typically give little insight into manners or pleasure. Indeed, why should they since they concern food provision and preparation, not eating? Nevertheless, they belong to a genre of writing which currently contributes significantly to the understanding of eating.

Thus advice about the various aspects of eating derives from reflections on other types of practices. Professional writers and organizations of various kinds explicitly and purposefully aim to inform and instruct the public about how to manage performances. Organizations include ministries of state, quangos, corporations involved in the food industry, commercial publishers and voluntary associations founded by enthusiasts. Their combined effect is to objectivate practices and to encourage their institutionalization. All are agents committed to the development, enhancement and promotion of either the practice as a whole or more frequently some particular version of it. They seek to define the Practice and prescribe acceptable performance, often in a competitive context. Every practice is subject to internal controversies over standards and procedures, and engaging in dispute is both a commitment device for participants and a perpetual fount of innovation. Practices are thus not metaphysical entities, but constructions moulded by interested stakeholders. Intermediation processes and their outputs disclose hidden interests, reveal trends and fashions and account for current orthodoxies. Best practice is often no more than the temporary victory of sectional opinion in the course of recent controversies. There is, then, competition over recommendations about how eating should be organized. Authorities vie over the best ways to arrange meals, design menus and manage bodies.

The influence of the different authorities claiming legitimacy over popular understandings of how people should eat fluctuates over time. Religious authority, expressed in the form of taboos against particular foods and periodic observance of fasting and feasting, was for long a major arbiter. Injunctions were transmitted very effectively by oral means. Even now, in an increasingly secular Europe, there is significant observance of alimentary rules like those of the Roman Catholic Church which urged weekly abstention from meat on Fridays (Sutton 2001). Secondly, medical discourses also have had extensive influence on western habits (Turner 1982), with the development of the science of nutrition being a particular form of specialization. Food has often been, and is becoming again, a primary tool of medical intervention to maintain and improve health. The state increasingly intervened in the later twentieth century to add weight to the disciplinary injunctions of medical and nutritional sciences. Other forms of authority wax and wane in their influence. Codifications of social etiquette, particularly significant during western modernization, became less so in the later twentieth century during a period of general informalization of manners. Meanwhile, many aspects of the process of food consumption are increasingly judged against aesthetic standards of appearance, style and taste. This is partly the result of the increasing role that commercial communications play in presenting and representing eating.

Perpetual and often intense controversy does not portend incipient anarchy. In one sense there is no essential contradiction between different codifications: one can eat healthily, tastefully, *en famille* and have fish on Fridays. Indeed, probably achieving balance, avoiding being excessive in any dimension, is the dominant common sense in relation to the potential quandary raised by competing discourses. The principal rationale in France is the pursuit precisely of balance, a characteristic considered inherent in its meal format and meal system (Darmon and Warde 2014). Nevertheless, people often act zealously in promotion of one or other of the frames. The nutritional frame – in the form of adherence to government rules of healthy eating, calculation of weight management and many types of specialized proprietary diets – has recently captured substantial segments of the British and American populations. In this context, neither religious doctrine, nor rule of commensality which requires all companions to eat the same foods, nor the exquisite flavours of rare items should be permitted to distract dedicated followers of nutritional regimes. However, in the main, antagonism is neutralized by the fact that advice is rarely imperative or authoritarian in tone.

Contemporary sources regarding what to eat tend to offer recommendations rather than authoritative rules, reflecting the ideology of consumer choice which dictates that preferences and decisions should be at the discretion of the client. That does not, however, preclude rule-like instructions in the etiquette book, nor strong guidance about what not to eat in diet regime manuals. Indeed, one crucial feature of all texts is an implicit message that products and tastes which are not mentioned, those which are excluded in the process of selection and compilation, are of lesser worth. Another reason for mildly tempered advice is that such volumes are competitive, and recognized to be so by their authors and many of their readers, and an overly authoritative tone is unlikely to convince. Objectivation, when considered as the outcome of cultural intermediation, is subject to competition within economic and cultural fields. One result of constant rivalrous codification and evaluation of performances is the permanent potential for turbulence and sometimes also systematic shifts in the standards and the content of Practices, even if the outcomes of such contestation are initially unpredictable.

Processes of cultural intermediation are fundamental to the codification and coordination of Practices. Codification is an expert process, usually literary in form, which renders procedures explicit and subject to an accumulation of accredited, if also contested, wisdom about how best to do something. Coordination involves making explicit a set of procedures, understandings and indeed creating and reinforcing the *illusio* of the field (Bourdieu 1990 [1980], 2000 [1996]). If integrative Practices always have some form of textual representation, they also typically have formal organizations dedicated to their promotion and regulation. This is true for eating, although in a weaker form than for some other practices.

Coordination and Regulation

One appeal of considering Practices as entities is that processes involved in their social coordination can be brought to light. Practices are subject to differing degrees of both social coordination and authoritative regulation. The sharing of practices is not simply, nor even primarily, a function of the circulation of ideas, for it also depends upon authoritative direction and correction. Authority is sometimes backed up by the force of law; many common practices are partly circumscribed by legal regulation. Practices are often in addition regulated by organizations created to deal with the governance of the activity and the everyday performances of its practitioners.

Think of occupational associations and trade unions, the governing bodies of sports, scientific and medical colleges, therapeutic communities, trade associations and the multitude of voluntary associations of enthusiasts for recreational activities like fishing, dancing and motoring. These pillars of civil society, which develop from being mutual associations to becoming bureaucratic organizations, typically evolve from facilitating desirable levels of cooperation among participants to the wielding of power through making and enforcing rules about procedure. Their effects are difficult to measure or to estimate, and their operations less transparent than the published texts discussed above. They nevertheless play an indispensable role in the formalization and codification of Practices, their propagation and their regulation.

Practices become institutionalized. Institutionalization is a central, if sometimes elusive, concept in sociological analysis (Berger and Luckmann 1966; Hodgson 2006; Martin 2004). It refers to both organizations (e.g. mental institutions) and to ways of doing things (e.g. the institutions of electoral democracy). For Berger and Luckmann, institutionalization was fundamental to society, the consequence of reciprocated habitualization and the basis of the objective features of social arrangements. Like other post-war sociologists, they understood the process of objectivation in the terms of role theory, which has been eclipsed in more recent micro-sociology, condemned for presenting performances and interaction in too rigid a manner. Nevertheless, their definition of institutionalization as a 'reciprocal typification of habitualised actions' which set up 'predefined patterns of conduct' and preclude many theoretically possible alternative courses of action is the basis of a serviceable working definition (Berger and Luckmann 1966: 72). Institutionalization potentially makes way for new positions devoted to the social coordination of performances. Organizations emerge devoted to the management and reproduction of practices. Integrative practices always have institutionalized forms and agents explicitly and overtly devoted to the regulation of the practice. The process of institutionalization thereby portends incipient regulation which may be more or less formal.

The existence of dedicated organizations indicates that a significant degree of institutionalization has been achieved. While theoretically the perpetuation of a practice requires only continued performances, its consolidation and its trajectory are much influenced by organized promotion and regulation. Institutionalization engenders mechanisms which offer generalized reassurance and feedback to practitioners. In the process people are encouraged to conceive of what they do as that which they ought to do; normal behaviour comes to be judged effective and is accorded moral or aesthetic value. Normal procedures are seen as best, or at least respectable, conduct in light of the standards of the practice. Institutionalized patterns of conduct assume to themselves a degree of legitimacy. They acquire authority, at least 'for the time being', by virtue of the fact that they are accepted and reproduced in the performances of members of the relevant community or population, much as do traditions. Not that typified and reciprocal expectations automatically acquire legitimacy, for legitimacy must be gained and can be contested, denied or later rescinded. Nevertheless, to paraphrase a proposition of Karl Marx, we are born in historical time into communities with already institutionalized ways of going on and these are impossible to avoid and difficult to repudiate.

Eating is not currently strongly subjected to bureaucratic organization or authoritative regulation, certainly when contrasted with many other everyday practices. Compare eating with motoring, for example. Regulations and organizations strongly define motoring, its standards, its justifications and its conditions for flourishing as a practice. Driving a vehicle is founded upon an enforceable legal framework of acceptable behaviour. It is taught commercially in schools of motoring and competence is tested and licensed by the state. The infrastructure of road systems and traffic signs powerfully channel performance. The *Highway Code* publicizes rules for drivers. Organizations of the state in negotiation with the motoring lobbies (automobile associations, guilds of truck drivers) produce a working consensus about acceptable parameters of the activity. Although there are different styles of driving, few motorists flout the norms of traffic management; norm and normality are in close alignment. Eating, by contrast, is more loosely framed, more a matter of convention than authoritative regulation, neither formally taught nor accredited, occurring mostly in private, not requiring constant and second-by-second adjustment to the actions of strangers, and not, despite the attempts of social movements and consumer organizations, subject to direction and control by powerful organizations of practitioners or regulatory agencies.[2] In comparison with motoring, eating is both weakly regulated and weakly coordinated.

It is partly the pressures exerted by the four key component practices which make eating difficult to coordinate at the level both of individual performance and collective institution. Each of the component integrative practices has its own logic and its own different coordinating agents and organizations. This may give the impression that eating is disorganized. There is no overarching discourse or regulatory framework. Moreover, even the component parts are not very heavily regulated and policed. Most of the 'rules' of etiquette, taste and nutrition are discretionary conventions rather than enforceable edicts. Missing breakfast, offering a dinner-guest snack foods, eating cheese sandwiches for Christmas dinner or using the knife to eat peas may all be transgressions of convention but are not in contravention of any law. Even so, while not grounds for severe punishment, miscreants might suffer less than subtle social disapprobation.

Arguably, therefore, the degree and manner of organization or disorganization of eating is historically particular. The component integrative practices have evolved over many decades, and some over centuries. They have come together sufficiently for eating to be recognizable 'out there' in performances. In some circumstances, they come together to constitute an entity, which is socially coordinated in such a manner that an organized nexus can be identified. At other times and in other places, coordination is weak. There are certainly historical and regional variations in the ways that these four integrative practices are put together. France has exhibited a high level of social coordination, where, until recently, there were formal, institutional, intellectual and artefactual modes for specifying how these component activities should be organized and arranged in some authoritative manner, a combination of regional produce (terroir), French cuisine (cooking), the bourgeois family meal and intellectual and sensual interest in eating and taste codified as gastronomy (Ferguson 2004; Trubek 2000; Warde 2009). By contrast, in the United Kingdom, now and in the past, eating has been a less strongly coordinated practice. For instance, food supply is mostly organized by supermarkets, with some government regulation, and some effects from contestation by social movements for safe and healthy food. Supermarkets make for a fissiparous domain, driven by selling not eating; major suppliers do not care what people eat, but rather aim only to provide customers with choices. Meals have in the past provided a strong temporal and social structure to eating; but while etiquette, manners and rules about companionship and regular mealtimes may once have held sway, they are currently often flexible and informal. Moreover, although elements of a system for the judgement of taste may have emerged recently as a function particularly of the expansion of eating out (Warde 2009), the terms for comparison of objectives and standards are not yet widely established. Cooking, despite having several agencies at work effecting its formalization, *inter alia* recipe books, educational institutions and the celebrity-chef system, is perhaps most highly organized as a Practice. Generally speaking, however, because these integrative practices have developed at different speeds and in relation to different logics, they remain weakly coordinated.

One reaction to these observations might be to investigate the effectiveness and configuration of agencies specifically seeking to promote coordination. Few agencies are operating in the United Kingdom which might accomplish what the literate tradition of gastronomy achieved in France (Ferguson 2004). Perhaps the Slow Food movement could be taken as a latter-day attempt to frame the constituent components into a coherent compound practice of eating. It seeks to influence supply, cooking techniques and the temporal rhythms of eating convivially in the light of an intellectual justification for reform of the eating habits associated with fast food and industrial farming (Petrini 2001). A more prosaic and mundane form of coordination is fostered by the catering trades which create a partly integrated system of supply, preparation, social format and aesthetic standards, institutionalized through restaurant guides, celebrity chefs, the wholesale trade and innovation in relation to the combination and presentation of food. As a consequence, eating out tends to have greater coherence than does domestic practice (see Warde 2004).

Conclusion

This chapter has examined eating as an entity, as a constituted, compound Practice. The process of Practice constitution has been conceptualized in terms of objectivation and institutionalization. Particular attention has been paid to quasi-scholastic reflection on performances, the core activity of cultural intermediation. Texts objectivate performances. Cultural and bureaucratic intermediaries are agents of objectivation, authors of the formalization of practice which is a general feature of modern societies. Intermediation is a controversial, competitive and noisy process. It supplies a record of how things are done, a description of what is available, what is possible, what is worthy of attention and what might matter. The circulation of information that accompanies objectivation is one reason why people who are not food journalists, scholars or critics to some degree possess competence in discussing and making judgements; they derive a normative understanding, and often a template for action, which bears an affinity to the codified versions of the practice. But the understandings to hand contain contradictory injunctions, are not equally accessible to all and are therefore likely to be valued in different ways by people with different social trajectories and experiences.

While it is vital to consider the literary mediation and objectivation of constituted Practices, the role of both informal-mutual and imperatively coordinated organization must also be recognized as part of the process of institutionalization. How those integrative practices are ranked and aligned varies from country to country, and indeed within countries in relation to population segments. However, although many organizations are dedicated to steering the conduct of eating, they perhaps have less direct effect than is the case with many other practices. This is partly the result of eating being a compound practice. The integrative Practices from which eating emerges have developed increasingly differentiated codifications of appropriate standards of performance. In addition, the ubiquity and frequency of eating tends to reduce the possibility to regulate imperatively, as does the fact that eating in most of its manifestations is conducted in private space. The result is that eating is comparatively weakly coordinated and regulated. The absence of a dominant authoritative regulatory framework is one source of the impression of gastro-anomie. Nevertheless, most people adopt an orderly and practical mode of going about eating. The puzzle lies in fathoming how this is achieved. Theories of practice find answers in the procedural nature of everyday expertise, in habituation and routine, which is examined below.

6

Habituation

Preamble

If performances are not the result of actors consciously implementing rules prescribed in formulations of Practices, how are they orchestrated or aligned? When Teri (see pp. 77–8 above) organizes an evening meal, how does she know how to do it? The most straightforward and orthodox answer to the question would be that she had internalized knowledge about the Practice during processes of formal education and informal socialization. The orthodox solution has been to postulate that people assimilate cultural knowledge, primarily general values and norms, which are then the basis for, and a guide to, voluntary decisions and conscious acts implemented in the social situations and practical predicaments which they encounter.[1] So Teri would know a set of rules about how she ought to behave in line with a commitment to certain values and her performance would be explained in those terms.

However, this model is gradually losing ground. A number of objections have been raised in the light of what I will call the new behavioural bent (NBB). Across the social and cognitive sciences, there are increasingly calls to take note of unreflective and repetitive mental and bodily processes. The model of the thoughtful and deliberative actor is not consistent with the evidence of the fluency of everyday conduct. Cognitive science suggests that this is the product of a distinct and dominant system in the brain characterized by automaticity. The view is summarized simply by Thaler and Sunstein (2009), who reiterate claims of cognitive science to the effect that the brain has two systems generating behaviour, one 'automatic', which is uncontrolled, effortless, associative, fast, unconscious and skilled, the other, 'reflective', controlled, effortful, deductive, slow, self-aware and rule-following. The first is far more important such that a great deal of behaviour is governed by mental processes which are automatic, intuitive and emotion-driven, and which therefore involve little deliberation or rational thought. The result is said to be biased judgements, difficulties in resisting temptation and a strong tendency to social conformity. In this account, consumers certainly are not rational, calculating, self-aware, independent-minded agents. And the brain is not a repository of internalized knowledge but rather a rapid processor of connections and patterns. Much of what appears to have been learned by a competent actor is not retained in the form of explicit knowledge, and people often cannot articulate how they accomplish their acts. Others maintain, in addition, that useful knowledge is absorbed by and embedded in the body, and that the distinction between mind and body is misplaced.

In these respects, the portfolio model of action, and hence much of the conceptual apparatus commonly used to explain consumer behaviour, is being gradually eroded by developments across the social sciences surrounding the nature of cognition and its relationship to action. However, this has not yet been thoroughly assimilated by sociology, nor explicitly by theories of practice, despite very significant consequences for explanations of how people get by in everyday life. I will pursue the implications of two of the key points. First, the importance of deliberative thought in everyday life is exaggerated. We deliberate less frequently and less efficaciously than we are pleased to imagine. Second, the degree of personal control and initiative available to the individual is overestimated, leading to neglect of the importance of context, an external, collectively accessible, social and cultural environment wherein the mechanisms steering competent conduct are to be found. These two central insights have been elaborated and incorporated in many ways into competing theoretical and disciplinary traditions. For the sociology of food, they open new avenues for describing and accounting for recurrent aspects of eating; for to emphasize automatic and reactive aspects of conduct conjures up concepts associated with habituation.[2]

Mindlessness and Automaticity: A Critique of Deliberation

The relevance of this general academic ferment for an understanding of eating comes first of all from its challenge to the assumption that people are meaningfully *choosing* what they eat. In a hugely instructive and entertaining book, on the basis of many small-scale experiments, some in a laboratory furnished as a restaurant, Wansick (2006) shows how little people reflect about their eating and how this has consequences neither intended nor desired. His book contains no explicit theory, although it shares in and draws upon behavioural theories in psychology. Its culmination takes the form of instructions about how to eat less. Its recommendations draw upon the exposition of a programme of often ingenious experiments to investigate how behaviour is influenced by the situations or conditions in which it occurs. With 'the crisis of obesity' as a background – almost no one in America at the beginning of the twenty-first century wants to be, or intentionally sets out to become, obese – the overall thesis is that much behaviour is outside, or only at the verges of, the boundaries of deliberate, rational or prospective thought. We eat in a state of distraction.

Most of Wansick's experiments show that people are not reflective when engaged in ordinary or familiar activities. My favourite reported experiment concerns the consumption of tomato soup. Tables seating four people are arranged in the laboratory set up as a restaurant. They are each served a bowl of tomato soup. Two people have ordinary soup bowls, the other two have a bowl attached under the table to a pump which, unbeknown to the diner, steadily refills it. On average, those people with the doctored bowls eat 73 per cent more soup. One lesson is that appetite is often not actively and consciously regulated so people easily eat beyond satiation; one experimentee, when asked what he thought of the soup, remarked 'filling'! Although in a harmless way, this case involves tricking or deceiving the subject, for no one in their mundane past experience (except perhaps in their dreams) has ever encountered a self-replenishing food receptacle. A phenomenological account would observe that mostly our social world is 'taken for granted', such that we are very rarely required to reassess or reaffirm beliefs based on prior experience. Hence we are easily prompted by the signs and symbols populating the social environment to behave without thinking or reflecting rationally. Nevertheless, at the same time the experiment indicates how people are led, and misled, by their matching of visual prompts and conventions. Soup bowls typically contain a portion suitable in size for a single person, and it is customary to eat until the bowl is empty.

Many small double-blind experiments show that different information influences consumption level. The same (free) wine accompanying a meal was presented in bottles with labels attributing origin either to North Dakota (unknown as a wine-producing region) or

California, resulting in much more left undrunk in the first than in the second case. The same dish, with a plain description, turns out to be significantly more appreciated than when it is given a more detailed and enhanced name. Caviar, escargots and sweetbreads sound more delicious than fish eggs, snails and calf thymus (Wansick 2006: 134). Sensory judgement is seriously affected by the accompanying or surrounding material artefacts and textual messages.

Although Wansick thematizes mindlessness, he actually employs various other explanations for the prevalence of automaticity. What is presented at the table steers our behaviour – people eat more if the plates are larger or if food not initially distributed is put on the table. Thus Wansick shows how different contexts offer a predictable propensity for people to eat and drink in quantities greater than is advised by the science of nutrition, and probably more than they themselves would want to eat if they stopped to calculate the effects of what they were doing or were inclined to do. Lives are conducted in a state of partial distraction which opens us to persuasion. Wansick, for example, reports that Campbell, the soup manufacturer, had an arrangement with radio stations that on rainy days their soup would be advertised before noon. In such respects, features of an external environment – of material objects and their arrangement, media messages and interaction with other people – steer behaviour. Very significantly, companions tend to converge in their behaviour with the consequence that the collective norm outweighs personal preference.

Wansick uses the term 'habit' only occasionally. This is perhaps quite proper since laboratory experiments are isolated events and furnish no evidence about sequences of actions that recur frequently and in a similar manner over an extended period of time. However, it is not hard to extrapolate from studies of, say, eating chocolate in the experimental situation to other situations of everyday life. The mechanism identified will have predictable and repeated consequences, depending upon the parameters set: keeping chocolates on a high shelf in a cupboard in the least used room of the house will reduce their consumption, leaving them on the table where you work will do the opposite. Wansick analyses our foibles as non-rational one-off acts that we might, with a little more thought, make different decisions about. This is partly for humorous effect; showing that we do not pay attention and are therefore subject to unintended consequences allows us to laugh kindly at ourselves, or more likely at other people, without attribution of stupidity or gluttony. It is also, however, partly a result of a predilection within psychology for versions of decision-making models of action. Repetition can be presented as the equivalent of many identical decision-making episodes, the favoured strategy of a dominant model of behaviour (like the Theory of Planned Behaviour) which seeks to predict actions by way of values, attitudes and intentions.

Overall, Wansick shows how little we mostly think about food and food intake. Hence there will be a significant propensity to habitual behaviour and a strong tendency for people to repeat their actions when in similar situations. As long as the environment and the cues it emits remain the same, behaviour is likely to be repeated. People react to food as it is made available, in relation to the form in which it is presented and represented to us – via labels of dishes, loaded plates, unacknowledged encouragement and so forth. Features of the environment conspire to determine levels and quality of consumption. And the consumer readily accedes, automatically and without deliberation.

Wansick's experiments demonstrate primarily that, in a state of mindlessness, the environment steers behaviour. His account is more plausible than its converse – that people have an internalized propensity or disposition to be greedy and therefore eat from large plates. To the extent that contributions to the obesity debate are polarized between accusations of gross moral turpitude on the part of fat individuals and the vile obesogenic forces in the environment, Wansick comes closer to the latter.

One might have therefore expected habit to play a significant part in this analysis of conduct. It mostly does not. In a paper with Sobal (Wansick and Sobal 2007) about how people ignore and deny the effect of environmental cues on food intake, the problem is introduced in terms of the hundreds of decisions which people fail to recognize that they make every day. For Wansick, the objects of analysis are essentially rational and irrational (or perhaps non-rational) decisions. Tellingly, though, Wansick (2006) does make use of the term 'habit' in his advice about behaviour change. Habit appears, almost exclusively, when he is discussing (especially in chapter 10, pp. 208–24) how to eat fewer fattening foods. In his view, when it comes to correcting behaviour (at least in relation to obesity), it is what we do repeatedly that is either beneficial or harmful. Repetition matters. Thus the advice he gives to the seeker after weight loss is to adjust material circumstances and reform habits. While proposing practical steps, not unlike many other weight-control dieting books, he asserts that 'There's only one thing that's strong enough to defeat the tyranny of the moment. Habit' (p. 218), and that 'The best diet is the one that you don't know that you're on' (p. 219).

In this respect, Wansick resembles others in the behavioural movement who are very averse to abandoning the model of the rational and calculating self-interested actor. They identify behaviour which is non-rational against some universal yardstick of rationality with which all behaviours are compared and measured. The point of an intervention is to return the actor to the straight and narrow path of effective self-regarding conduct, rescuing him from irrational or non-rational tendencies. The trope involves putting actors back in charge of their own strategic conduct, restoring their sovereignty so that they might seek what they ought to prefer (or really would prefer if they had better information or could anticipate future consequences, and so on). They attribute non-rationality to the manner of the operation of the mind, which encourages biases, usually entailing misperception of self-interest. Mindlessness tends to engender the repetition of bad (non-rational) behaviour which is thus not intentionally motivated. Yet still the actor could do otherwise by dint of reflection and therefore can be held responsible for it. Obesity may then be seen as a moral failing. However, this argument is scientifically problematic. If the brain prefers and will always have first recourse to automatic engagement via System 1, expecting people to override their mindlessness and cease to operate in anything other than a habitual manner is otiose. First, and probably less important, it presupposes both ideological agreement on a definition of substantive rationality, which is always politically contestable, and also an optimal instrumentally effective strategy which is likewise susceptible to dispute. Investigation of practices indicates frequent contestation over which strategies are optimal for effectiveness. Second, if it is postulated that most behaviour is habit-like, which is implied by the dominance of System 1, it seems fundamentally contradictory to invoke a model of individual deliberative decision making to explain behaviour. Surely it is perverse to make the latter the template for all forms of behaviour. This raises a question of why aversion to other forms of habitual, collective and situational explanation is so great. Why, despite the dependence of the behavioural bent on the role of mindlessness (in System 1), and when mindless repetition is staring analysts in the face, is there extreme reluctance to abandon the notion that people are making decisions?[3]

Habit and Habituation?

The more it is posited that people are predominantly mindless, the more attention must be drawn to analysis of repetition.[4] The puzzling paradox revealed by the NBB is that people deliberate very little but nevertheless align purposeful and competent action to practical and social settings with great skill and rapidity. Explanations of the wondrous capacity of people to display practical competence over a huge range of activities remain weak and contested. From the orchestration of a family meal or a dinner party to the prevention of tomato soup spilling onto white shirts, major feats of coordination are achieved with little attention or effort. The most commonly accessible concept to describe this facility is habit. However, habit is a difficult and contested term, with most authors being at pains to avoid the concept, or to use it in only very restricted circumstances. Nick Crossley (2013) suggests three powerful reasons for resistance to analysis in terms of habit. First, it has strong overtones of the now largely discarded behaviourist school of thought in psychology associated with B. F. Skinner. The stimulus–response model, based on operant conditioning, seems to fit laboratory rats better than the average human. Second, antipathy arises from the hugely influential Kantian philosophical tradition which sought to present humans as different from animals because of the separation and autonomy of their minds from mere animalesque bodies. Third, it is hard to find a consensual definition of the term. As Crossley (2013: 138) puts it, concepts of habit have been formulated in a variety of different ways by philosophers and theorists and 'the case of "habit" is further complicated by the fact that it belongs to everyday language, wherein its meaning is variable and imprecise'.

In the absence of a satisfactory agreed definition of habit, Charles Camic (1986: 1044) offered a generic operational definition, used in his review of sociological usage and vocabulary over time: 'the term "habit" generally denominates a more or less self-actuating disposition or tendency to engage in a previously adopted or acquired form of action.' The scope of the phenomenon is nicely captured by this working definition. The domain is one of activity occurring without deliberation or calculation prior to the episode, where conduct in manner similar to previous occasions is automatically or reactively actuated. More succinctly, the components are lack of deliberation, automaticity and repetition.[5] These three components or dimensions of habit and habitualization appear in various guises in the discussions among scholars across several disciplines. Camic, along with many other sociologists, considers action of this type to be of immense importance in accounts of human conduct and social ordering. We might recall Weber's observation that:

> in the great majority of cases actual action goes on in a state of half-consciousness or actual unconsciousness [*Unbewusstheit*] of its

subjective meaning. The actor is more likely to 'be aware' of it in a vague sense than he is to 'know' what he is doing or be explicitly self-conscious about it, In most cases his action is governed by impulse or habit. (Weber 1978: 21–2)

Let us examine the conceptual underpinnings of such accounts of habit.

Competing accounts of habit deal in different ways with these three components. In doing so they explore aspects of conduct which are not to be located in the commensurate processes of deliberation and reflection, explicit decision making about objectives and the projective planning of means to a determined end, which subtend and define the portfolio model. In this and the subsequent section, I will briefly outline some current alternative understandings of the conjunction between lack of deliberation, self-actuating tendencies and repetition. At least six approaches can be identified. Introduced in the preceding section of this chapter, the first draws upon cognitive and neuro-science to explain the prevalence of automatic and unreflective action. A second is a new psychology of habit seeking to revive the concept to explain the prevalence of repeated behaviours. A third approach decentres the individual mind and finds the wellsprings of action distributed between personal properties and the encompassing environment. A fourth account, deriving from pragmatist philosophy, takes habit as the central mode of human action and deems foundational dispositions to repeat procedures automatically, providing they do not fail. Fifth, developments within the sociology of culture in the United States have pushed further a notion that culture is not something that resides in the heads of individuals but rather is publicly available in an extraneous environment and the tools thereby provided steer conduct. Finally, there are the classic accounts of practice theory, already discussed, of Giddens and Bourdieu, for whom institutions and routines, or learned social *habitus*, respectively, are at the core of practical competence and social organization. From reviewing these accounts, I draw some lessons about which types of mechanisms and processes would be most compatible with contemporary theories of practice.

In empirical psychology, the term 'habit' was promoted by William James (1981 [1890]) in the late nineteenth century but it became more or less defunct after the demise of Skinner's behaviourism after the Second World War (Darnton et al. 2011). It was revived by Triandis (1980) and has recently blossomed in a new research programme. There is now a cottage industry within psychology theorizing about the role of habit in the determination of individual behaviours. The point of departure, as Verplanken, Myrbakk and Rudi (2005) remark, is that in the world in general repeated behaviour prevails over new. They defend a definition of habits as 'learned sequences of acts that have become automatic responses to specific cues, and are functional in obtaining certain goals or end states' (Verplanken et al. 2005: 231). Such a definition attributes repetition to responses to 'specific cues' and is built upon a dualism which distinguishes habitual from intentional action. James said that the term 'habit' applied best to simple acts – twiddling thumbs when bored, attacking one's food with the spoon always held in the right hand, swallowing[6] – and it is those which Verplanken and colleagues appear to address. For them, habits are mindlessly accomplished, triggered by external cues and frequently repeated in an identical manner. The scientific objective is therefore to identify and predict the origins and outcomes of simple and single, isolable, units of behaviour. However, not much of sociological interest occurs at this microscopic level of granularity, although it is possible that a series constructed of a significant number of such habits may constitute performances worthy of analysis. Other psychologists suggest that repetition is not in itself enough, specifying that, while a habit typically refers to behaviour that is frequent and automatic, it should also occur in a stable context (Neal, Wood and Quinn 2006). This view produces a more open or extensive sense of what is to be explained, and that does suggest the importance of sequence.

Habit refers to the often strong link between past behaviour and present behaviour, and can be shown in path-dependency models to have a strong independent effect upon behavioural outcomes, particularly in stable situations. Oulette and Wood summarize such a view of habit as follows:

> Past behaviour directly contributes to future performance in contexts that support the development of habits. Behaviors that are well practiced and performed in stable contexts are likely to be repeated because they can be performed quickly, relatively effortlessly, in parallel with other activities, and with minimal or sporadic attention (Bargh 1989; Logan 1989). Conscious deliberation and decision making are not required for performance of such acts. Although habitual behaviors may be intentional and goal directed, the controlling intentions are not typically accessible to consciousness, because with repeated performance (a) intentions themselves tend to become automatic; (b) intentions tend to be specified in an efficient, stable and general form that emphasizes the goals met by the action rather than the action details; and (c) intentions, much like the actions they direct, tend to be combined into broader and more efficient units that refer to sets of behaviors that occur together rather than to individual actions. (Oulette and Wood 1998: 65)

Claims that 'conscious deliberation and decision making are not required for performance of such acts' and that past behaviour contributes to future behaviour are not recognized in many models of consumer behaviour, as for instance in accounts in economics, where each purchasing decision is considered independent. More importantly, the final point in the passage implies that to analyse 'unit acts' rather than sequences of actions is problematic, thus distancing effective explanation of behaviour from decision making, for example at the point of purchase or in a situation of interaction. People have suites of integrally associated actions which constitute building blocks for performances.

Arguments deriving from neuro-science and economic psychology, the doyen exemplars of the NBB, and also those of the new social psychology of habit still conceptualize actors as individuals with integrity and autonomy, whose identity is bounded as it were by their skin. Aware of the extent of interdependence in human societies, some traditions in social science have always sought to challenge the analytic power of this now commonsensical view. Recent practice theories which insist that actors are bearers of practices offer just one of many versions of the claim that individuals are indissociable from their environment or habitat, and that to take this into account in explanation of conduct requires conceptual reframing to temper rampant methodological and ontological individualism.

'Social ecology' perspectives emphasize the symbiosis of actor and environment achieved through habit, as for instance in Alva Noe's book, *Out of Our Heads: Why You are Not Your Brain, and Other Lessons from the Biology of Consciousness* (2009). Highly critical of a very common (mis)interpretation of the implications of research in neuro-science, he insists that the brain does not cause behaviour but is merely a conduit which offers specific affordances for carrying out action.[7] He suggests that the human brain has evolved in particular environmental niches, such that it facilitates a particular tranche of capabilities. It predisposes people to be creatures of habit whose span of activity is encompassed by the necessity of inhabiting what might be described as their own familiar social environment.

Capacities for deliberation and intellectual endeavour are built upon, and are therefore secondary to, acquired basic habits and procedures. He says that: 'the hallmark of expertise is its fluency: it is engaged and, precisely, nondeliberative; the expert eschews just the kind of distanced, careful contemplation that, according to the intellectualist, is definitive of our truest nature' (2009: 99). Noe makes a more general case that, in a life without habits, 'Each day would be like one's first day in an unfamiliar country. No familiar pathways or tested strategies for getting things done would be available; no routines would be in place to serve as anchor. We would scan, interpret, evaluate, decide, execute, reevaluate.' Rather, it is the relationship between habits and the situation or environment that underpins expertise: 'Only a creature with habits like ours could have anything like a mind like ours. But habits, at least many of them, are situational or environmental' (2009: 125). He elaborates, when concluding: 'Habit and skills, however, are world-involving. Just as my habitual route to work is shaped in part by the landscape in which I find myself, so in general our habits are made possible by the world's being as it is (even if it is also true that our action shapes the world in turn)' (2009: 127).

Overall, Noe offers a strong, pragmatist-inspired, holistic version of habits as the means through which humans inhabit their local environments. In all cases, this allows for greater complexity of the environment – it is not merely a repository of cues. No strong separation is made between intention and habit. Rather, intention is subsumed in the recognition of the appropriateness of a course of conduct in a particular situation.[8]

Noe's dispute is with brain scientists and their inclination to fall back on evolutionary psychology to explain behaviour; hence he gives little clue as to how to isolate and explicate particular social acts or courses of action. He is especially persuasive in regards to his critique of models of action based upon internalized and endogenous properties of individuals, but the terms of his analysis are less helpful in relation to the particularities of activities like eating. His account pays little attention to repetition per se. In that, he may be well in line with contemporary pragmatist social philosophy which uses the term habit freely, but insists upon it as a source of versatility and even creativity.[9] For pragmatists, habit is not defined by its regular exercise in familiar circumstances, as with the psychologists, but instead almost entirely by its self-actuating character. Individuals will live through their store of capabilities which they generate automatically in skilled streams of conduct – until interrupted. In sympathy with pragmatist accounts, the supposition is of continuous, but not conscious or deliberative, monitoring of action, which surfaces when things go wrong.

Ultimately, *contra* the pragmatists, it is difficult to see how habits can exist without repetition and without acculturated adjustment to a relevant environment. However, all in all, environment, while also a rather difficult concept for the social sciences, very importantly gives some background support for sustaining an account of habitualization.

Environment and Habits

Accounts of habituation are heavily dependent on a plausible portrayal of an exogenous environment. Of course, no social scientific account of action entirely ignores the external setting, but it may often be attributed a very minimal role. In circumstances where there is no personal contemplation of action, and where there are no plans and conscious decisions, some form of impulse or trigger is required to account for a person engaging in a course of action. If that is not to be an internal mental event, one way to explain the capacity for competent and fluent performance in the absence of deliberation is to emphasize the role of the external environment in steering behaviour.

The social environment provides cues. Symbolic communication, the actions of other people and configurations of material objects, when perceived as relevant, variously and selectively, prompt activity. For example, people may repair to eat not only in response to pangs of hunger, but because they are looking at the clock, passing a patisserie, fulfilling a social engagement, reading an advertisement, missing an accompaniment to a drink or feeling unloved. All occasionally serve as triggers to an act of eating. Such a simple model might be suspected of excessively behaviourist overtones. Yet situation is a sociological concept par excellence. Context, setting and situation comprise significant parts of explanations of actions in several sociological traditions. Sociology might even be defined as the study of the relationship between social positions and social situations. Sociology requires an equivalent concept to 'environment', but one which is more detailed and complex than those typically invoked in explanations based on individual intentions and decision making. To generate an account of eating which captures the habitualized aspects of performances requires greater clarity about what relevant phenomena occupy the 'environment' and how they impinge on, or instigate, performances.

An influential article by Ann Swidler (1986) instigated a long series of attempts to reformulate for sociological purposes a concept of culture which repudiated Parsonian orthodoxy, which had assumed 'that culture shapes action by supplying ultimate ends or values towards which action is directed, thus making values the central causal element of culture' (Swidler 1986: 273). The idea that culture is something collected and compiled as (especially propositional) knowledge within the minds of individuals is rejected. Revised accounts of how culture works seek to abandon the paradigmatic models of instrumental or strategic action in favour of others in which automatic or habituated responses and reactions play a greater role. The argument was specifically opposed to the view that culture is a set of internalized and coherent values and norms, learned in a process of socialization, which were privileged causes of action. Swidler argued that culture does not affect action in that way. Culture does not reside within the individual in a coherently formulated and organized manner. Rather, it is accessible to actors mostly in fragments; cultural traces available to the individual are used more like 'a tool-kit', items which can be called upon when forming a strategy for action. Because internalized content is fragmentary and unorganized, the impetus to action tends to come as cues from the external environment which, for Swidler, consist of codes, recognizable contexts and institutions to be found in public texts and public spaces. Since eating is cultural activity par excellence, such an account deserves careful consideration.

The persuasiveness of such an externalist account requires that the environment contains all the symbols, clues and affordances necessary to generate effective conduct. To conceive of the actor as having internalized very little knowledge might suggest explanations in terms of habit and response. Swidler, however, has little truck with habits, and posits a more mentally flexible or reflective (partly calculating) actor who navigates a course of action in relation to codes, situations and institutions. Ultimately, for Swidler, it seems that an active, purposeful individual (albeit not one who has earlier internalized a coherent set of values and norms to be applied in sovereign manner) determines which aspects of the environment shall be judged relevant and compelling. Swidler's actor is in the end an observant, alert, discriminating, virtuoso, using a tool-kit purposefully. This suggests that Swidler remains uncomfortable with mechanisms of cues and triggers which are key to ecological explanation and prefers to retain powers to initiate conduct for the individual.

Paul DiMaggio (1997) drew on evidence from cognitive psychology to elaborate Swidler's rejection of the idea of culture being a seamless and unified web of beliefs internalized by whole populations. In a nutshell, he propounded a view of the individual as a collector of vast swathes of fragmentary images, opinions and information which are given some degree of stability and consistency through the interplay of personal schematic mental organization and 'cues embedded in the physical and social environment' (1997: 267). He situates this in relation to the two different modes of cognition, discussed above (pp. 100–1), emphasizing the importance of the 'automatic' mode in 'routine, everyday cognition [which] relies heavily and uncritically upon culturally available schemata' (1997: 269). It simplifies cognition and is highly efficient, and is therefore made use of on most occasions, despite its not always being accurate. Thus a great deal of behaviour is governed by mental processes which are automatic, intuitive and emotion driven, and which therefore involve little deliberation or rational thought. DiMaggio argued that this research strongly favours the tool-kit view over the model of the mind as a receptacle of an intricate cultural world-view.

DiMaggio thus views culture as operating through the interactions of vast amounts of information, a restricted number of mental schemata (which condense and organize such information) and an external or objectivated symbolic universe. Schemata, he says, can be activated through conversation, media use or observation of the material world, but, whichever, he concludes that 'selection is guided by cultural cues available in the environment' (1997: 274). DiMaggio admits that the conclusions he draws for the sociology of culture involve speculative interpretation of the evidence of cognitive psychology; nevertheless, he makes a wide range of insightful extrapolations to issues of collective identity and memory, social classification and the logics of action. For present purposes, however, it is the role of the environment which should be stressed. If this account is remotely accurate,[10] the skills and competences exhibited in individual performances do depend much more than previously thought upon the way in which the external social and physical environment, with its complement of items of objectivated public culture, is organized and made accessible. Later development of Swidler's basic position has produced more radical stances, giving to the public environment much greater autonomous effect (e.g. Martin 2010).

With respect to eating, the relics of past performances litter the environment. Some are purposefully compiled records of how and what to eat, for example recipe books and restaurant guides as was discussed in chapter 5. Some are commercial prompts, such as advertisements, restaurant menus displayed in the street and discarded packaging. Others are accidentally or casually deposited and constitute little more than ephemeral detritus. All are substantial artefacts of public culture which provide essential evidence for a practice-theoretical account. They constitute the environmental cues used practically as triggers for and parameters of streams of conduct. Familiar, recognizable and well-understood settings help maintain flow. The sedimentation of prior practice, manifestations of the achievements or accomplishment of experience, constitutes an environment that has been created through the collective cumulation of multiple, uncoordinated but mutually referential performances, the availability of which mostly makes life more predictable, easy, fluent, secure and satisfying. The contents of the public cultural environment are the key feature of the human ecological situation alluded to by Noe (2009), which make it possible to navigate, more or less effectively in everyday life, around the many Practices that require perpetual articulation and implementation.

Between Environment and Habit

The relationship between persons and their environments has been subjected lately to further elaborate conjecture. It is increasingly widely contended that the orthodox account of the individual is flawed and that it is necessary to postulate an intricate and intimate relationship between person and environment in order to explain human conduct. Formulations vary, but increasingly it is suggested that it is remiss to postulate that a human skin is the key barrier between person and environment. One alternative is to posit that the person is part of his or her environment because he or she is inescapably and irreducibly dependent upon its properties and affordances (Ingold 2000; Kaufman 2004; Latour 2005; Noe 2009).

Another is to suggest that the person incorporates aspects of the environment, as is intimated in concepts of 'dispersed cognition' or 'distributed agency'. Wilhite (2012: 90), for example, espouses a concept of distributed agency and argues that 'agency in consumption habits is distributed among body, material context and social context'. He finds sources of habit, and the knowledge that it unconsciously draws upon, both in embodied skills and in the material artefacts and tools which constitute the capacity for action. He particularly emphasizes the interfacing of habit and technology; machines script how we carry out particular procedures, and we tend repeatedly to revisit the paths previously trodden, even when other options are available. Habits are not perpetuated by personal decisions, but through repetition, particularly in the case of strongly embodied habits. He distinguishes strong from weak habits in terms of degree of reflection involved and thus the extent to which they might be tempered by 'cognitive choices and verbal communication'.

It is a moot point – to be discussed further in the next chapter – whether these modifications and alternatives to established disciplinary accounts of habit can better serve practice-theoretical approaches to eating. Both alternatives interest theorists of practice and both claim that a plausible or proper description of action will overspill the boundary, sacrosanct to orthodox Enlightenment accounts, between the conscious individual and features of the surroundings.

To ignore the skin barrier promises new ways of linking context and conduct. The relationship between environment and individual is more intimate and intricate than portfolio models propose. It is the context which makes the conduct possible and sensible – and indeed the conduct would not have arisen but for the specific context inspiring it.[11] Potential benefits might be revealed by considering the failure of antagonistic accounts of habit and environment to resolve debates about the nature and cause of obesity in the contemporary West.

Environment, Habits and Obesity: An Illustrative Case Study

Much ink has been spilt in attempts to describe and explain the increasing prevalence of obesity in the West since 1980. Some commentators consider it one of the greatest contemporary social problems, others think it overblown, an instance of moral panic (Campos et al. 2006). The causes and the implications are highly contested. Causal explanations tend to emphasize one or other of two forces. The dominant account finds individuals lacking in foresight and willpower with respect to maintenance of body weight, sometimes tantamount to accusing the overweight of gross moral turpitude in their refusal or their inability to control their gluttony. The challenger position attributes overeating to an obesogenic environment, to malign aspects of the production, promotion and sale of food. Scholars attached primarily to rational action models and neoliberal politics promote the former moralist position, while those influenced by political economy, the NBB and epidemiology more often favour the latter.

Few accounts entirely ignore either individual behaviour or the socio-economic context. Moralists recognize that personal self-discipline is compromised by institutionally supported temptations; and proponents of the environmental case very rarely absolve entirely the overweight from personal responsibility for their inadequate body management. Few, however, question that there is a crisis requiring resolution via policy intervention. Equally few postulate that the problem is related to anything more than a balance of the exchange between eating and exercise. Most are relatively uncritical of the common-sense political framing of the problem as a rise in measured BMI, due to an unbalanced intake and expenditure of calories, which imposes an avoidable costly burden on public health. The behavioural and nutritional scientists who address the issue typically consider a narrow range of factors relating to individual choices. By contrast, Guthman (2011) is notable for identifying a great many potential contributory factors which are institutional in nature, rather than personal. She brings into question some of the orthodoxies such as the validity of the BMI measure and the assumption that being overweight is any form of illness. More significantly, she points to phenomena like the urban environment, the food system and food policy as autonomous forces driven by capitalist economic arrangements. Other potential wider causes include the pharmaceutical properties of manufactured food and drink. In addition, medicines and chemical compounds suspended in public water supplies are rarely considered, yet they may be key components of obesogenic environments. Even less attention is given to the joint or mediating influences of other practices not directly associated with food, like drinking, leisure and recreational pursuits, and socializing rituals; it is too often implausibly assumed that people are focused single-mindedly on dietary guidelines to the exclusion of other competing ends and purposes.

If, as seems likely, many factors influence the increase in average body mass, it is worth considering which one a practice-theoretical account might emphasize. Such an account might first note that obesity is one of the most unambiguous and intractable instances of the value–action gap. Everyone wants to avoid being overweight – there is a very high degree of consensus on preferred body shape and, whether for health, aesthetic or economic reasons, that means being slim relative both to current body size and to a national average.

A theoretically instructive example is the individual explicitly seeking to exert control by restricting level of consumption. Large proportions of western populations occasionally, and sometimes more or less permanently, consider themselves to be on a weight-loss diet. Yet a very small percentage of dieters are successful in their efforts in the long term. The level of failure arouses suspicion about the accuracy of the calorie intake and energy expenditure balance theory. It should be so much easier for people to lose weight than it appears to be if restricting calories is the main avenue for success. Failure by someone who has resolved to reduce their weight and who is prepared to go to considerable effort to achieve a target or goal (in an activity not subject to zero-sum competition) is surprising. It suggests that weight-loss diets may fail for reasons other than dieters not being able to limit sufficiently their recommended calorie intake. Secondly, high failure rates suggest limits to strategies and campaigns which require careful calculation, perpetual self-monitoring, meticulous planning and single-minded pursuit of the goal of reducing weight. Such circumstances should be conducive to weight loss according to orthodox rational action and economic accounts of behaviour. Yet effective action seems out of reach (Darmon 2009; Lhuissier 2012). At the very least, this is puzzling if individuals are assumed to have sovereign control over their own destinies. Failure at the individual level may be better explained in terms of the habitual, distracted, repetitious and self-actuating features of action and the ways in which these aspects of performance are facilitated and steered by infrastructural forms and environmental cues.

Eating involves many embodied repetitive procedures which occur with very high frequency, for example forking and spooning, tasting and swallowing. Wansick's experiment with the self-replenishing soup bowl illustrates well a process whereby people automatically continue with an entrained process of shovelling until the bowl is empty. No doubt his subjects did not think about the mechanical action or the quantity being removed until long after the amount anticipated was passed. Usually, faced with a bowl of soup, people do not ask 'Have I had enough?' because enough is primarily determined by eating what is on the plate. A plateful is a conventional unit directive of how much should be eaten, though there is evidence that dishes are getting larger over time (Wansick 2006: 68). This is apparent in commercial settings where the standard size of cups of coffee, soft drinks and glasses of wine have increased in the last decade or two in the United States and Britain. It can also be seen in the size of hamburgers and portions of fast-food chicken. There are differences from country to country, and differences according to restaurant status, where one rule of thumb appears to be that the more prestigious the place, the smaller the portions. Conventionally, however, in either case, the customer eats the amount served. So eating is underpinned by some embodied habits directing physical movement, temporal extension and also flavour appreciation. That is not to suggest that obesity is a consequence merely of habituation of the body; there is more to eating than that. However, embodied procedures are particularly powerful and many are entirely automatic.

Availability of equipment is a key feature of settings for food preparation and consumption, with everything from the domestic stove and industrial oven to the nature of the table setting – or even access to a table – having an impact upon what it seems appropriate to eat. Infrastructural objects may be more constraining than directing, but arrangements for food storage and meal delivery exert pressure in particular directions. Importantly, much infrastructure is not amenable to rearrangement by an individual. So while my chocolate can be put in the furthest recess of a basement cupboard to avoid easy temptation, I have little effective control with respect to a great many other contextual factors, for instance the dominant regime of provision, suburb–supermarket–car–refrigerator–microwave, or the location of food shops which attract my attention on the journey to work. Public infrastructure does not dictate habits, but it does emit cues that are responsible for physical and symbolic channelling of trajectories through many attractive opportunities to eat which may stimulate, bring forward or create previously unfelt wants. In this regard, theories of practice concur with arguments about the obesogenic environment.

The social settings that comprise the 'environment' steer trajectories and communicate messages immediately relevant to any individual's current purposes but also express collective conventions and preoccupations. Customs are visible through observation of others' behaviour. Although mealtimes are a little less rigid than in the mid-twentieth century, temporal rhythms persist (Kjaernes 2001; Lhuissier et al. 2013; Southerton et al. 2012). Temporal routines remain geared to the rhythms of employment, study and household obligations and recreations (Brannen et al. 2013; Grignon 1993; Yates and Warde forthcoming).

The collective legitimacy of particular meals and meal formats finds public expression; despite some degree of informalization, a broad template for eating events pertains and its characteristics are given publicly signified authorization. Laporte and Poulain (2014) argue that a main reason for the French being less obese than the British is the continued availability of regular and structured lunches in workplace canteens in France. Lunches prepared by professional chefs, on the template of main meals whose structure is modelled with nutritional balance in mind, compare favourably with the British reliance on sandwiches. Routines serve not only to facilitate the spatio-temporal coincidence of commensal groups but also to deliver emotional security and social assurance to the individual who can both feel content that their own performances are acceptable in the eyes of others and can also anticipate effectively the conduct of others.

No legal or social authority exists to enforce through punishment common patterns of eating behaviour, but convergence occurs nevertheless. Christiakis and Fowler (2007, 2009) demonstrated contagious effects through social networks on levels of obesity. Their analysis of the Framingham longitudinal data examined connections between friends and showed that if Alter, defined as a mutual friend, became obese, then Ego's risk of obesity rose by 171 per cent. The association diminished with more distant friends. However, the effect was of the same strength whether or not the friends met frequently, and also extended beyond the immediate contact, affecting persons at three removes from Ego. Eliminating implausible and unsupported hypothetical explanations, they concluded that 'the spread of obesity may rely less on behavioural imitation than on a change in an ego's perception of the social norms regarding the acceptability of obesity' (2007: 377).[12]

Embodied habits, temporal routines and established norms within social networks are factors particularly emphasized by theories of practice. They are important factors affecting large sections of the population and push eating beyond the control of individuals. Because of their particular emphases, theories of practice may help better understand the trends, circumstances and perhaps the causes of obesity, in particular by emphasizing the situational entailment of courses of conduct. A coherent practice-theoretical account is likely to find its explanation partly in embodied habits but more generally in the affordances of the social and cultural environment, in both material and communicative aspects of the settings in which the practice of eating occurs. The account emphasizes the force of repetition in several different forms. First, while most eating habits are hard to break, embodied habits are particularly difficult. Second, deliberation is rare; as the behavioural accounts insist, constant explicit monitoring of conduct is costly in both time and energy and even then far from guaranteed to be successful. Other forms of repetition besides habit – for instance the greater or lesser degree of routinization of mealtimes, content and formats – steer behaviour. Moreover, and most importantly, other people also have habits and observe routines. These operate vicariously as steering devices by virtue of the need to anticipate and synchronize with them. In the light of these observations we might expect that some common strategies for remedying the crisis of obesity, or for individual weight loss for that matter, would be unlikely to succeed and that others, more conscious of the role of habituation, might prove more efficacious.

Conclusion

These accounts all contend that habitualization is of crucial importance in the explanation of everyday conduct. They emphasize different combinations and powers for the three key features of habit – mindlessness, self-actuation and repetition in everyday life. Schematically, both Noe and the psychologists, from opposite ends of a continuum, suggest that all are necessary to a proper depiction of habit. Some see the possibility of slipping easily or frequently from System 1 to System 2, such that habit is not necessarily a recipe for constant identical replication. Others see different degrees of self-actuation, with much dispute over the mechanisms involved. Yet others divide over the nature of repetition, some like the pragmatists finding it not a very compelling or defining feature, while it seems much more important for sociology and theories of practice – as we will explore in the next chapter. Nevertheless, disputes aside, examination of those positions bequeaths some relevant insights into aspects of practices.

The competent automatic conduct apparent in everyday performances would be impossible without much repetition on the part of actors. Habits, routines and conventions are learned mostly in the course of the accumulation of practical experience. Playing a larger role in the direction of everyday conduct than does scholastic reflection, practical experience delivers and enhances an understanding of the constraints and potentialities of different types of cultural and material setting. Repetition is insufficiently examined as a process or as a concept. It is not simply equivalent to habit. Repetition creates typical and effective procedures which lie behind the patterns displayed as part of the process of becoming more expert. It is not just a matter of displaying competence in personal performances. Repetition also has emergent effects, including the externalization of social arrangements for coordination, regulation and transmission of practices. Repetition is by definition sequential, but it also occurs in the context of other practices.

Habits and habituation cannot be comprehended in the absence of an external environment which is responsible for instigating and accommodating performances. The process is more complicated than is suggested by the automatic triggering of behaviours by cues in the environment, as is suggested in psychology's models of the unit act. However, the general picture, in which actors, armed with sophisticated acquired competences, are stimulated by properties of settings, seems accurate. The goal, then, is to depict the relevant anatomical features of the environments which encase eating.

While the external environment plays a very powerful role in explaining repetitive action, explicating the idea that cues trigger behaviour is difficult, as is specifying the relevant features of the environment. Any environment comprises the sediment from many kinds of practices. Hence, it takes an eye trained in the relevant practices to exercise the selective perception required to instantly decode cues necessary for competent performance. Some cues may have regrettable consequences for particular individuals – leading them into temptation and reinforcing bad habits. However, there is no alternative other than to inhabit culturally framed environments which contain the potentially confusing signs and residues of multiple actors and multiple practices.

The objectivation of culture occurs not only through intermediation processes of codification and regulation, but also through everyday repetition of actions which leave traces in the physical environment and a public stock of fragments of informal and often frail knowledge. Frail knowledge emerges from hearsay, chatter and opinion, often obtained at second or third hand as commentaries upon commentaries. Fragmentary items of information are obtained as a result of passing contact, in circumstances of distraction, in the course of movement through public space, by means of much casual observation of and interaction with other people, and through exposure to mass media communication. Such products of the objectivation of culture are very selectively perceived and decoded, case by case, instance by instance, in contexts where they might be relevant to practical performances. These are not the effects of the reading of instruction manuals and guides to services and do not involve conscious processing and internalization of explicit culinary knowledge. Nevertheless, they perpetuate, through the domain of public culture, understandings of the nature of particular practices and reveal something about the standards to which performances should aspire.

7

Repetition and the Foundations of Competence

Preamble

Repetitious conduct is absolutely central to theories of practice. To say that practices exist as entities requires the positive identification of similarities of response in similar practical situations (thus confirming the existence of some things *shared* – understanding, procedure and commitment).[1] Demonstrating the existence of a Practice requires both that individuals repeat themselves over time and that such conduct can be observed to be repeated across populations. The extended discussion in the previous chapter of recent social science treatments of the concept of habit did not ultimately provide sufficient grounds for adopting it as a general model of action. No doubt there are strongly incorporated habits of the body which individuals repeat very frequently, automatically and mindlessly. However, the phenomena to which the term is applied go well beyond those, are very heterogeneous and are attributed to different mechanisms and forces. For sociological purposes, a more varied set of concepts for dealing with the repetitive character of conduct is required to encompass the flexibility and virtuosity displayed in the ease and effectiveness of competent performances.

Scholars have not been very precise about the nature of different concepts governing repetitious action. Everyday language possesses a number of concepts to describe the operation of mechanisms lying behind the regular (and therefore statistically predictable) repetition of acts and courses of action. Concepts of habit, usage and custom, routine, convention and ritual are applied to many domains of activity, although unsystematically. These concepts generally perform two roles. First, they suggest that repetition has different types of rationale. Second, they situate individual action in a collective context. Occasionally, it is implied that people have routines, conventions and rituals which are totally private and personal. However, these concepts more usefully identify ways in which the individual is connected to, and orients her or his action towards, collective temporal rhythms (like household or community mealtimes), normative principles of social groups which are repeatedly acknowledged (not to eat the dog) or formalized sequences of conduct which are repeated in similar form on appropriate occasions (like the Thanksgiving Dinner, say). In the food domain, normally none of these types of conduct are obligatory, in the sense that non-observance puts the agent at risk of severe punishment.[2] Nevertheless, they steer conduct, their repetition occurring in similar, but not identical, ways among multitudes of persons, all of whom depend on appropriate sequencing for their acceptable enactment. People become accustomed to doing things in a particular, accredited manner in accordance with practical sense.

Disposition is one concept offering a nuanced appreciation of practical sense and the importance of repetition for mundane competence. The effortless stream of conduct which can be replicated across non-identical situations is the essence of competent performances. This raises two pertinent theoretical questions. First, what is the basic anatomy of performances? Second, how do people come to approximate in their performances the injunctions of a Practice such that they come to be carried out in recognizably similar ways? Cognitive science, pragmatism and the sociology of culture give clues as to the operation of practical sense.

Practical Sense: Experience and the Command of Procedures

Cognitive science highlights the automaticity and speed which render acts non-rational. People very rarely sit back to think about what they should do next. Almost always they are sure how to continue with the sequences of action in which they have engaged. They are able instantaneously, without deliberation, to continue their course of action, directing their behaviour in pursuance of implicit objectives or purposes, without hesitation and generally effectively. Such feats are accomplished not because they 'think quickly'; it is not a matter of complex deliberation and rational calculation about utility of the kind associated with the scholastic model of thought. People simply do not weigh up all the pros and cons, select optimal over satisficing strategies, consider the environmental consequences of apples over bananas, which of several possible values to optimize, or whether there is adequate justification for their preferred response to the ongoing situation. According to Haidt (2007, 2012), this even applies to moral acts which are accomplished without recourse to ethical mental processing. Cognitive science suggests that the wonder of the flow of mutually adjusted, purposive human conduct is *not* to be explained in terms of a human capacity for exceedingly fast complex rational thinking as actors are presented with continuously evolving situations.

One avenue for loosening up the strong accounts of habit is to focus on dispositions. Dewey considered it a possible synonym for habit, though he did not prefer it, while Bourdieu made it central to his definition of *habitus*. Disposition implies direction, although without providing an originating motive or a precise purpose for a course of action. It typically indicates what, if called for by circumstances, an actor might be likely to do. It refers not only to an outcome if and when barriers are removed but is also an affordance for a preferred performance. Nevertheless, dispositions per se give no inherent substantive account of purposiveness. While all versions of the portfolio model of action postulate goals that are determined prior to an act, the concept of disposition presupposes nothing much more than some learned, but mostly non-conscious, inclinations. Disposition conveys a much less pressing or determinate sense of purpose than is normally captured, for example, in the concept of strategy, where the actor fits a means to an end which is immediately in view and relatively precisely articulated. The purposeful impulse of a disposition, by contrast, may be concealed because procedures selected and repeated over time, in a more or less similar manner, have become sedimented to the extent that the actor is largely unaware of, and might find it difficult to reconstruct, its explicit purpose or rationale. The intimation of purposiveness in weak strategic action is one that sociology has often deployed, to describe how some institutional arrangements make it seem as if instrumental conduct was planned, orchestrated and decided upon, when in fact no explicit or intentional formulation or agreement ever occurred. Rather, dispositions generate welcome outcomes merely as the outcome of a concatenation of circumstances (including capacities, obligations, constraints and interests) and loosely apprehended objectives, embedded through many repeated episodes.[3]

A second virtue of the concept is that disposition describes a propensity to repeat acts when appropriate circumstances present themselves. It is not necessary to explain behaviour in terms of its regularity or as a universal constant and predictable enactment in response to a cue, as in models of strong habits.[4] The disposition persists without the interval between repetitions being specified.

Moreover, disposition does not lead to the expectation that action will be identical on every occasion when the disposition is put into practice; rather, it retains the possibility of improvisation to meet new, although not totally unprecedented or foreign, circumstances. For a theory of practice, disposition is suitable precisely because Practices prescribe a limited (though not necessarily narrow, as for instance with the range of acceptable dishes) set of possible responses. Individuals are not free to do just anything; responses to a range of relevant and potentially efficacious lines of action are constricted and confined. Being competent in a practice means having a feel for what courses of action would be appropriate. When conjoined with a set of dispositions and predispositions, conduct is mostly steered effectively. The more efficacy attributed to disposition, the less a concept of decision is needed. Past experience is the tacit guide or steering mechanism intimating how to turn a particular situation to advantage in light of the standards of the relevant practice.

Dispositions should be considered as elements or foundations of practical reason. The inspiration for concern with practical reason, practical sense or practical consciousness was scepticism about the universality (ontological or theoretical) of reflective calculation. Giddens, though giving little role for calculation, did not abandon reflection or reflexivity and increasingly saw this less as a matter of the monitoring of behaviour and more as a matter of masterful projects. The pragmatist insistence that reflection is mostly a matter of alighting upon corrective measures when a course of action goes awry gives a significantly different impression from the celebration of virtuosity conveyed by concepts of reflexive agency. Bourdieu also was sceptical about the extent of reflection. An automatist *avant la lettre*, he did not need the individual to explicitly articulate his or her own goals because these derived from collective sources and were inherited by virtue of position and learned from experience. Experience is accrued in particular social circumstances, and understanding the meaning of experience is a collective interpretation gained, promoted and diffused by the people and institutional messages at hand in such contexts. That is one respect in which social differentiation of position matters.

For most practical purposes, reflective calculation, the strategic deliberation about proper next steps in a course of action, is not required. Reflective deliberation is not precluded; practised more by some than others, it is almost certainly called upon by everyone occasionally. However, this does not entail that people act usually in a decision-making mode, which is precisely Whitford's (2002) criticism of the portfolio model. Mental faculties and capacities are permanently operative – people think all the time, and their minds do not turn off – but the process does not conform to the logic or the temporal phasing implicit in the portfolio model. The sociological practice theorists do not so much challenge the existence of deliberation as the over-dependence of many accounts of action on reflective calculation. What the concept of practical consciousness does for Giddens and what practical sense does for Bourdieu is to register the claim that for practical purposes we mostly do not need, and certainly do not frequently have recourse to, extensive deliberation or bouts of reflection. Rather, people have available a repertoire of procedures which are brought into a stream of activity without the need to stop to think about how they are done or whether they will work. Mundane effectiveness in the conduct of activities in everyday life is the consequence of having at one's command suites of procedures, sanctioned by and vouched for by a collectively maintained Practice, which require no reflection about their implementation *in situ*.[5]

The analysis of habit in chapter 6 indicated that people display competence through repetition of simple and effective actions carried out mindlessly. Practice theory suggests that competence is demonstrated in the same mode or manner, in a state of distraction, with regard to much more complicated episodes of conduct. Probably the most useful single concept to capture the phenomenon is routine, which carries overtones of activity extended in a patterned manner in time and space.

Routine, Custom and Convention: Some Concepts Governing Repetition

Routine is first and foremost conceptualized in relation to time; it indicates temporally regular repetition of particular series of actions. Habit, by contrast, at least understood as a disposition to action, does not require temporal *regularity*, for I may have a disposition which is rarely, if ever, exercised. So while habits do tend to be repeated, typically because acquiring habits requires repetition to form the habit initially, nothing is implied about frequency, regularity or sequencing. Routine has been a more popular sociological concept,[6] partly because in a rationalized and bureaucratic world governed by clock-time, the patterning of conduct accords with imperatives of temporal organization. Temporal routines are both personal and collective, entailing repetition and rhythm, frequency and predictability. Collective routines which are mandatory or binding generate very strong patterns of individual behaviour and result in reproduction of practices through simultaneous repetition (e.g. the schedules of the monastery as depicted by Zerubavel [1981]). Office and factory hours and mealtimes play a similar role as *Zeitgeber* in industrial societies (Grignon 1993).

Whereas habit is normally understood to be not easily accessible to consciousness or planned alteration, routine usually implies a minor role for choice or design. Individual routines are sometimes interpreted as decomposed plans, initially intentionally established, and subsequently followed because they express and meet the purposes that caused their adoption. However, they may equally emerge without personal deliberation. Collective routines are neither strategically determined nor decided upon by individuals. They are, in origin, supra-individual, affected by organizations and authorities, but more or less binding for individuals. They often stabilize personal habits. Regular mealtimes are a good case in point. When deeply entrenched collectively, individual behaviour is disciplined by customs and conventions by which most people abide and, through their obedience, reinforce. Once established, routines have steering power. As Southerton (2013) argues, timing and practice are recursive; routine is not simply an observed temporal pattern but also has emergent properties. Ehn and Lofgren (2009: 100) describe routines as organizing and disciplining principles of everyday mundane activity and make instructive use of the metaphors of 'routes' and 'pathways' to analyse the effects of routines.[7] They ask: 'When is a chosen route repeated enough to become a trail, and how are trails redirected, narrowed or broadened in ways that slowly may change them? One important aspect of comparing routines with paths is that once the path is established the moment of conscious choice is diminished. Most routines are likewise performed without second thoughts' (2009: 100).

If the first association of the concept of routine is with issues of timing, the term is also used in a second sense, equally valuable to a theory of practice, to refer to the practical, sequential organization of performances. An example would be 'the song and dance routine'. A song and dance routine is, literally and figuratively, a set of steps, in sequences, of shorter and longer duration, which sum to a performance. The repertoire of a performer on stage might be broken down analytically into a list of movements comprising a series of practical procedures, accomplished in sequence. The order matters, and typically the arrangement of the elementary units has been previously planned or scripted so that the relevant steps can be orchestrated effectively on the stage. They can also be isolated for coaching purposes. The process implies a learned series of actions, which can be repeated whenever a performance is called for and for which specific sequence of procedures the performer is highly prepared and especially proficient. Such 'routines' when delivered on stage are not experimental but, rather exemplary, polished, practised through sufficient prior repetition backstage. The component elements might be seen as procedures, not usually rule governed, but a series of well-practised, accomplished and reliably repeatable moves which are at the practical command of the performer. Procedures are manifestations of practical consciousness, units of activity chronically available to the actor, which can be enacted, without more thought or further design and without the actor necessarily being able to explain how the component steps could be imitated or learned by another. These practical routines are the means by which people mostly get most things done, in more or less the same way as before, effectively, if not necessarily with optimal efficiency.

In such performances, time is often critically important. Proficient timing of the component elements or procedures is a source of fluency or competence. A reassuring point of commencement, proceeding in a sequence which fixes the flow of component procedures, operating at a rehearsed tempo, marked out and measured by suitable temporal duration, serve to integrate movement with timing. The routinization of procedures, because of its complexity, entails more than the frequent repetition of simple habits. It is more complicated than an unreflective capacity to put one foot in front of the other when walking; left, right, left, right. Oulette and Wood (1998) recognized this when describing how a fluent habitual performance transcends its component elements and may obliterate any capacity to report or describe their orchestration. Even if learned by following rules, the action could no longer be decomposed into the basic or rudimentary parts, either by the actor or the audience. Routines build upon repeated spatio-temporal sequencing, yet still allow for improvisation.

Studies of eating based on time-use data continue to demonstrate societal patterns in the timing of meals. The three-meal pattern of twentieth-century Europe is still strong. Evidence from France, Spain, the Nordic countries and Britain indicates that most people have three meals a day and that these are concentrated at three time peaks (Lund and Gronow 2014; Lhuissier et al. 2013; Southerton et al. 2012). The hour of each meal varies between countries, as does the degree of concentration at a given hour. In our study of Britain in 2012 (Yates and Warde 2015), a very large majority of people (approaching 90 per cent) claimed to have a regular pattern, mostly of three meals per day. On the weekday prior to the survey being administered, 79 per cent of the population had eaten three meals.[8] Only one person in ten reported that on the days of the survey they had diverged from their normal pattern. They were mostly people who had *not* taken three meals, implying that the approaching 90 per cent of the population subscribe to a routine involving three meals. On the reverse of the coin, 10 per cent declared that they had no usual or regular meal pattern, and on the weekdays surveyed another 10 per cent of people had for one reason or another been diverted from their normal course. As regards timing, at population level three peaks occur during the day when a substantial proportion of people are eating, although the pattern is less homogeneous than in some other European countries. Also, when compared with 1955, while the rhythm of 2012 is similar, there were minor shifts and less pronounced peaks in mealtimes. Nevertheless, the overall picture is one of a population-wide dominant routine, a moderate amount of adaptation and deviation to deal with special circumstances on a daily basis, and a small but not insignificant minority lacking any 'usual' pattern.

Routines may then be seen both as temporal regularities and as bundles of activity whose effectiveness derives from their sequencing. They can be decomposed into a series of consecutive procedures which an individual actor has become accustomed to perform in a given order. Collective routines may usefully be referred to as customs, which under certain circumstances may become ritualized. While there is no greater consensus on the application of the term 'custom' than of 'habit', it is generally defined as a typical or habitual practice backed neither by moral force nor a claim to reason. A custom describes merely the usual, how people in a certain population go about specific activities. As with all these conceptions of repetition, custom has both a personal and a collective intimation.[9] Customs tend to beget conventions because the way that things are done sometimes provokes discussion and may even require justification in some situations, although the grounds for observance are primarily that 'this is how it is round here'. Since the usual is rarely condemned, there is a mild injunction to answer the question 'How should one behave?' as a statement in the form of a convention. Conventions are a guide to competent procedure and simultaneously a tool of justification. Thus, for example, explanation of the frequent presence of turkey at Thanksgiving Day dinners in the United States and Christmas dinner in Britain is primarily in terms of national customs. An annual alimentary routine subtends custom and convention lying behind the (entirely non-compulsory) simultaneous consumption of many millions of turkeys.

Habituation might thus be thought of both as the general default mode of human action and as imparting a significant degree of consistency and effectiveness to behaviour in familiar situations. Anticipated outcomes are accomplished as people get by, with low levels of reflection, in an effective manner in relation to unstated and weakly defined or held objectives. This does not imply an absence of mental processing, only that the procedure is passive monitoring rather than calculation, steered by cues in the external environment, propelled by routines, which results in actions consistent with prevailing conventions. One implication is that other people are neither perplexed by the activity, nor will they intervene in order to alter or abort the action.[10] Although insufficiently frequently recognized, the impression that individuals have that they are in control of their actions depends primarily on their conviction that other relevant agents will act predictably, as if in a habituated manner, which is the fundamental basis of an orderly environment for normal and confident personal conduct.

Transmission of Competence

Eating Training

People, then, learn through exposure to, and particularly through repetition of, sets of procedures, consistent with shared understandings of a given Practice, from which arises a practical sense, operating through sedimented dispositions, which jointly function to select sequences of conduct effective in the face of the ever-changing situations in which they find themselves. This poses questions about how injunctions associated with Practices are imparted, to the proficient as well as to novices, such that agentic competence is available to hand for the mounting of fresh performances.

One of the most powerful sources of habituation is the repetition of bodily motions. The physiological elements of eating – seen in chapter 4 to be a complex set of actions including looking, smelling, tasting, conducting food into the mouth, chewing, swallowing, ingesting – are key props of habituation in the domain of eating. They subtend food preferences, speed of eating, manipulation of cutlery and size of appetite. To the best of my knowledge, not much scholarly work has been devoted to how people come to develop their particular versions of what Mauss (1973 [1935]) called body techniques in the domain of food. Certainly, techniques vary between individuals and across cultures. Many of the techniques must be learned in early childhood subject to intermittent and mostly unsystematic training offered by parents. Manners regarding the manipulation of implements, movements of the mouth, and so on, might be subsequently refined.

In some circumstances, people train their bodies purposively, intensively to produce precisely the type of automatic action that is generated instantaneously in the remarkable manner described by behavioural economists and cognitive scientists as the processes of system 1 of the brain. One of Bourdieu's favourite metaphors came from sport where 'the feel for the game' – an embodied sense of how to react, highly tuned in professional athletes, exhibiting a high degree of skill, capability and facility for being in the right place at the right time, adjusting the body perfectly for its next manoeuvre – equally well applies to other activities of everyday life. The flowing improvisation of the skilled cook, the jazz musician or the accomplished conversationalist is often attributed to possession of exceptional talent. However, these are more likely the result of progressive training. In an important article on Olympic swimmers, Chambliss (1989) debunks the idea of talent in favour of an account of the perfecting of technique, incrementally, little by little, as a function of attention to fine detail in training sessions. A similar account of the learning of bodily habits can be found in Wacquant's (2004) notes of an apprentice boxer. Maybe more germane is a similar account of step-wise improvement, from threshold to threshold, through practice, in the apparently more cerebral skills of the jazz musician, recounted by Sudnow (1978). Tellingly, however, he entitled his book *Ways of the Hand*, the fundamental message being that, at a phenomenological and practical level, ability to play recognizable jazz was experienced as a manual skill wherein the hands moved automatically ahead of, and independently of, any specifically focused mental engagement.

The result of training is to make embodied procedures available, always at hand, for instant and automatic inclusion in a stream of conduct. The bodily techniques of eating, including sensory responses of taste, as well as the manipulation of the fork, are probably similar, laid down in a procedural memory through countless repetitions.

Regarding eating, learning is largely informal; eating has not yet appeared on the school curriculum, although cookery lessons and domestic science are taught in some schools which, by addressing directly food preparation and nutrition, transmit some relevant information and instruction regarding what to eat. However, the school dining hall is probably more relevant to learning than is the classroom.[11]

Bodily techniques learned over time from experience might best be re-described as procedures – things that the actor can effortlessly and automatically repeat, at least in familiar surroundings. Such procedures subtend the necessary improvisation that the subtle, and not so minor, differences in situation require of a competent performance. These procedures have to be worked up. They are to some extent imparted by forms of coaching, which might entail advice imparted by a human trainer, or be the material artefacts bequeathed in the process of objectivation of a Practice. An article entitled 'So, how did Bourdieu learn to play tennis?' (Noble and Watkins 2003) described the activities of the professional tennis coach, who intervenes in the mechanical re-fashioning of bodily procedures by means of both verbal instruction (enunciating 'coaching rules') and simultaneous synchronized physical demonstrations which invite imitation. Technical improvements in performances can be achieved through both formal and informal instruction, though almost always only in association with much repetition which, it is said in tennis-playing circles, grooves a player's strokes. Professional assistance in improving eating techniques is not so commonly called upon, although cookery lessons, wine appreciation classes and weight-loss courses do flourish.

No doubt people sometimes set out intentionally and purposefully to improve their performances and do so by seeking relevant knowledge and taking the advice of coaches. That this has become the prototypical model for altering the capabilities and behaviour of individuals is, however, problematic. When governments issue nutritional guidelines or devise labelling schemes in order to get citizens to 'eat better', they overestimate the general efficacy of the model. Behaviour change initiatives, which give people information in the hope that they will act accordingly, drinking no more than a given number of units of alcohol or eating at least five portions of fruit and vegetables per day, are notoriously prone to failure. Re-education often stalls in the haze of distraction and the conspiracy of social circumstances; as Wansick might have said, obstacles within the infrastructure of the organization of eating prove too great, and the casual and contingent cues from the environment, only half digested, spread the seeds of failure. Coaching does not guarantee success.

For example, the evidence of weight-loss programmes indicates that the process of trying to tame the body through a regime of restricting food intake includes a good deal of re-education of the students in relation to many aspects of the compound practice of eating. As Muriel Darmon (2009) well demonstrated in her observation-based account of a course for working-class women led by a middle-class teacher, instruction involves moralizing, counting and calculating, protocols for self-discipline, self-delusion and other disciplinary techniques applicable to other aspects of life. No doubt information and advice about other aspects of the properties of foods, fashion and style are also imparted, but 'improvement' is directed at developing understanding and commitment not only to aspects of the integrative practices most closely tied to eating but also of other social and moral domains (Darmon 2009; see also Lhuissier 2012).

The indirect consequences described by Muriel Darmon imply that many instances of welcome change are not the result of an explicit search for improvement. One source of change not easily amenable to coaching solutions is when the dynamic or force for change actually lies in some distant practice. A qualitative study of changing habits among Anglo-French couples, conducted by Isabelle Darmon and myself, shows that moving in with a new partner is often a source of significant change (Darmon and Warde forthcoming; see also Marshall and Anderson 2002). In a majority of cases, the British partners were subjected to a (not at all unwelcome) period of eating in a French manner, with French dishes and often French meal formats and patterns. One might say that love rather than education was the source of significant change. This was overlain for half the partners by the fact of going to live somewhere new, with somewhat alien institutional arrangements. Britons, for example, commented ruefully on the problems of eating very extended and formal meals with their French in-laws. Interviewees' stories of the ongoing evolution of household arrangements also indicated that changes in employment for one or other partner was a point of change because mealtimes were disrupted by longer journeys to work, longer absences from home or new hours of employment. However, the arrival of children was the most significant source of adults changing their eating habits, involving as it did new nutritional calculations, revised eating schedules, and memories of the current cook's childhood food experience (Darmon and Warde forthcoming). Thus the common patterns of adjustment reported were often a result of changes in practices other than those directly associated with eating. The evidence also affirms what critical reflection on research on behaviour change indicates, that alterations in key parameters of everyday life offer brief periods, so-called windows of opportunity, for effective behaviour change.

These considerations indicate how important it is to understand the interdependence of practices. Alterations to the routines of more or less adjacent practices have knock-on effects. When explicit strategies for changing behaviour acknowledge, as most do in an unsystematic way, that work schedules, family agreements, shopping routines and the like are key foundations for stability or change, they bear witness to the importance of the juxtaposition of Practices. If the social world is comprised primarily of practices, analysing their interdependency is critical, for effective triggers for change may often be found in relatively distant practices. This reopens the question of the boundaries of practices and it problematizes the injunction to examine the practice as a unit of analysis. One possible conclusion is that focus on a single integrative practice (for instance, the overwhelming attention paid to the nutritional properties of the items to be cooked when people try to achieve weight loss) is unwise. Since eating is a compound practice, recommending changes to only some parts of the practice of eating while ignoring the others is a likely source of failure.[12]

Clues and Cues in the Environment

The external environment of action always plays a significant role in the explanation of habituated forms of action. Triggers that initiate a rehearsed sequence of action and the feedback information which reassure the actor in the course of the action are essential aspects of the external situation steering performance. Relevant features of the environment include material objects, infrastructures, messages and people, the complexity of which some American sociologists have tried to analyse as culture.

Paul DiMaggio's (1997) account of how an external social environment steers behaviour, discussed in chapter 6 (p. 112), can be readily applied to explain the ways in which individuals can become, even while mostly in a distracted state, oriented towards conventional eating patterns. He argued that 'individuals experience culture as disparate bits of information and as schematic structures that organize that information' (1997: 263). Hence, because of the need to explain why in specific situations particular schematic structures are activated, a supra-individual, institutional and external symbolic universe plays a very important role. In this view, the environment consists of public culture, a multitude of signposts or steering mechanisms to guide practical conduct. Action is thus informed by shared and institutionalized cultural forms of knowledge, most of which are likely to be unsystematic and contingent, among other reasons because those forms are inconsistent, contested and unequally distributed.

If culture is public property rather than a body of personal knowledge, then it is available to people in the environment of their daily life – in their homes, in the street, in the shops – through signs, concepts and artefacts. Many instances of such phenomena – artefacts, symbols and signs, singular and collective behaviour of observable others – are incidental and often produced without any intention to steer behaviour. The many references on the city street to culinary activity are mostly devoid of intended normative force. They are not the conduits for commands in respect of enforceable behaviour. They are rather hints and clues, traces and sediments, congeries of unplanned and unorganized activity. Nevertheless, such non-scholastic, informal communication is probably a very effective part of the transmission process. Even those dwelling in social circles where food is not a regular topic of discussion are unlikely to escape endless prompts about normal ways to eat. One avenue is through exposure to media. Food has become a staple element of television scheduling. Popular genres include celebrity chefs teaching the preparation of particular dishes, competitions among amateurs assessed by their proficiency and inventiveness, and semi-humorous competitive cooking against the clock. There are channels devoted twenty-four hours a day entirely to cookery programmes. Advertisements and advertorials for particular foods and brands abound. Furthermore, advice and information about food, cooking and eating is peppered across the internet. All the elements that comprise the information load of the publishing and television industries can be found repeated and elaborated online as broadcasts, blogs, encyclopaedia entries, promotions and advertising for shops and restaurants. The published ephemeral literature on food is enormous. Chefs write autobiographies. Tourist boards invent local food routes. Government departments publicize regulations and health advice. Political criticism is addressed to the state and the food industries. It would be very odd to consider all this publicly and almost universally available information and commentary to have no impact upon individual performances, despite its not being studied, consciously absorbed or intentionally taken into account by the actor (Ashley et al. 2004; Naccarato and Lebesco 2012; Rousseau 2012).

As a result, people casually encounter advertisements for ice cream and soft drinks, cookery books on the shelf or in the bookshop, menus at restaurant entrances, equipment in the window of a cookshop, strangers eating in the street or peering at exotic produce in an Asian grocery store. These, the bric-a-brac of publicly available material culture, are the products of a multitude of episodes of externalization through performances, not necessarily of eating per se, but rather of adjacent and associated practices. Shop-owners engage in the economic activity of trying to sell foodstuffs or kitchen utensils; public hygiene regulations are inscribed on certificates on the wall of the butcher's shop; lorries with supermarket or branded product logos pass by; discarded pizza crusts lie in the gutter; and the doors of a weight-loss clinic announce its services. A jumble of signs relate to past and future eating. It is rare to contemplate them in a scholastic manner. People barely, if at all, take conscious notice and only occasionally register such information. But if usually mere background, signs may, under certain conditions, trigger a response. If I am hot and on holiday, an ice-cream stall may rivet my attention; if I am hungry, a restaurant's name board and the view through the window may attract me; a glance into my refrigerator may impel me to go shopping to buy food. The material environment, and the strangers passing through it, are stocked and stacked with potentially relevant cultural information. When proceeding upon courses of action, such signs and symbols receive at best fleeting recognition and mostly practical disregard. No set of rules to govern behaviour could be derived from such signs. The messages are largely incoherent and contradictory, in no small part because they derive from practices with tangential, contrasting or competing logics – economic agencies seeking to make a profit from customers, symbolic representations of domestic affection and care, reminders of personal strategies for avoidance of health risks. In much the same way that advertising normalizes capitalist economic exchange rather more than it sells specific goods (Schudson 1993 [1984]), the multitude of passing references to food announce normal ways to eat rather than spur particular actions. However, the more one accepts the arguments of Swidler and DiMaggio, the more these casual and unsystematic hints and cues circulating in public space should be thought of as influencing performances.

Situations and Response to Environment: How are Skilled Procedures Triggered?

Habituation is an essential aspect of the recursivity at the core of practice theories, whereby repeated and successful performances generate the observed and known regularities which are institutionalized as norms or conventions of appropriate behaviour and their associated practical procedures. Conventions and procedures may then be subsequently transmitted to novices primarily through training (and through re-education to old lags) such that subsequent performances will bear recognizable similarities and approximate the standards of the Practice.

The extent to which objectivated understandings, procedures, rules, standards and judgements constitutive of Practices are transmitted to individuals is highly variable. Nevertheless, the means of transmission of learning or re-learning processes are readily identifiable. Broadcast and narrow-cast media output, advertising, public information campaigns, word-of-mouth recommendation, conversation, advice and correction in relation to a specific performance are among the mechanisms which circulate recommendations about competent performance. The result could never be uniform adoption of procedures and judgements because access to such mechanisms are socially differentiated: which newspapers are read; which TV channels and websites are viewed; which friends are consulted; which locations are frequented; and which advisors are trusted? This does not, however, prevent the generation and reproduction of broadly commensurate impressions that certain ways of doing things are better than others. There is usually a huge amount of redundancy in those messages and many cues are signalled. Some minimal shared recognition of the nexus of understanding, procedure and engagement is normally common currency among the participants of a practice.

A further question that arises is *how* habitualized procedures are deployed, or put into operation. Knowing what to do, instantaneously, *in situ*, is something magnificent to behold and it is not clear that social science really yet has an adequate account. One type of explanation consistent with theories of practice goes as follows. People learn multi-functional or multi-purpose procedures which can be applied in different contexts. The repetitious use of these procedures because they prove generally successful – at least they satisfice, for otherwise they are dropped – converts them into consolidated dispositions, manifest as a tendency to prefer some categories of procedure over others. Those procedures are triggered in response to patterns perceived in familiar environments, which imply suitable directions for the continuation of a course of action, for example the prolonging of a conversation or interaction, or the savouring of a dish. Generally, this is achieved very fluently and confidently because of a familiarity derived from prior repetition in similar circumstances.

People are not often bewildered. Bewilderment occurs when the signs in the environment are incongruous, when what should follow does not, when it is not clear how to go on, or because an anticipated pattern is not forthcoming. People deploy what they have learned not primarily by consulting a stock of knowledge and deliberating, but rather through automatic implementation of sequences and previously rehearsed responses to clues made available in familiar settings which generate fluent practical action. These are not exactly, and certainly not exclusively, habits in either of the strong senses of the term and are probably not best described as habits *tout court*. But they are fundamentally founded upon a capacity to implement procedures embodied as a result of extensive prior practical experience.[13] That does not, however, entail that responses will remain fixed for all time.

Learning New Tastes: The Case of Exotica

One frequent objection to theories of practice is that, because they emphasize habit and routine, they cannot easily account for change. Chapter 5 showed that if Practices are considered entities, an internal dynamic can be detected, arising from controversy, competition and pursuit of excellence, and impelling personal and collective development of procedures, often in the name of improvement or progress. Conventions, routines and habits shift in relation to new affordances and standards. A second source of movement is change in the environmental setting to which performances are adapted. Changes in other practices, ones external to eating – sometimes global cultural trends and shifts in aesthetic sensibility, sometimes economic changes in supply, sometimes changing employment patterns – steer performances in new directions. The 'strong' environmental accounts reviewed in chapter 6 suggest that as the properties of the social and material environment change – with different equipment and infrastructure, revised patterns of temporal ordering, re-classification of standards, new agents involved in coordination and regulation – capacities, and thus performances, will adapt and evolve. This gives some insight into a mechanism behind some of the more remarkable transformations in eating habits in recent decades. Let me take the example of the growth of restaurants distinguished in the marketplace by their provision of 'foreign' cuisine. How can we best explain the growth in the preparedness of a local population to consume vast quantities of previously unfamiliar foods?

In chapter 1, I observed that scholars of consumption and food have, quite rightly, paid much attention to three processes: globalization, commodification and aestheticization. The separate and combined effects of those processes upon contemporary eating practice are profound. For they have transformed the environmental settings in which eating takes place. Strong environmental accounts emphasize the importance of the people, things, orders and pathways which populate public culture. Being adapted to a familiar setting, being familiar with its prevalent operations and having a capacity to navigate it with practical procedures embodied and embedded through repetition, performances flow smoothly. However, what happens when unfamiliar items appear in an environment to which the actor is accustomed? At an abstract level, probably people try initially to hold onto their precious learned procedures and commitments. To ignore the potential interruption is one common response. Another is to find ways to incorporate the potentiality of the innovative elements into a slightly revised set of procedures. Sometimes, by contrast, actors are forced to abandon previous practice very quickly in the face of a very radical alteration in circumstances. More often, there is a process of collective adaptation, with different degrees of rapidity, to the features of the changed setting. Patterns can be detected in this process, and the adaptation of the British population to the availability of prepared 'foreign' cuisine is a fine example.

The current period of globalization has ostensibly diffused a knowledge and appreciation of different cuisines across the world. By cuisine I mean not just cooking, but all that the composition of meals entails for a social collectivity – tools, recipes, condiments, typical ingredients and the organization of eating.[14] Cuisines are now typically accorded spatial delimiters and are most frequently identified as national – French, Italian, Greek, Thai, and so on. The circulation and reception of different cuisines means that some have come to be recognized by many people as 'foreign', arguably the most appropriate term to capture the idea that, while people mostly could not describe the defining principles of their 'native' cuisine, they nevertheless operate with a general sense that such exists and can identify deviations from it (Ashley et al. 2004: 76ff).

A significant, rapid but uneven spread of foreign, or 'ethnic', restaurants has occurred in affluent cities and towns across the globe. The number of different cuisines represented in any western city is growing apace, suggesting an increasing willingness to experience the cuisines of the world. In the West, this is a function partly of the growth of eating out in general, although there are major differences between countries; for example, a much greater proportion of Britons eat out regularly in restaurants than do Norwegians or the Dutch. As the restaurant trade has expanded, it has differentiated its offerings. One major dimension of practical and aesthetic differentiation is cuisine type. Variation between restaurants is signalled by devotion to specific national cuisines.[15] A systematic spatial dispersion of different types of restaurant on any scale of map – international, national or urban – is detectable and symbolically marked. In the United Kingdom, when asked what types of restaurants were liked most, Britons opted overwhelmingly for cuisines other than British. Survey responses indicated that, when presented with a list of a dozen types, almost half nominated one of three most popular foreign restaurants as their favourite (46 per cent said Italian, Indian or Chinese). Conversely, very few (4 per cent) selected these as their least favourite. Since few such restaurants existed in the recent past, it must be that the local populations have developed new and matching tastes and preferences.

Reactions to foreign foods in Britain passed sequentially through four distinct stages: rejection, naturalization, improvisation and authentication (see Warde 2000). Asian food initially met with a considerable degree of hostility and rejection, expressed sometimes in racist fashion (Hardyment 1995: 129–31). Subsequently, however, the population increasingly frequented Indian and Chinese restaurants and takeaway establishments, if we are to judge from the rapid growth of such businesses in the 1970s and especially the 1980s (Burnett 2004). In the years between 1965 and 1980, Asian restaurants and takeaways both created dishes that were particularly palatable to British tastes, modifications which made them fit locally with British tastes; such restaurants also included popular European dishes on their menus.[16] As experience of dining out grew, an aesthetic space became available for more 'authentic' Asian cuisine, resisting thereby tendencies to global uniformity. However, in the interim, improvisation by British chefs increasingly incorporated the ingredients, combinations and flavours of exotic cuisines into their menus. Many of the most celebrated restaurants of the 1990s typically constructed menus which can best be described as eclectic in relation to culinary pedigrees (see Warde 2009).

The result of intermittent exposure to exotic cuisines and their vendors was that people became familiar with the tastes of new foods for which they would have had no vocabulary, expectations or standards for judgement two decades earlier. Britons from the 1970s onwards learned alternatives which fostered an appreciation of foreign cuisine. One effect was to subject food to aesthetic standards and to regularly classify foods in terms of national cuisine, the catalogue of which simultaneously came to include 'British'. For, as Panayi (2008) nicely demonstrated, cuisines, as represented both in cookery books and on restaurant menus, acquired nationality in the post-war period. Before then, the culinary origins of the dishes were a matter of very little concern. Identification of 'foreign' cuisines also permitted the emergence of a new orientation towards eating whereby social distinction came to be attached to an appreciation of variety (Warde, Olsen and Martens 1999). (This tendecy became identifiable in other domains and is now referred to as 'cultural omnivorousness' [e.g. Peterson and Kern 1996].)

An interesting debate might be had about the social origins of the tendency to dispersion of 'foreign' cuisines. Several explanations are promulgated to account for new tastes among local populations. Mass tourism is one, migration another, and new cultural and aesthetic conventions a third. All have some credibility, but probably the last is most persuasive, and indicative of the ways in which intermediation and a changed social and material environment can familiarize people with the new elements of practices and thus alter conventions and habits. Of one thing we can be certain: that it was not Britons deciding individually that they wanted to eat Chinese food that led to the spread of the Chinese takeaway and restaurant businesses in the United Kingdom.

The first and least satisfactory explanation is the growth of mass tourism. Many Britons first took vacations abroad in the 1970s, mostly in Europe at that point, with Spain and France particularly popular destinations. They were thus exposed to unfamiliar food, to different degrees, and reported different levels of pleasure or disgust. Perhaps some returned with new preferences. However, holidays are neither sufficiently frequent, nor do they last long enough, to have a profound impact on habits. Moreover, holiday destinations do not correspond to reported favourite cuisines. Probably the main impact of holidays was to make people a little more aware of, and perhaps more inquisitive or less fearful about, foreign foods.

The most widely canvassed explanation is in terms of migration and the opportunities the food trade offers for small businesses. This seems most true of the United States, where most of the evidence comes from, which saw a steady flow of new sources of immigration through the nineteenth and twentieth centuries. New migrants, living among others from their country of origin, spawn businesses for the import of foods and serving of meals from the home country, supported initially from within that ethnic community. Subsequent expansion depends upon attracting customers from the country of destination, and gradually greater familiarity is established (Gabaccia 1998). The tendency for restaurants with cuisines of former imperial dependencies supports this to some extent; Indian restaurants flourish in Britain, Indonesian ones in the Netherlands. However, the dispersal of foreign restaurants is not proportionate to ethnic group density. More significantly, chefs are versatile and there is little correspondence between the cuisine offered by restaurants and the country of origin of its chef. Food products and the recipes for their preparation flow even more freely than do people.

The rather rapid and general shift in tastes in Britain requires a rather more general environmental explanation. Contemporary urban living is strewn with artefacts and representations of culinary variety. Advertisements, television programmes, shopfronts, restaurant interiors, the shelves of supermarkets and grocery shops, store cupboards, along with popular literature about diet and cookery, supply constant cues for the recognition of the multicultural and international character of contemporary food consumption. For many, awareness is reinforced by past experience of eating such foods not only in public places but also when bought ready prepared and eaten at home. Economic considerations in the catering and food manufacturing sectors lead some professional cooks and chefs, who have the time, the skill and the financial incentive, to experiment, while others imitate their innovations. Gradually, new features among the cultural fragments scattered in the environmental setting prompt different behaviours. Further commodification of the food preparation process, when combined with globalization and aestheticization, spreads the taste for the exotic. Understandings, procedures and standards change as a result of shifts in the environment. Aspects of the practice of eating incorporate new elements, in this case new tastes and flavours, but also new eating techniques, like the ability of Europeans to use chopsticks. Aesthetic standards shifted, new environmental cues aided recognition and provided collective impulses to try new foods.

Reflection and Personal Projects

The previous section described some of the ways in which practices might change and evolve, instigating fresh trends and tendencies in behaviour as new accommodations with the environment generate different performances. Such an account emphasizes the dynamic properties of the external environment and the specific attempts by the organizers of Practices to steer and coordinate activity. Giving priority to those mechanisms is one distinctive feature of practice-theoretic analysis; the focus on repetition and the role of external situations in behaviour provides an important corrective to dominant approaches based on personal and individual choice. Theories of practice, because suspicious of orthodox or portfolio accounts of action, are reticent about explanations in terms of individuals deliberating and devising projects and plans. The obvious riposte from an advocate of an orthodox voluntarist position is that this creates a false impression that people are never able to exercise conscious control over their personal destinies. This is alien to current common sense wherein individuals are attributed personal responsibility for the full range of their behaviour, and where notions like identity projects and lifestyle choice abound. Where, it might be asked, is reflection and agency in this account?

Theories of practice attribute less weight to the role of deliberation – to explicit calculation and projection – in everyday life than many other theoretical approaches. However, emphasis on the effortless exercise of judgement in the moment is in no way to deny the ubiquity of mental reflection. While it is observed that much reflection is shallow and inconsequential, serving to affirm and entrench already established habits and routines, momentary pauses for thought are common. The presentation of a menu in a restaurant often occasions pause for thought in order to select dishes. Uncertainties and indecision may delay reactions about how best to proceed. Moreover, intermittent bouts of deeper reflection occur as people review past performances and dream or project future ones. Processes of evaluation and re-evaluation of past performances reflect on proficiency and effectiveness, sometimes with a view to improvement on subsequent occasions, sometimes as affirmation of a task well done, sometimes as justification for a mistaken decision and sometimes as part of a resolution to behave differently in future. Reflection nourishes hopes and plans for future performances.[17] Deliberation involving dreaming and planning is especially interesting when it prefigures innovative performances in the future.

Episodes of reflection and deliberation occur repeatedly – and are especially consequential – when impediments arise in the orchestration of performances. The most immediate instance is when a routine performance goes wrong and a diagnosis of error is required. A menu felt to lack aesthetic or nutritional balance, a meal taken so late that it hinders digestion and sleep, and a dish containing a displeasing mix of flavours are sources of reflection on experience from which something might be learned. Second, sometimes the circumstances that had surrounded previously congenial routines disappear, as when resources become depleted, the commercial environment changes or others in the social circle adopt new convictions. Examples might include receiving a medical diagnosis, for which part of the cure is a change in diet, or migration, when new surroundings disrupt previous routines and require serious modification to find acceptable substitutes. A third important ground for deliberation is when called upon to give a justification of past conduct. Although challenges are comparatively rare, habits like eating unseasonal fresh food or animal flesh, or discarding edible food as waste, are open to ethical objections and may require explicit justification. Such circumstances provide occasion for re-evaluating performances in the past and making projections into the future. Theories of practice are here distinctive only because the thinking involved is considered to be rooted in and circumscribed by the procedures and preoccupations associated with the orchestration of performances.

As was remarked in chapter 2, one of the attractions of theories of practice at the point of their development in the 1970s was their promise to overcome structural determinism by establishing a feasible concept of agency. Agency, especially in relation to anticipation of radical political change, was frequently equated with individual empowerment, a proclamation that collective destinies were in the hands of individuals committed by personal ethical or political engagement. A parallel notion in studies of consumption was 'the active consumer', a figure who exerted a much greater degree of control than had been allowed in previous accounts which had rendered them passive recipients of pressures exerted higher up the supply chain. Capacity for innovation can, however, be mis-specified and exaggerated.

Individuals do sometimes embark upon projects with a conscious intention to change aspects of their own and others' practices. Most obviously, people determine to participate in previously unfamiliar practices, for example to embark upon specialized dietary regimes like vegetarianism. As Boyle (2011) notes, this involves both a shift in behaviour and a conscious adoption of a new identity, that of having become a vegetarian. As he observes, given many different 'levels' of vegetarian observance, novices rarely adopt the more extreme and taxing versions, like veganism or fruitarianism, although some will progress to these later. To become a recruit, and to participate in a specialized mode of activity, is to join in a collective movement with its own rules, motivations and justifications. Thereafter, a 'career' becomes a possibility. Being a member of such a movement may inspire a desire for improvement or refinement of personal performances, which may well involve reflection on current performances and purposeful greater immersion. It also sometimes nurtures ambitions to take part in the organization of the practice and its diffusion to a wider public. The sociological concepts of enthusiasms and of social worlds capture nicely the different stages and levels of engagement with purposeful collective endeavours in everyday life (Gronow 2004; Longhurst 2007; Unrah 1979). Practice theories put recruitment, participation and the continual adjustment of procedures at the core of understanding. However, participation in a collective venture still takes explanatory precedence over personal deliberation and self-determination. The careers that people pursue usually take the forms that are indicated and afforded by the organization of the practice. Agency need not be conflated with reflexivity, nor should it be reduced to individual empowerment founded on a capacity for self-determination by means of personal reflection.

Personal evolution or transformation in eating habits is also usually more a matter of shifting allegiance between already established alternative types of practice than of radical innovation. Eating is an especially unlikely candidate for a model of pioneering. Children have well established eating patterns long before they have any capacity to conceptualize, countenance or practise significant alternatives. Changed habits must always be a process of modification, for it is impossible to engage in eating completely afresh. Even a process of radical conversion is often a matter of selection among optional modes of eating. The proliferation of well-advertised specialized diets is a feature of current times; there are many options associated with, and motivated and justified by, religious conviction, health concerns, political commitment and aesthetic consideration. Becoming vegetarian is an interesting case because it does not require additional economic resources. While it might be considered a project of the self – certainly in interviews vegetarians frequently talk in retrospect about the process in terms of a considered personal project for which they have reasons and rationale (e.g. Beardsworth and Keil 1997: 235) – it is also socially structured. It is organized and coordinated by the apparatus of a long-established social movement which is keen to attract adherents; it could therefore be considered an episode of social mobilization. Its spread is in part a matter of infrastructure; the facilities and atmosphere are more conducive in the United Kingdom than in France, for example. It also proves attractive to a particular group within the population – young people, especially young women, are the most likely converts. Transitions or careers are patterned, with defection a permanent possibility; many convert, but the proportion of vegetarians in the British population seems to remain constant.

The concept of conversion, while often used, may be misleading, intimating conscious deliberation when in fact the process of adjustment is often neither abrupt nor decisive. When individuals embark on projects to change their practice, they are more likely to succeed if they have explicit social support than if they are reliant purely upon will-power or intention. The evidence is that weight-loss diets, which are mostly unsuccessful in the long term, have more chance of being effective if they are pursued in association with others, in classes or clinics, where personal endeavours receive social support. A favourable context, involving a collective programme and peer approval, makes individual change in behaviour much more likely.

Conclusion: Repetition in Practice

Any version of a theory of practice requires a convincing account of the role of repeated and similar performances by individuals and across populations. Practice theory has not yet alighted on an agreed vocabulary for dealing with the many repetitious aspects of conduct. Bodily techniques are most readily understood in terms of habit; repetition makes for automatic reactions. However, the phenomenon of repetition is so extensive, portentous and complex that it cannot be encapsulated or exhausted by any established version of the concept of habit. Concepts of habit generally prove too restrictive. Concepts of custom, routine, convention and ritual, which recognize habituation as a collective or social property, and which thereby decentre deliberation and decision from explanation, increase conceptual flexibility.

The inescapably temporal aspect of repetition aids the conceptualization of the sequential and serial nature of conduct, and pulls analysis away from the typical focus on the unit act. Streams of conduct are an appropriate object of sociological explanations of practice, particularly with respect to eating, through the idea of orchestrated performances. Theoretically, it seems valuable to locate competence in the combination of dispositions and procedures. Disposition intimates purposive inclination which, once triggered, is consistent with the self-actuating tendency subtending habituation. Embodied procedures, mental as well as physical, are vehicles for instantaneously matching dispositions to situations requiring action.

On the basis of practical understanding, procedures are called up from a learned repertoire to fit unfolding situations. Practical sense and grooved procedures, often involving facility with equipment of many sorts, steer competent performances. Eating occasions, menu selection and the processes of incorporation are orchestrated in light of established routines and conventions encountered and enacted in the form of a long series of performances.

For the nexus of understanding, procedure and engagement, which constitutes any Practice, to appear in competent performances requires opportunities for learning, including learning to recognize and read features of the encompassing environment. However, once the strong distinction between mind and body is disturbed, processes of repetition and sensitivity to an environment come to have greater significance for the explanation of many types of social action. Consequently, the environment or setting plays a critical role in explanation. Knowledge, once thought to be internalized, finds its efficacy through the clues and cues, affordances and hindrances, which shape and steer conduct. The capacity to 'read' situations in relation to the logic of particular practices becomes crucial to the construction of performances. Environments are complex, but practical sense is precisely adept at recognizing cues and negotiating passages in pursuit of ordinary purposes inscribed in Practices. Explicit cultural intermediation plays a part, but not mostly in a doctrinal or scholastic way. Its impact on the understanding of practices, procedures and standards, as reflected in the ways that people talk about and justify their eating habits, is far from negligible. However, it is only one among a heterogeneous array of forces the exact influence of which cannot be precisely measured.

This chapter has referred intermittently to differential competence in the compound practice of eating which is displayed in performances. Injunctions associated with Practices are imparted to participants at all levels of competence, from novice to expert, such that capacity is available to hand for the mounting of fresh performances. The short version of an explanation of how practices are transmitted is that people learn through experience, and particularly through repetition, sets of procedures, consistent with shared understandings of a given Practice, from which arises a practical sense, sedimented as dispositions. Practical sense functions to select sequences of conduct effective in the face of the ever-changing situations in which they find themselves.

In this light, we can finally better appreciate the nature of performances. Performances are sequences of conduct, invoked practically in relevant situations by skilled agents, instigated on the basis of dispositions, deploying habitualized and routinized procedures, embodied through experience, imitation and repetition, adjusted to environment and situation, effectively deploying objects and tools, collectively sanctioned or approved in light of explicitly evaluated standards shared by others in the same social circle. Thus convincing and concise explanations will focus on dispositions (understanding and norms), command of procedures (primarily embodied and involving use of material prostheses), and the cues to routines and conventions in a public cultural environment which act as trigger and reassurance about how to go on.

8
Conclusions: Practice Theory and Eating Out

The Promise of a Theory of Practice

Theories of practice offer a distinctive perspective on the operation of the social world. When applied to eating they draw attention to the phenomenon of habituation, to what Camic (1986: 1044) described as more or less self-actuating dispositions or tendencies to engage in a previously adopted or acquired form of action. The recurrence of previously acquired forms of action may be accounted for in terms of a range of mechanisms, including routine, social networks, environmental cues, and institutionalized systems of reward, which steer behaviour such that individuals predictably repeat performances in similar ways. Consequently, practices are reproduced through the reinforcement of notions and enactments of appropriate conduct. Appropriate conduct is founded not so much in values, attitudes, calculations, and conscious design of strategies as in learned procedures. Command of a range of techniques and procedures constitutes a repertoire of alternative ways to carry out a suitable flow of action in light of the standards of a shared practice, which make for reliable and predictable performances. This is not a matter of following rules, or of bringing to mind explicit tenets or techniques which have been formalized as Practices. Rather, it is an essentially embodied (though not thereby unconscious, nor bereft of mental process) capacity to respond in a given ongoing situation by implementing procedures anticipated as being suitable on the basis of previous experience for the generation of an effective stream of action. Such experience may not be solely the personal or immediate experience of the actor. Previous experience is collectively as well as individually stored, and it is gained in collectively monitored circumstances. Effective and relevant performances are triggered by dispositions and recognition of the demands of particular situations. Repetition is important in the process of learning procedures, but is not sufficient since different situations pose different challenges and improvisation is normal. Dispositions are generative and, so long as they are not monolithically wedded to a single procedure, facilitate the generation of different responses depending upon the prevailing circumstances or situation. Lines of conduct may thus be perfectly effective without entailing deliberation or calculated decision-making processes.

In these ways, the elements of activity emphasized by theories of practice, as against the portfolio model – especially habituation, practical reason, routine and convention, limited deliberation, the encompassing flow and sequence of action, and dispositions – are brought to the forefront of analysis. With these particular emphases, it is possible to found a more elaborate, comprehensive and credible theoretical account of eating.

The theoretical analysis commenced by constructing eating as a scientific object. This involved identification of three component elements of the activity of eating which are generic to its understanding in most, if not all, situations, even if my specific terminology is tailored to contemporary settings. A study of eating must examine social occasions, food selection and processes of bodily incorporation. Examination of the ways in which these elements are orchestrated in the myriad quotidian performances of food consumption provides the basis for describing and analysing eating as a social practice.

Theories of practice propose that human activity can best be understood as a recursive process whereby the repetition of performances, in a similar fashion, by a great many different actors, establishes a way of doing things which is constraining upon others who seek to participate in that activity. Establishing which members of which collectivities feel subject to any particular constellation of constraints is a complicated, but ultimately empirical, matter; for example, national, regional, religious, political, class, gender and ethnic affiliations exhibit statistically significant associations with different ways of eating.

A thriving practice not only requires reaffirmation by existing participants but also a flow of new recruits. Because learning must occur in the image of current orthodoxies and their attendant controversies, there is a tendency for path-dependent reproduction of the practice over time. Nevertheless, for a great many reasons reproduction will be imperfect and the associated performances are frequently highly differentiated. Individuals forge their trajectories in the everyday world through engagement in a swathe of already established practices. Those practices are founded upon shared understandings, familiar procedures and commitment to collective norms and standards. Thus, as Reckwitz put it, all practices are *social* practices.

Almost everyone on the planet with the means to do so eats once or more each day. Because they live under very different circumstances, the form and content of what is eaten, and thus performances of the practice, vary enormously. Events, menus and styles of bodily incorporation – the elementary units of eating – take many different forms and guises. Performances require permutation of available options within each of those elements in order to achieve overall orchestration in a manner which will satisfy self and others that eating is being at least adequately carried out under prevailing circumstances. The orchestration achieved in performances is an impressive practical accomplishment. Such performances are unique particulars. Each occasion is different. Yet they typically exhibit patterns; individuals repeat themselves over time and significant features of behaviour are exhibited in a similar manner by members of social groups. An acceptable interpretation of those patterns, one which goes beyond explanation in terms of individual choice and decision, is a major preoccupation of theories of practice. Singular performances are normatively framed; some pathways are prohibited or discouraged, others obvious and well-worn by virtue of their adoption as common and collective habits and routines. Performances are semi-public and serial. They occur in sequence, and the biggest problem in the coordination of eating well lies in achieving meaningful, practicable and justifiable sequences. However, the understanding deriving from past experience, embodied in skilful procedures and awareness of standards, may be sufficient explanation for people mostly going confidently and assuredly about their daily routines. For, even though individual performances are hugely varied, they are nevertheless readily acknowledged by lay actor and social scientist alike to be instances of eating. A key problem is therefore how that mutual understanding is established and sustained.

Mutual understanding is the most fundamental condition of existence of a Practice. In the first instance, it arises from observation and recognition of a frequently repeated activity. The identity of the Practice is partly collectively affirmed by means of shared conventional linguistic usage. More importantly, it is a result of accumulated practical experience and extensive discussion and justification of various actual and potential performances. On the strength of these, individuals may become, by degrees, knowledgeable participants able to make credible judgements. More important is that they prove themselves practically capable and competent. What people actually do is very varied, involving much improvisation and exhibiting structured differentiation rather than strict obedience to common rules. However, most people experience order and continuity; they have a sense of what is usual for them and typically explain exceptional instances as deviation from the normal.[1]

Performances, when widely repeated, create the impression that there are proper ways to go about the business of everyday life; effective or admissible procedures and legitimate and justifiable objectives are woven into shared understandings which are taken for granted in given social circles. The consequence is a sense of an external, 'objectivated' social reality, whose features people mutually recognize, and around which they organize their conduct and their interactions. Having isolated elements of a performance, many indicators are available to help to identify a Practice – things, appetites, conventional understandings, evidence of participation in collective routines and rhythms. Despite being in one sense a reified and contestable impression delivered by many actual performances, the implicit conventions exert power, in part by defining often an orthodoxy regarding how people should proceed in their daily lives. This is the essence of the process of institutionalization.

Such a way of addressing the matter is currently rather unfashionable, as sociology has lost confidence in using supra-individual concepts to explain behaviour. The fear is of illegitimate abstraction, of suggesting the presence of collective entities whose existence cannot be empirically demonstrated or examined. However, this concern is exaggerated. Practices are subject to purposeful direction, coordination and regulation by different stakeholders, some of whom are active participants, others of whom are engaged in commentary, in the widest of senses, on performances. Examples include associations and organizations devoted to the practices of eating, and published texts describing and prescribing how performances may be staged. Agents construct Practices, with the intention of authoritatively steering performances, and do so through the creation of supra-individual institutions, infrastructures and artefacts which steer conduct.

In chapter 5, I argued that, in general, practices are subject to differing degrees of both social coordination and authoritative regulation. At present, eating in Europe is not subject to very high levels of either coordination or regulation. Eating is treated mostly as a personal and private matter, witness the widespread objection to the state or experts telling people what to eat. It has also been subject to processes of informalization in recent decades. It therefore escapes the authoritative steering of behaviour which obtains in respect of, for example, driving or the taking of medicines. Nevertheless, as the Eliasian accounts of informalization stress, people may not therefore do just as they please. Informalization often requires greater personal self-discipline, greater nuanced understanding and interpretation of what kinds of behaviour will be acceptable (Wouters 2008). Moreover, alternative modes of conduct thrive, so questions of where and what to eat and how to comport the body become more open to judgement and are likely to require more elaborate justification.

In the absence of authoritative regulation, a good deal of controversy surrounds how best to behave. Controversy is fuelled, structured and exploited by the activities of cultural intermediaries. They create visual and written texts which may be studied and which may have direct effects on changing or reaffirming a reader's engagement in the Practice. Interviewees do sometimes report transformative moments, when for example a television programme or a public meeting converts them to radically new ways. However, the impact of intermediaries is mostly indirect, as weak messages are diffused in media products, the built environment and the happenstance of casual conversation. Modern media, in liberal state regimes, positively validate pluralism and court disputation for its entertainment value, notwithstanding a substantial bias towards preferred hegemonic understandings and minimal coverage or suppression of alternatives perceived to be unpalatable. Controversy is a feature of twenty-first-century media culture.

In the domain of food, component integrative Practices have their own internal well-worked debates and disputes. For example, discussions about taste often revolve around what is distinctive about national cuisine, what is authentic national cuisine, whether there is improvement over time and how ideals should be attained. Professional interests are at stake and the level of conviction behind recommendations of best practice is often very high, although the extent to which the intermediaries wish to impose their opinions and solutions on the general public varies. One optional lay response is to follow zealously the recommendations of a single authority; particular dietary regimes or taste movements attract enthusiasts. Most commonly, debate is framed *within* the terms of single integrative Practices. However, because eating is a compound Practice, with contention over the degrees of priority and credibility deserving to be accorded to, say, nutrition, rather than taste or commensality, complications arise. The resulting cacophony constitutes public culture as a rich pool of fragmentary resources.

Usually, in everyday life, most people respond in a pragmatic fashion, mildly aware of disputes and disagreements as they forge practical compromises informed by limited and imperfect information. That is to say, they rarely reflect or deliberate in depth or detail. The nature of these processes, whereby the texts and artefacts arising from the articulation of Practice come to have an effect upon subsequent performances, was examined in chapter 5. All – especially exponents of theories of practice – agree that proficiency and fluency of conduct can scarcely ever be accounted for in terms of following rule books or memorizing codified rules prior to embarking on a course of action. A big question, then, concerns how the objectivated Practice is imparted to the agents which are its bearers, those who are delegated to recursively carry out performances in a manner suitable to reproduce and reform that Practice.

Chapter 6 outlined the general conditions which lie behind the capacity of agents to mount credible performances. People do so fluently and without hesitation. That admirable capacity cannot, however, according to theories of practice, be adequately described or explained by orthodox accounts in the social sciences. The supposition that populations learn rules, values or norms which they subsequently consult in order to make discrete decisions about what to do moment after moment, the form in which action is understood by the Portfolio model of the actor, is found wanting in several respects.

One tranche of reasons adduced, deriving from research in cognitive science and the sociology of culture, includes both the apparent automatic implementing of the vast majority of human action, for people do not stop to think very much or very often, and the intricately entangled relationship of the individual to the social environment, which makes available the multiple artefacts of an external public culture. The strong argument is that the brain does not, and cannot, operate as a storehouse of all the relevant knowledge, information and inspiration which would be required for the average human being to carry out the many complex activities which s/he constantly successfully accomplishes. The wondrous practical competence of my interviewees must therefore be located elsewhere. Theories of practice postulate that these capacities are subtended by repertoires of strongly embodied procedures, by mechanical aids which extend the powers of the individual body and by the steering properties of a social environment which includes other people, symbols and symbolic prompts, and material infrastructure. In Martin's (2010: 240) provocative analysis, culture lies not in our heads but in material objects and the behaviour of other people. Internally, culture exists as unorganized fragments which can be assembled for particular purposes; culture constitutes 'a set of potentials for experience' but outcomes owe a great deal to the chance matters of 'what is available'. The practice of eating is no exception to the general rule, with automatic and vicarious cultural competence endowed by the environment, rather than the individual actor, forming the grounding or foundation of performances.

The capacity for conducting complex activities without deliberation derives from command of versatile procedures which make observable fluency possible. Procedures are embodied and are imparted primarily through practical training, involving enormous amounts of repetition, though not necessarily identical replication nor in identical circumstances. The capacity to act appropriately is thus a product of an individual's specific range of experiences. This is one source of the distinctiveness of performances by different individuals. However, the process of learning is not, usually, a matter of trial and error on the part of autonomous individuals. Rather it occurs in a context of a social imparting of aspects of a shared practice. Sometimes this is by means of verbal instruction alone, sometimes words and practical demonstration, sometimes in the autodidactic mode of reading a manual. However, from the point of first exposure to a practice, the novice is influenced by clues and cues about how other people, and particularly how other competent actors, navigate and traverse the sequences of actions that comprise recognizable performances of the Practice.

This very abstract account of processes finds particular manifestations in social environments of eating. Representations of how to eat arising from the intermediation processes are ubiquitous, populating the public environment in a multitude of forms, not only as media products but also in the visible performances of other people, the commercial infrastructure of the city and frequent conversation about food and eating. Carrying on competently does depend upon an awareness of the definitions of relevance inscribed in public cultural forms, and an ability to deal with them instantaneously (discarding the vast majority as irrelevant), and sometimes subsequently to exercise the capacity to deploy and redeploy the procedures learned and embodied from prior experience. While shaped or framed by cultural intermediation, no determinant effect on any particular performance is entailed. One reason is that people do not follow rules, nor directly and faithfully implement recommendations of the sort laid down in the advice manual. A second is the need always to make a course of action fit a particular situation. The third is that the advice in circulation is almost always multiple, contested, competing and contradictory.

The advice of intermediaries circulates and comes to the attention of individuals in fragments, which are unevenly diffused to people in different social locations. It may still, however, affect aspects of subsequent performances, the best indication of which is how people talk about eating. When they talk to the sociologist in the artificial context of an interview, or when they converse with friends or household members about what to have for dinner, they display a repertoire of understandings and 'knowledge' of conventions and standards. They divulge the normative dimension of the activity, which is circulating in public codes and discourses, and upon which individuals draw when required to engage in discussion about their conduct.

However, most people spend little time justifying their diet or their food preferences to sociologists, or indeed to anyone else. According to recent work at the intersection of the sociology of culture and cognitive science, people spend very little time on reflection in the course of everyday behaviours like eating. The challenge thus posed to the model of the sovereign or expressive individual is conducive to the intuition of theories of practice. Practice theories do not deny the operation of individual deliberation, but characteristically stress the greater, and often unacknowledged, power and relevance of embodiment and automaticity. They can accommodate habituation, but without postulating an overbearing role for strong habits. They espouse concepts of habit, routine, procedure, sequence, disposition and convention, relying on them to convey the nature of practical sense or practical consciousness. They make competence in respect of how to do things the key principle of social organization. Practical competence involves the learning of effective procedures and strategies, founded in much repeated experience, which mostly short-circuits processes of deliberation. Thus the theoretical stance revolves around the notion that there are different modes and rhythms of repetition, the distinctiveness of each being captured in terms of procedures, and key concepts include a distinction between strong and weak habits, extension of powers in the environment through embodiment and equipment and practical and temporal routines. This brings collective institutions to the fore.

Social institutions are the emergent consequence of the multiple performances of activities which, in order that they may be intelligible to persons for whom they are relevant, objectivate the principles or logic of Practices and hence inform subsequent performances. Without some awareness of its principles, observers could not recognize the performance as specific to that Practice. Practices have institutional form and are not imaginary reifications; institutionalization takes the forms of organizations, binding injunctions (laws, contracts) and regulative intervention which exercise agency irreducible to the behaviour of individuals. Individuals mostly do not give shape to their performances after giving conscious consideration to the welter of forces operating extraneously or externally; rather, their performances are intricately woven into a web of potential and meaning afforded by their interconnection with facilitating entities in their environment.

An Application: Eating Out

The account in the previous section contains many observations and injunctions applicable to any practice. Corroborating the value of the general framework is perhaps best accomplished through the illustration of a particular case. Since my general claim is that the conceptual lens of theories of practice will provide a thorough and integrated account of the bundle of activities associated with eating and will generate new insights, I present a schematic outline of eating out as an illustrative case.

Although eating is primarily associated with domestic settings, people have always eaten away from home. Agricultural workers transported food to distant fields. Institutional settings like monasteries, hospitals, military establishments, factory canteens and schools have provided alternatives. Also, travellers have always required meals, which have occasionally been provided as a social obligation of hospitality or charity but more usually in European history have involved personal and private arrangements mediated by payment to inn, hotel or restaurant. The restaurant took shape during the eighteenth century and evolved a myriad of sub-types subsequently (Haley 2011; Spang 2000; Van den Eeckhout 2012).[2] The frequency of eating away from home on commercial premises has increased significantly in the last 30 or so years. One crucial aspect of this has been that eating out has become a very popular recreational activity (Burnett 2004). People eat away from home not just because of travel and work commitments, which prevent a return to the domestic table, but for recreation and pleasure. In Britain, the Food Standards Agency estimates that in 2014 one meal in six is taken away from home (FSA 2014). The majority of these will be eaten on premises dedicated to the sale of prepared foods, although only a minority will be purely social and recreational events. This represents significant growth.

Expenditure on food away from home increased from 10 per cent of the average household food budget to almost 30 per cent between 1960 and 2013 (Family Spending 2013; FES 1960). Eating out is an increasingly important modality of contemporary eating, and it might be considered a significant challenge for theories of practice because of their emphasis on habit, routine, collective rhythms and restricted choice. Or put another way, eating out in a commercial setting might easily be imagined to display the fundamental characteristics of consumer choice – individuals can choose between restaurants and between items on the menu, unrestrained by any obstacle other than an ability to pay for the labour and materials provided by an enterprise. On the contrary, more can be seen about this activity through a practice-theoretical lens.

There are many ways in which to eat meals away from home, including picnics, consuming takeaway food walking down the street, standing at the bar in the railway station café, and sitting in a Michelin-starred restaurant. They signify different types of event, and they will typically result in different types of dish being consumed. One source of typicality is the sequence and frequency of different events. Eating breakfast on the way to work is habitual for a small proportion of the population, and attending upmarket restaurants for dinner is very infrequent and therefore rather special for most. The food supplied at each of these different occasions is unlikely to be confused.

Eating-out establishments operate in accordance within a widely recognized temporal schedule. Inscribed within that is an echo of the same hierarchy of occasions which regulates the pulse of the domestic calendar. The timing of particular events and the matching of dishes to social occasions echo domestic patterns. Mealtimes constrain the rhythms and routines of eating across social circles. Catering outlets serve customers within those parameters. Restaurants have restricted opening times at which they present dishes suited to particular meal events. With the exception perhaps of the British 'all-day breakfast', individual commercial eateries rarely offer breakfast and morning coffee and lunch and afternoon tea and dinner and midnight feast. Through specialization, they steer customers towards tempering their selection of food to fit the occasion. People know where and when it is fitting to order porridge rather than steak tartare. Moreover, given the many different types of commercial establishment, the potential customer has, before crossing the threshold, in principle dismissed an enormously larger set of options about food and ambience. Considering all dimensions of the eating occasion, the degrees of freedom are many fewer than when eating at home.

Outlets almost universally use menus to list composed dishes, narrowing radically the range of items from which to select. If Giard (1998) noted that domestic dishes rarely have names, those appearing on commercial menus can almost always be found in a cookery book and will be prepared in accordance with a recipe. Names imply some kind of culinary pedigree and some degree of standardization of expectation about what will be served. The type of establishment creates expectations about what it would be appropriate to eat, anticipations which are symbolized also by decor, the arrangement of furniture, table decoration, china and glassware, staff dress, menus, opening hours, and so on. The setting is laden with cues. The environment frames and constrains performances. Restaurants also standardize requirements for embodied performance: sitting at a table is usual; predictable and standard eating implements are provided; portion size is carefully controlled; and the fact of putting people on public display constrains their bodily as well as their interpersonal manners. The manner of provision powerfully constricts performances.

Restaurants have been responsible for some of the most radical changes to eating patterns. Their operations conform to the key features of eating and they encourage performances corresponding to a template of shared understanding, procedure and standards. Customers orchestrate their performances in light of the identifiable features of the environment and evidence from research on eating out indicates that they share the understanding, procedures and standards which signify their engagement in a Practice. Almost everyone in Britain integrates episodes of eating outside the household into their alimentary regimes. In the CCSE survey of 2004, only 4 per cent of the British population claimed never to eat away from home. Eating out involves spending time and usually money, mostly on a highly discretionary basis (for there are alternative modes of provision), in an activity offering considerable variation across sites, formats, time slots, styles of cuisine, symbolically identifiable and valorized dishes, companions, prices and much else. However, no one has difficulty in seeing what happens in a café, canteen or friend's house as instances of eating.

The following analysis is based upon two studies in which surveys, face-to-face interviews and focus group discussions reported on experiences of eating out. One examined eating away from home in England.[3] The study involved 35 semi-structured interviews with inhabitants of Preston in the north-west and a survey of 1,001 individuals living in three cities – London, Bristol and Preston – the fieldwork being carried out in 1995. The other involved focus groups conducted during a preliminary phase of the CCSE study of the distribution of cultural capital among the British population.[4] The focus groups operated during the summer of 2003 and were designed to prompt discussion about a broad spectrum of cultural activity and taste. Ten groups, living in various locations around the United Kingdom, discussed eating out. Groups contained members sharing particular socio-economic, demographic and identity characteristics.

Interviews in 1995 revealed clearly that people generally recognize at some level that they are involved in the same activity, in a practice of eating out. When asked, people offer a comparatively small set of reasons for wanting to eat out and invoke an equally narrow set of considerations when evaluating their experiences. They have a shared set of understandings about what eating out involves, how to recognize it and delimit it. Interviewees defined eating out as occurring away from home, involving none of their own labour, requiring payment, being a social occasion, itself relatively special, and involving eating a meal rather than a snack. Not everyone mentioned all six features, but this characterization nonetheless constituted shared and coherent understanding (Warde and Martens 2000: 43–7).

A shared knowledge of the procedures associated with eating out was uncovered in response to questions about the last meal that interviewees had eaten away from home. Evaluation of the nature and quality of the service relationship indicated the existence of a widely shared template of how such an event should be conducted (Warde and Martens 2000: 121–34). Features used to evaluate the experience delivered by a commercial establishment included dress codes, rituals of ordering and payment, temporal rhythms, and menu and meal structure. People clearly had different levels of tolerance for formality. Some felt very uncomfortable in, and therefore avoided, formal places, while others said that sometimes they deliberately sought out such places, though this depended upon the type of occasion.

Interviews also exposed significant agreement about the range of prospective purposes and satisfactions. Reasons given for eating a main meal out were quite closely related to understandings of the activity – a change, a treat, an opportunity to socialize, a celebration or a social obligation (Warde and Martens 2000: 47–51). In addition, the survey revealed that eating out was, almost always, highly enjoyable. Eighty-two per cent of people agreed with the proposition 'I always enjoy myself when I eat out'. Only 7 per cent disagreed. Moreover when asked 'How much did you enjoy the overall occasion when you last ate out?', 82 per cent said they liked it a lot and a further 14 per cent said they liked it a little. Satisfaction seemed little dependent upon the type or source of the meal eaten. Concern was mostly that the meal was appropriate to circumstances (people recognized that different venues were suited to different kinds of occasion) and not obviously spoiled in any way. Otherwise, cheap or expensive meals, traditional English or Thai cuisine, couples or families, daytime or evening all delivered similar and overwhelmingly positive experiences in that people claimed to enjoy themselves when eating out. People were concerned with the quality and quantity of food, with value for money, with aesthetic features of the food and the occasion and with having an enjoyable and sociable time. The last of these, the company and the conversation, were most appreciated.

Interviews revealed the existence of common standards, indicated for example by a typical range of complaints. Neither the sociology of consumption nor theories of practice fully exploit the potential of complaints and complaining behaviour. From a theoretical point of view, the event of issuing a complaint strongly indicates the existence of shared understandings, among diners and between supplier and customer, of standards of performance which are expected in a given setting. The topics of complaint were predictable: unhygienic behaviour by staff, poor ingredients, food undercooked, overcooked or at the wrong temperature, staff clearing up too soon and dishes not arriving at the table simultaneously for all diners. These are mostly matters of the service provider failing in some regard with respect to the expectations of their customers (Warde and Martens 2000: 178). In many instances, interviewees reported a sense of grievance but refrained from complaining. Such restraint was often explained in terms of the wish to maintain a harmonious atmosphere around the table. One complex but telling example was a woman who felt a complaint would have been justified but that it would have been impolite to her host had she, a guest, made one. This also underlines that, because most people eat in company, many features of the occasion are outside the control of participants. An intriguing feature of the survey was the frequency with which people played no part in decisions of when and where to eat out. Only 45 per cent of respondents claimed to have been involved in the decision about whether to eat out on the last reported occasion, and 20 per cent replied negatively to the question: 'Did you have any say in the decision to eat there?'

Nevertheless, the practice is not engaged in, nor experienced in the same way, by all. People are positioned within a practice. The bases of positioning include unequally distributed economic resources, cultural experiences and cultural competencies. Interviews indicated not only shared understandings and common procedures but also differentiation by class, gender and ethnic group. Registers of evaluation, for instance, varied from group to group and were used differentially to legitimate and justify normal behaviour. The manner of organization and engagement in the practice also varied, exhibiting locally distinct, but nevertheless collectively shared, norms.

Differentiation was made very apparent in the focus groups of 2004. The poorest groups almost never ate at a restaurant of any kind. Working-class groups had more experience. A group of younger skilled manual workers, who were friends and regular companions, announced a liking for Chinese, British (which they enumerated as steak, chicken, ribs or pub food) and Indian meals, the last especially after an evening of drinking. The men said they preferred a takeaway curry to going to a restaurant. Apprehensiveness was expressed about not 'fitting in' to restaurants. One woman said, 'None of us wants to make a pillock of ourselves,' a point which was followed by a discussion of an uncomfortable episode when a group member had eaten with a brother of higher social rank 'in a really posh restaurant', having to eat 'posh food' and sensing that he was being told: 'Come on, now. You've got to eat this properly.' Possessing appropriate levels of social and cultural competence and confidence is necessary to enjoy diversity of experience (Bennett et al. 2009: 165).

A more affluent self-employed group exhibited much greater fluency in discussion, suggesting prior experience of conversing about their tastes and a preparedness and capacity to justify them. People of higher social class also had more experience. Middle-class members felt more at home in restaurants, and a wider range of restaurants lay within their field of vision and experience. Every group exhibited knowledge of foreign cuisines, but different ones were mentioned at different levels of the social hierarchy. An implicit hierarchy of taste exists. At the top are 'posh' restaurants and those selling exotic foreign cuisine; then come more popular foreign cuisines, especially Italian; these are followed by pub and Indian restaurants; then there are fast-food restaurants; and, finally, takeaway outlets – Indian and Chinese, fish-and-chip shops and street stalls selling burgers.[5] No group experienced the full range. Different contexts attract a different clientele.

Awareness of options often transcends direct experience as a result of the intensification of cultural intermediation. In one focus group, where all members regularly spent recreational time together, one man, in a discussion of favourite types of restaurant, nominated 'Mexican', to which his friends jokingly countered that he had never been to a Mexican restaurant in his life. Celebrity chef cookbooks, restaurant guides and reviews, in print and online, are part of the apparatus which has, for example, generated the community of 'foodies'. Observed throughout the West, they have absorbed, cultivated, discussed and transmitted a body of knowledge, a series of fashionable tastes and a set of aesthetic standards (Johnston and Baumann 2010). A substantial body of comparatively well-informed customers and amateur cooks, they operate with symbolic codes which entrench the credibility of evolving procedures and standards governing dining out, especially of the food content. In the United Kingdom at least, the *Good Food Guide* (*GFG*), that product of a social movement of the professional middle class, has been defining standards of cooking and service for the upmarket sector of the catering trade since the 1950s. A classic form of cultural intermediation, the *GFG* has both tracked and influenced the trajectory of the practice for both restaurateurs and diners. Gradually, its role as a weapon of a consumer movement has diminished, such that it now primarily runs a reputational contest for the industry. While continuing to contribute to public discussion and understanding of aesthetic standards, its influence is no doubt declining relative to television and internet sources.

People select among restaurants on the basis of their appropriateness for a specific type of occasion. Environment matters. Judgements about which venue is suitable for particular purposes differ between groups; the place to go to celebrate a special occasion is differentiated by class and ethnic group. Shared local conventions are reaffirmed by repeated performances among known others. Yet one cannot say that these performances are the autonomous creations of their participants. A widely held set of social conventions govern performances. The predictable regularities involved in eating out are not the result of negotiations on site – in restaurants – between diners, or between customers and providers. Nor are they the result of unconstrained individual choice of behaviour or reflective decision making. There is instead something resembling a recognizable instituted practice, in relation to whose conventions competent actors are able to orient their social performances. The script is not written *in situ* in each restaurant anew. There is a set of widely recognized, institutionalized procedures for conduct, the product both of the intentional design of specific sites and of a generally diffused notion of the conventions of the practice. While the experience of the particularity of a given meal may be a function of the symbolic interaction which constitutes it as a singular event – and interviewees showed high levels of recall of the details of their last meals out – a normative and disciplined understanding is equally apparent. Hence, although particular performances and justifications may operate in accordance with localized conventions, the possibility of local improvisation remains constrained by the wider institutionalized framework. The components of that framework include the understanding of the rules governing economic transactions in a consumer culture, the conventions of eating a meal and codes for personal conduct in public space.

To summarize, typical of any practice, eating out has shared understandings, common procedures, a set of conventions governing performances and shared standards and justifications. Understandings, procedures and engagements are socially differentiated; not everyone engages in the practice in the same manner. Specific experiences of eating out overlap only narrowly for members of different social groups. Performances of eating out are differentiated by social group – by social class, ethnicity and gender. The practice is thus compartmentalized. These differentiated patterns of eating out – frequency, use of resources and preferences for venues and dishes among different social groups – provide evidence of social distinction attached to some forms of eating out. Currently, the appreciation of many varieties of ethnic cuisine confers distinction (Warde et al. 1999). Income matters, but so does cultural capital. Accommodation to levels of economic and cultural resources occurs within the bounds of local circumstances and local networks of associates. As focus-group discussion indicated, shared social and normative understandings regulate group behaviour. Yet, while there is not a uniform way to eat out, nor to talk about it, there is a generalized recognition of its variety, imperatives and constraints. Witness the orderliness of restaurants, where both parties to a form of commercial exchange accommodate one another in accordance with the shared conventions of a normalized and widely instituted practice. Eating out is a particular orchestrated meeting of context and personnel, with many elements regulated from without. It is more regularized than eating at home because of the way that the environment shapes social interaction. This is partly a matter of deliberate design. The existence of the patron is critical to the pattern of consumption within any establishment, for many aspects of appropriate performances are designed into the business model. Differentiation results from the restaurant trade being subject to deliberate market segmentation. The restaurant experience is consequently rather less affected by informalization than eating at home, leaving the customer with less discretion.

Finally

Looking at eating out from a practice-theoretic perspective throws new light on existing empirical evidence and suggests different types of explanation of observed patterns. Modes of provision, the restaurant setting, the constrained interaction in quasi-public space among clients and staff and the widespread shared understandings of the underlying conventional standards of competent performances make for a strongly framed account. The commercial sale of meals frames a specialized version or sub-type of the general practice of eating. It can be seen to have had significant impact on other forms of eating. In Britain, it has been an avenue for significant innovation in the content of the family meal; it is now common for households to eat ordinary dinners accompanied by rice or pasta rather than potatoes, a change which can be attributed to the lessons learned by exposure to restaurants and takeaway outlets (Marshall and Anderson 2002; Yates and Warde 2015). It has had perhaps even more effect on patterns of domestic entertaining, for which it is a partial substitute. Thus some people find cooking for visitors very anxiety-provoking because they anticipate failing to live up to the standards established by commercial producers (Mellor, Blake and Crane 2010). It also has had effects upon the people who engage enthusiastically, the 'foodie' being a particularly instructive example of how a set of activities can escalate into a shared practice which absorbs people's interests, developing commitment (or *illusio*) regarding conditions and standards of excellence and generating a generalized appreciation extending to modes of discussion of many aspects of dealing with food. Eating out is a truncated form of the wider practice, enhancing the ability to pass judgement on the qualities of ingredients and the cooking of dishes. It thereby increases awareness and knowledge of those aspects of the compound practice of eating, and encourages intermediaries to supply ever more information about its organization and coordination. The effects include a more sophisticated, expert and dedicated body of enthusiasts and fellow travellers whose impact has driven evolution in the catering trades.

Of the outstanding recognized challenges to theories of practice, one of the most pressing concerns the relationship between different practices. The requirement to identify practices as the fundamental meso-level units of analysis raises the stakes regarding definition of the boundaries of practices and also awkward questions about the relationship between them. Some of the issues were alluded to in earlier chapters (3, 6 and 7). The concept of a compound practice throws light on how integrative practices, as they develop, are subject both to internal evolutionary pressures and to pressures arising from adjustments in other adjacent, and sometimes indeed rather distant, practices. Thus, for example, mealtimes accommodate the schedules of schools and places of work. Outcomes of fields of forces are often unpredictable because unanticipated and unintended consequences abound. This, however, only serves to underline once again the value of institutional analysis. The success of historical analysis in the social sciences results from specificity regarding the underlying conditions making particular patterns of behaviour possible. Because describing events unfamiliar in the present cannot so easily appeal to common sense (that things are the way they are because they have to be), professional historians draw more complex pictures of context in order to explain unfamiliar aspects of behaviour. The social scientific analysis of the contemporary world has a more difficult task in rendering the familiar strange enough to show how and why behaviour is shaped by prevailing constraints. Sociology might revert to using the terms 'conditions of existence' and 'conditions of possibility' to indicate that certain phenomena and patterns of activity are only possible because of prior institutional forms consistent with and conducive towards a specific range of outcomes.

Some of the general claims made in this book are conjectural. It may well turn out that some of the cognitive science is inadequate, or that the radical anti-idealism proves unsustainable. Nevertheless, it will remain necessary to find conceptual tools which are able to deal with habituation, to diagnose its overwhelming preponderance in the practical, collective, sequential, automatic and repetitive aspects of action in general and of consumption in particular. Possibly, combining recognition of habituation with other accounts of mental faculties of memory and reasoning might provide a more parsimonious explanation of the processes lying between strong habit and deliberative decision making. It also remains possible that occasions of deliberation, although small in number, are more momentous in their consequences than those which are repeated more or less automatically as a function of embodied habit, routine, disposition and convention. I suspect not, but I do no more than claim that my application of a theory of practice is one way to make more coherent sense of prominent aspects of the activity of eating. Significant insights into current eating behaviour – obesity, eating disorders, gastro-anomie, specialization of diets, eating out and 'foodie-ism' – can be generated by examining performances considered to be the enactment of procedures, embodied by agents, using equipment, regulated by collective and conventional standards, activated and propelled by setting (people, infrastructure, symbolic signals, collective routines) and, in distraction, continuously monitored.

Notes

Chapter 1 Introduction

1 I use the term 'Practices', with a capital 'P', to refer to the notion of a practice as an entity, rather than simply behaviour. The distinction is explained more fully in chapter 3.

Chapter 2 Towards a Sociological Theory of Eating

1 Charting the inequality of access to desirable goods and services has been a principal contribution of sociological work in the field. On acquisition more generally, see Warde (2010).
2 Murcott et al. (2013) catalogue developments in social research and easily fill 500 pages about research in these previously less prominent social scientific fields, but a substantial proportion is devoted to production rather than consumption. See Pritchard (2013, pp. 167–76) for a review of different approaches continuing to address the question of the role of food in the global (and national) economy, of food security and sufficiency of production required to ensure the survival of the world population.
3 Previously one could find only occasional articles, beginning in the 1990s, in mainstream sociological journals, and typically they were using food consumption as illustration of some conceptual framework or in the context of debates about culture, taste and aesthetics.
4 Note, Abbott (2004) distinguishes three types explanatory programmes (syntactic, semantic and pragmatic), each of which has very different objectives.

5 Though, at the time of writing in 2013, there are estimates that a million people in the United Kingdom are making regular use of food banks run by charities as government policy fails to ensure collective security for the poorest sections of the population.
6 An exception was the examination of eating disorders in the 1990s.

Chapter 3   Elements of a Theory of Practice

1 'The dispersed practice of X-ing is a set of doings and sayings linked primarily, usually exclusively, by the understanding of X-ing. This understanding, in turn, normally has three components: (1) the ability to carry out acts of X-ing (e.g. describing, ordering, questioning); (2) the ability to identify and attribute X-ings, in both one's own and other's cases; and (3) the ability to prompt or respond to X-ings' (Schatzki 1996: 91).
2 Some contend that there is nothing else except the individual performers reflecting upon their performances (and the performances of others); philosophical accounts of practice and performativity and sociological interpretations with strong notions of agency veer towards such a view. The issues at stake have a long history in social scientific debate about methodological individualism, which I cannot resolve here.
3 Even Bourdieu, while empirically interested in many of the elements that might define a Practice, rarely addresses a practice as a coherent entity, instead emphasizing *praxis*.
4 It should be noted also that I use coordination in a different manner from Shove, Pantzar and Watson (2012) in their influential account of practice theory.
5 The idea that a Practice is more than the sum of the individual doings and sayings involved suggests a criterion of complexity. Elias (1969 [1939]) is particularly well known and celebrated for having indicated the historico-cultural importance of belching and scratching in his account of the civilizing process and the refinement of manners in Europe in the early modern era. But while these activities had significance in the broader matter of civilizing manners, no one has found them worthy of description or in-depth investigation. We might conclude that some activities are too simple to be considered as Practices.
6 Note the history of the learning of cookery: what was once primarily a process of watching mother was complemented or circumvented by commercial apprenticeship, home economics training (various levels), Cordon Bleu finishing schools and evening classes, catering colleges and televised cookery demonstrations.
7 These are the products of other practices (practices of cultural intermediation, for example) and they exhibit some properties that Bourdieu attributes to scholasticism.

8 Arguably, assemblages do for DeLanda (2006) the same as *habitus* for Bourdieu, local groups for Gary Fine (2010), interaction ritual chains for Randall Collins (2004) and discourses for Foucauldians.
9 A term coined by Hindess, the 'portfolio model of the actor' was defined by Whitford (2002: 325) as one in which 'individuals carry a relatively stable and pre-existing set of beliefs and desires from context to context. Given the situation, they select from this portfolio "those elements that seem relevant and [use] them to decide on a course of action".'

Chapter 4   Elementary Forms of Eating

1 The *Oxford English Dictionary* (OED 1989) distinguishes two headline meanings: 'to consume for nutriment' and 'to destroy by devouring'. The first is elaborated as 'take into the mouth piecemeal, and masticate and swallow as food; to consume as food'. Its primary intransitive usage is defined by OED (1989) as 'to consume food, take a meal'. The close connection between food and meal is both historically informative and a problem for precision in social scientific analysis. Secondary meanings include to consume, to corrode and to taste.
2 Nor was food a focus of attention for the many students and researchers with whom he collaborated.
3 Probably this depiction of the French bourgeoisie no longer holds in the twenty-first century. Bourgeois manners have disintegrated and degraded, but not without some elements having been dispersed and diffused to other social groups; there seems to be no substitute dominant template. Debates about gastro-anomie and informalization are testimony to the sensitivity about deviations from late nineteenth-century French bourgeois norms (see Kaufmann 2010).
4 A third objection might be that postulating 'a cultural frame of reference' does not give a persuasive enough account of how that actually gets to affect performances (or actions) substantively.
5 The data were produced by the research team for the ESRC project *Cultural Capital and Social Exclusion: A Critical Investigation* (Award no. R000239801). The team comprised Tony Bennett (Principal Applicant), Mike Savage, Elizabeth Silva, Alan Warde (Co-Applicants), David Wright and Modesto Gayo-Cal (Research Fellows). For the main results of the study, see Bennett et al. (2009).

The data were collected in 2003–4 from focus groups, a national random sample survey and follow-up semi-structured interviews with selected respondents and their partners. I quote extensively from the information provided by the third of these instruments where people were asked to describe the previous day's 'main meal', most of which occurred on a weekday. Evidence was provided by 24 households for 46 meal occasions: some households reported on more than one main meal, sometimes because partners had not eaten together the previous day, sometimes because an earlier meal was introduced as typical of a routine and most often because different household members had eaten different dishes. From this it is possible to understand something of the experience of eating at home in the contemporary United Kingdom. Some interviewees were also asked a little about aspects of eating away from home.

6   The challenge is to recognize the irregular, on-the-run, occasional, contingent events as part of the overall system – while not assuming that, for example, snacks are without any spatio-temporal pattern (see Yates and Warde, forthcoming).
7   Somewhat more minor issues of location have revolved around whether eating took place in a dining room or a kitchen, at a table or on the sofa.
8   Also, the equation matching event to food content seems to be solved differently if the meal is taken in a restaurant or café.
9   This was a small study recording meals taken by people over the Christmas period in several European countries (Warde and Kirichenko 2012).
10 There is no compelling logic related to the food content that drives the connection or match. It is not that the event demanded X; rather that X was found suitable for the occasion.
11 Douglas uses letters of the alphabet to indicate the relative importance of food items and different courses in order to capture the structure of different events. So, for example, 'A proper meal is A (when A is the stressed main course) plus 2B (when B is the unstressed course. Both A and B contain each the same structure, in small a + 2b, when a is the stressed item and b the unstressed item in a course' (Douglas 1972: 68).
12 Although a customer might choose more than one from a single stage or miss out a stage.
13 One form of dish comprises a single foodstuff, like a raw apple or boiled carrots, let us call this a simple dish. Another form is compound, items like tomato soup or a hamburger, which involve preparation of a melded product from several ingredients, one with a recognizable identity, resulting from the conventional manner of its preparation, and a symbolic unity, signified by its having been named. A further form involves the alignment of more than one simple and/or compound dish, fish and chips for example, where items cooked separately and having a separate identity are presented together as the elements of a single 'course'.
14 Foodstuffs presented at table could be conceptualized as something other than dishes. We could eat nutrients – calories, vitamins, carbohydrates, minerals. It is a matter of contestation when such medicalization of diet is relevant, although it has become a dominant organizing principle in some countries and among some social groups. Discussion in terms of dishes is, arguably, a temporary victory for the cultural repre-

sentation of eating which corresponds to the currently popular genres espoused by professional food writers.
15 See note 5, ch. 4.
16 It should be emphasized that the interviews were not trying to obtain systematic information about everything that people had eaten. No doubt more probing would have uncovered additional items and perhaps even more courses and a greater variety of drinks. A couple of people drank wine, for example, but not many were asked about this. Dessert was an occasional treat for adults; one of 28 households admitted to jam roly-poly and custard, another had yoghurt, another fruit. A sweet was more regular for children, who had had apple and ice cream, instant whip and yoghurts. Only once, in a description of a Sunday dinner, was a starter or appetizer of any kind mentioned, Robert recalling that he had had soup.
17 Of the 25 main meals reported as having been eaten on the previous evening, eleven were 'cooked dinners' in Murcott's (1982) sense, containing meat or fish, potatoes and vegetables.
18 I am indebted to a conversation with Bodil Christensen and Linne Hillersdal (2012) for a rare account of the social consequences of bariatric surgery. Typically, online information about the surgery (e.g. Wikipedia, consulted 11 November 2014) make mention of the medical side effects of the operation and the physiological effects on subsequent eating, but without any reference to the social or culinary consequences.
19 But not Chinese takeaways, where you can always eat dishes respectably with the wooden fork provided!
20 Fletcher advocated 'thorough mastication', 'chewing each mouthful of food until it has absolutely no taste and was involuntarily swallowed, which normally meant chewing at least one hundred times' (Levenstein 1988: 87).
21 Social tension may have physical manifestation, as pain, for example, because diaphragms become more rigid in states of anxiety.
22 Southerton (2006) argues that, at more highly salient events where the meal is the fulcrum around which other activities are arranged, the organizer more readily recalls what happened.

Chapter 5 Organizing Eating

1 They tend to be linear and not to present alternative ways of doing or judging; advice is thus typically not open to contestation, though this may be truer of older manuals than contemporary ones.
2 Although driving styles vary, there is a fair level of consensus about what it means to be a good driver. By comparison, what it means to eat well is much less clear.

Chapter 6   Habituation

1. A somewhat analogous logic of internalization is sometimes applied to practices by emphasizing the learning of 'know-how' rather than 'know-what', of embodied rather than scholastic knowledge and of rules of performance rather than values and norms. The connection between Practice and performances is then relatively straightforward; individuals are taught the Practices current in their social environment through engagement in formal or informal learning processes. They are thus equipped with the practical knowledge, normally adequate to the successful accomplishment of their objectives. This solution, however, has some unfortunate affinities with the portfolio model.
2. Berger and Luckmann (1966) did not follow through the account of habituation established in their account of externalization – objectivation when dealing with the third strand of their dialectic, namely internalization. Implicitly, they see learning as acquisition of the knowledge required to decide and direct action personally, rather than the cultivation of habits.
3. Among the reasons, no doubt, are some very prevalent notions of autonomy and responsibility associated with deep-seated western conceptions of the individual.
4. There is a widely canvassed alternative explanation of mindlessness which relies upon the existence of strong, internalized instincts, natural or genetic, which are assumed to be always underpinning behaviour. The position I find implausible. In any case it would not be relevant to the elaboration of theories of practice. The error seems to me to be the mis-estimation of the depth of culture, which is conceptualized as a thin veneer behind which natural species impulses and instincts drive behaviour. It seems more plausible to me that culture is a thick and complex emulsion which, although it may not entirely eliminate impulse and instinct, submerges and reformulates rather than merely channelling instinct. Performing automatically and mindlessly in a highly cultured domain – of which food consumption is one – is not like withdrawing one's fingers from a fire. Nevertheless, it is worth considering the relationship between hunger and instinct, where it seems that people move down the hierarchy of palatable foodstuffs and in, dire crisis, eventually succumb to ingesting the inedible.
5. Note that Camic says nothing in principle about the setting or environment supporting habit, being more concerned with identifying it as one type of action rather than revealing the mechanisms that allow it to function.
6. William James (1981 [1890]: 107) is credited with the founding definition of habit as 'sequences of behaviours, usually simple...that have become virtually automatic'.
7. 'Neural activity enables us to develop the forms of expertise that determine how we deal with the world around us, but the brain is never more than part of the story about how all this works' (Noe 2009: 127).

8 Pragmatists find a distinctive and powerful role for the concept of habit. The force of Whitford's (2002) pragmatist critique of the Parsonian account of socialization as internalization of values and norms is to suggest that an alternative to the hegemonic portfolio model can be found in the pragmatist conception of 'the actor' of Pierce and Dewey: 'In the pragmatists' theory of action behaviour is purposive and even derives from a process of choice, but actors' goals are no longer assumed to be strictly separate from the conditions of action' (326). Whitford thus feels able to contest paradigmatic privilege without giving up the idea that in some instances action is indeed rational. Dewey in particular offers a negation of the universality of the means–end dualism espoused by other accounts in sociology and economics, and he, like others in the pragmatist tradition (see Kilpinen 2009), puts habits at the core of the analysis of social action.
9 Noe is quoted approvingly by pragmatists (e.g. Gronow 2011; Kilpinen 2012) but without enthusiasm for his account of pressures from the environment.
10 It has probably become much more credible as a result of cognitive science investigation in the intervening 15 years.
11 It is intriguing to consider trying to identify the contexts in which the appropriate response is to employ a vocabulary and instigate procedures of 'choosing'.
12 They are at pains to note that in addition to the effects of network connections more general obesogenic features of the environment are relevant: 'Over the past twenty years, there have been enormous changes that promote inactivity – such as labour-saving devices, sedentary entertainment, suburban design, and the general transition to a service economy. There have also been dramatic changes in food consumption, resulting from the decreased price of food, shifts in nutritional content and portion size, and increased marketing' (Christiakis and Fowler 2009: 115).

Chapter 7   Repetition and the Foundations of Competence

1 This is equally true of the weaker models of practice theory which rely only on the mechanism of recursiveness.
2 Although you might get into trouble if you eat your neighbour's dog.
3 For example, Warde and Hetherington (1994), in discussing domestic divisions of labour, show that, while several different arrangements feature in the United Kingdom, they are rarely adopted by explicit negotiation and mutual decision, but rather emerge from complex situations of positioned actors, differential power and the consequences of other practices.
4 Verplanken, Myrbakk and Rudi (2005), for example, propose, as discussed in chapter 6, a strong view of habits as 'learned sequences of

acts that have become automatic responses to specific cues, and are functional in obtaining certain goals or end states'.
5 This model would have a potential problem in accounting for change were it not for the fact that the external environment changes frequently and that the situations encountered are rarely identical.
6 Giddens (1984) makes a powerful case for the importance of the concept of routinization.
7 Thanks to Dale Southerton for bringing this formulation to my attention.
8 About two-thirds declared three meals at weekends.
9 Of course, most customs in the post-Enlightenment world have been subjected to scholarly scrutiny, but for those who perform in a customary manner explicit justification is neither sought nor articulated.
10 Interventions designed by others to interrupt, reform or stop a course of action are particularly telling in relation to convention. Variations on a procedure are permissible, to greater or lesser degree, depending upon what act is in purview, but always within limits. At limit points, others intervene to correct behaviour, indicating that the bounds of acceptability have been reached. People may intervene in my behaviour in the street if I am drunk or abusive. My employer may sanction me for having made a series of mistakes. There are, that is to say, legitimate reasons for others to intervene and they will do so when it seems that conduct is beyond what is normally sanctioned as part of the practice. And of course very often actors who engage in self-monitoring become conscious that their behaviour would be found unacceptable, morally or professionally, by others, and/or that the course of action is unlikely to succeed.
11 The increasing range of research on school dinners shows considerable international variation in policy, rationale, distribution and implementation (see Truninger, Horta and Teixeira 2014).
12 Far less attention is paid to changing with whom one eats, or to altering ones definition of the pleasures of taste, when outlining the dieting programme. Exercise is important, but moving abroad or taking a cookery course might be more efficacious.
13 Lizardo (2012) proposes a strong argument that personal cultural capacities are embodied procedures directly obtained from experience without need to internalize symbolic content transmitted via cultural communications. See also Lizardo and Strand's (2010: 223) advocacy of 'tool-kit theory', which puts great stress on the cues and clues provided by the environment thereby 'offload[ing] a lot of the cognitive work that previous approaches inscribed in the mental make-up of the agent outside towards the world of institutions and external structure afforded by the environment in which the actor is embedded.'
14 This would be the orthodox understanding in the contemporary literature on gastronomy (see, for instance, Gault 2001).
15 The essence of cuisine type, incidentally, is flavour principles – the same main ingredients, and the same basic treatments, produce different

tastes in Greece, Spain, France, Britain and Finland because of prevalent combinations of spices and flavourings (Ahn et al. 2011).
16 Mechanisms of naturalization are described in detail by Wilk (2006: 112–21) regarding the formation of the cuisine of Belize, showing how creolization works to merge foreign and local culinary practices through blending, submersion, substitution, wrapping and stuffing, compression, and alternation and promotion.
17 The sociology of consumption paid considerable attention to daydreaming, thanks to Campbell's (1987) account of the role of the romantic ethic in consumer culture, as well as to the design of future projects.

Chapter 8   Conclusions: Practice Theory and Eating Out

1 Research on eating is inconclusive in respect of the *extent* of routines because not much evidence of sequences is available; the standard data collection technique is the recall of consumption during one or a few days, which makes it hard both to determine the degree of repetition involved for individuals and to evaluate whether accounts offering justifications of behaviour correspond to actual sequences of performances.
2 Beyond the West, the story was different (e.g. Wu and Chee-beng 2001).
3 The main results of this study, conducted with Lydia Martens, appear in Warde and Martens (2000) and the methodology is described in some detail in an appendix (pp. 228–33). The study was funded by ESRC, Grant No. L209252044.
4 See chapter 4, note 5, for further details of the study published as Bennett et al. (2009).
5 At every level of the occupational hierarchy, some individuals, except within minority ethnic groups, preferred British to foreign food.

References

Abbott, A. (2001) *Chaos of Disciplines*. Chicago, IL: University of Chicago Press.
Abbott, A. (2004) *Methods of Discovery: Heuristics for the Social Sciences*. New York: W. W. Norton.
Abend, G. (2008) 'The meaning of "theory"'. *Sociological Theory* 26(2): 173–99.
Aglietta, M. (1979 [1976]) *A Theory of Capitalist Regulation: The US Experience*. London: Verso.
Ahn, Y.-Y., Ahnert, S., Bagrow, J. and Barabasi, A.-L. (2011) 'Flavor network and the principles of food pairing', *Scientific Reports*, December, http://www.npr.org/blogs/thesalt/2011/12/20/144021294/what-a-global-flavor-map-can-tell-us-about-how-we-pair-foods
Appadurai, A. (1988) 'How to make a national cuisine: cookbooks in contemporary India'. *Comparative Studies of Society & History* 30(1): 3–24.
Appadurai, A. (1990) 'Disjuncture and difference in the global cultural economy'. *Theory, Culture & Society* 7 (2–3): 295–310.
Appadurai, A. (1996) *Modernity at Large*. Minneapolis, MN: University of Minnesota Press.
Ascher, F. (2005) *Le Mangeur Hypermoderne: une figure de l'individu éclectique*. Paris: Odile Jacob.
Ashley, B., Hollows, J., Jones, S. and Taylor, B. (2004) *Food and Cultural Studies*. London: Routledge.
Atkins, P. and Bowler, I. (2001) *Food in Society: Economy, Culture, Geography*. London: Arnold.
Bargh, J. (1989) 'Conditional automaticity: varieties of automatic influence in social perception and cognition', in J. Uleman and J. Bargh (eds), *Unintended Thought*. New York: Guildford Press, pp. 3–51.
Barthes, R. (1973 [1957]) *Mythologies*. London: Paladin.

Beardsworth, A. and Keil, T. (1997) *Sociology on the Menu: An Invitation to the Study of Food and Society*. London: Routledge.
Belasco, W. (2002) 'Food matters: perspectives on an emerging field', in W. Belasco and P. Scranton (eds), *Food Nations: Selling Taste in Consumer Societies*. New York: Routledge, pp. 2–23.
Belasco, W. (2008) *Food: The Key Concepts*. Oxford: Berg.
Bennett T., Savage, M., Silva, E., Warde, A., Gayo-Cal, M. and Wright, D. (2009) *Culture, Class, Distinction*. London: Routledge.
Berger, P. and Luckmann, T. (1966) *The Social Construction of Reality: A Treatise in the Sociology of Knowledge*. London: Penguin.
Binder, G. (2012) 'Theory(izing) practice: the model of recursive adaptation'. *Planning Theory* 11(3): 221–41.
Bourdieu, P. (1977 [1972]) *Outline of a Theory of Practice*. Cambridge: Cambridge University Press.
Bourdieu, P. (1984 [1979]) *Distinction: A Social Critique of the Judgement of Taste*. London: Routledge & Kegan Paul.
Bourdieu, P. (1990 [1980]) *Logic of Practice*. Cambridge: Polity.
Bourdieu, P. (2000 [1996]) *Pascalian Meditations*. Cambridge: Polity.
Boyle, J. (2011) 'Becoming vegetarian: the eating patterns and accounts of newly practicing vegetarians'. *Food and Foodways* 19(4): 314–33.
Brannen, J., O'Connell, R. and Mooney, A. (2013) 'Families, meals and synchronicity: eating together in British dual earner families'. *Community, Work and Family* 16(4): 417–34.
Brillat-Savarin, J.-A. (1994 [1825]) *The Physiology of Taste*. London: Penguin.
Burnett, J. (1989) *Plenty and Want: A Social History of Food from 1815 to the Present Day*. London: Routledge.
Burnett, J. (2004) *England Eats Out: A Social History of Eating Out in England from 1830 to the Present*. Harlow: Pearson Education.
Camic, C. (1986) 'The matter of habit'. *American Journal of Sociology* 91(5): 1039–87.
Campbell, C. (1987) *The Romantic Ethic and the Spirit of Modern Consumerism*. Oxford: Basil Blackwell.
Campos, P., Saguy, A., Ernsberger, P., Oliver, E. and Gaesser, G. (2006) 'The epidemiology of overweight and obesity: public health crisis or moral panic?' *International Journal of Epidemiology* 35: 55–60.
Caplan, P., Keane, A., Willetts, A. and Williams, J. (1997) 'Studying food choice in its social and cultural contexts: approaches from a social anthropological perspective', in A. Murcott (ed.), *The Nation's Diet: The Social Science of Food Choice*. London: Longman, pp. 168–82.
Carolan, M. (2012) *The Sociology of Food and Agriculture*. London: Routledge
Cervellon, M.-C. and Dubé, L. (2005) 'Cultural influences in the origins of food likings and dislikings'. *Food Quality and Preference* 16(5): 455–60.
Chambers (1972) *Chambers Twentieth Century Dictionary*, new edn. Edinburgh: W. & R. Chambers.

Chambliss, D. (1989) 'The mundanity of excellence: an ethnographic report on stratification and Olympic swimmers'. *Sociological Theory* 7: 70–86.
Charles, N. and Kerr, M. (1988) *Women, Food and Families*. Manchester: Manchester University Press.
Cheng S.-L., Olsen, W., Southerton, D. and Warde, A. (2007) 'The changing practice of eating: evidence from UK time diaries, 1975 and 2000'. *British Journal of Sociology* 58(1): 39–61.
Christensen, B. J. and Hillersdal, L. (2012) 'Mad og måltider på arbejdspladsen', in L. Holm & S. T. Kristensen (eds), Mad, mennesker og måltider: samfundsvidenskabelige perspektiver. 2. udgave edn. København, Munksgård Danmark, pp. 129–41.
Christiakis, N. and Fowler, J. (2007) 'The spread of obesity in a large social network over 32 years'. *New England Journal of Medicine* 357(4): 370–9.
Christiakis, N. and Fowler, J. (2009) *Connected: The Surprising Power of Our Social Networks and How They Shape our Lives*. New York: Little, Brown & Co.
Collins, H. (2010) *Tacit and Explicit Knowledge*. Chicago, IL: Chicago University Press.
Collins, R. (2004) *Interaction Ritual Chains*. Princeton, NJ: Princeton University Press.
Couldry, N. (2004) 'Theorising media as practice'. *Social Semiotics* 14(2): 115–32.
Counihan, C. (2004) *Around the Tuscan Table: Food Family and Gender in Twentieth-Century Florence*. New York: Routledge.
Crossley, N. (2001) *The Social Body: Habit, Identity and Desire*. London: Sage.
Crossley, N. (2004) 'Fat is a sociological issue: obesity rates in modern "body-conscious" societies'. *Social Theory & Health* 2: 222–53.
Crossley, N. (2013) 'Habit and habitus'. *Body & Society* 19(2–3): 136–61.
Darmon, I. and Warde, A. (eds) (2014) 'Introduction: towards dynamic comparative analysis', in 'Comparing foodways: the cross-national and dynamic comparison of eating practices', special edn, S10, *Anthropology of Food* [online].
Darmon, I. and Warde, A. (forthcoming) 'Trials of adjustment: household formation, re-location and changing eating habits among Anglo-French couples', mimeo, University of Manchester.
Darmon, M. (2009) 'The fifth element: social class and the sociology of anorexia'. *Sociology* 43(4): 717–33.
Darmon, N. and Drenowski, A. (2008) 'Does social class predict diet quality?' *American Journal of Clinical Nutrition* 5: 1107–17.
Darnton, A., Verplanken, B., White, P. and Whitmarsh, L. (2011) *Habits, Routines and Sustainable Lifestyles: A Summary Report to the Department for Environment, Food and Rural Affairs*. London: AD Research & Analysis for Defra.
Davis, M. (2012) 'A time and a place for a peach: taste trends in contemporary cooking'. *Senses & Society* 7(2): 135–52.

DeLanda, M. (2006) *A New Philosophy of Society: Assemblage Theory and Social Complexity*. London: Continuum.
De Solier, I. (2013) *Food and the Self: Consumption, Production and Material Culture*. London: Bloomsbury.
DeVault, M. (1991) *Feeding the Family: The Social Organisation of Caring as Gendered Work*. Chicago: Chicago University Press.
DiMaggio, P. (1997) 'Culture and cognition'. *Annual Review of Sociology* 23: 263–87.
Diner, H. (2001) *Hungering for America: Italian, Irish and Jewish Foodways in the Age of Migration*. Cambridge, MA: Harvard University Press.
Dixon, J. (2002) *The Changing Chicken: Chooks, Cooks and Culinary Culture*. Sydney: University of New South Wales Press.
Douglas, M. (1966) *Purity and Danger: An Analysis of Concept of Pollution and Taboo*. London: Routledge & Kegan Paul.
Douglas, M. (1972) 'Deciphering a meal'. *Daedalus* 101(1): 61–81.
Douglas, M. (ed.) (1984) *Food in the Social Order*. New York: Russell Sage Foundation.
Douglas, M. and Nicod, M. (1974) 'Taking the biscuit: the structure of British meals'. *New Society*, 19 December.
Ehn, B. and Lofgren, O. (2009) 'Routines – made and unmade', in E. Shove, F. Trentmann and R. Wilk (eds), *Time Consumption and Everyday Life: Practice, Materiality and Culture*. London: Berg, pp. 99–114.
Elias, N. (1969 [1939]) *The Civilizing Process, vol. I, The History of Manners*. Oxford: Blackwell.
Evans, D. (2014) *Food Waste: Home Consumption, Material Culture and Everyday Life*. London: Bloomsbury.
Falk, P. (1994) *The Consuming Body*. London: Sage.
Family Spending (2013) *Family Spending, 2013*. London: Office of National Statistics.
Ferguson, P. (2004) *Accounting for Taste: The Triumph of French Cuisine*. Chicago, IL: Chicago University Press.
FES (1960) *Family Expenditure Survey, 1960*. Department of Employment, London: HMSO.
Fiddes, N. (1991) *Meat: A Natural Symbol*. London: Routledge.
Fine, B. and Leopold, E. (1993) *The World of Consumption*. London: Routledge.
Fine, B., Heasman, M. and Wright, J. (1996) *Consumption in the Age of Affluence: The World of Food*. London: Routledge.
Fine, G. (2010) 'The sociology of the local: action and its publics'. *Sociological Theory* 28(4): 355–76.
Fischler, C. (1980) 'Food habits, social change and the nature/culture dilemma'. *Social Science Information* 19: 937–53.
Freidberg, S. (2009) *Fresh: A Perishable History*. Cambridge, MA: Harvard/Belknap Press.
FSA (2014) *The 2014 Food and You Survey: UK Bulletin*. London: Food Standards Agency.

Gabaccia, D. (1998) *We Are What We Eat: Ethnic Food and the Making of Americans*. Cambridge, MA: Harvard University Press.
Gault, H. (2001) *Restaurants de Paris*. Paris: Éditions Nouveaux Loisirs.
Gherardi, S. (2009) 'Introduction: the critical power of the "practice lens"'. *Management Learning* 40(2): 115–28.
Giard, L. (1998) 'Doing cooking', in L. de Certeau, L. Giard and P. Mayol (eds), *The Practice of Everyday Life. Volume 2: Living & Cooking*. Minneapolis, MN: University of Minnesota Press, pp. 151–247.
Giddens, A. (1979) *Central Problems in Social Theory: Action, Structure and Contradiction in Social Analysis*. London: Macmillan.
Giddens, A. (1984) *The Constitution of Society: Outline of the Theory of Structuration*. Cambridge: Polity Press.
Giddens, A. (1991) *Modernity and Self-Identity: Self and Society in the Late Modern Age*. Cambridge: Polity Press.
Giddens, A. (1992) *Transformation of Intimacy: Sexuality, Love and Eroticism in Modern Societies*. Cambridge: Polity Press.
Glucksmann, M. (2014) 'Bake or buy? Comparative and theoretical perspectives on divisions of labour in food preparation work'. *Anthropology of Food*, S10. Available at https://aof.revues.org/7691.
Goode, J., Theophano, J. and Curtis, K. (1984) 'A framework for the analysis of continuity and change in shared sociocultural rules for food use: the Italian-American pattern', in L. K. Brown and K. Mussell (eds), *Ethnic and Regional Foodways in the United States: The Performance of Group Identity*. Knoxville, TN: University of Tennessee Press, pp. 66–88.
Goodman, D. (2002) 'Rethinking food production-consumption: integrative perspectives'. *Sociologia Ruralis* 42(4): 271–7.
Goodman, D. and DuPuis, E. (2002) 'Knowing food and growing food: beyond the production – consumption debate in the sociology of agriculture'. *Sociologia Ruralis* 42(1): 6–23.
Goody, J. (1982) *Cooking, Cuisine and Class*. Cambridge: Cambridge University Press.
Gracia Arnaiz, M. (2009) 'Learning to eat: establishing dietetic normality in the treatment of eating disorders'. *Food Culture & Society* 12(2): 192–215.
Grignon, C. (1993) La règle, la mode et le travail: la genèse social du modèle des repas français contemporain, in M. Aymard, C. Grignon and F. Sabban (eds), *Le Temps de Manger: alimentation, emploi du temps et rythmes sociaux*. Paris: Maison de Sciences de l'Homme, pp. 275–324.
Gronow, A. (2011) *From Habits to Social Structures: Pragmatism and Contemporary Social Theory*. Frankfurt am Main: Peter Lang.
Gronow, J. (2004) 'Standards of taste and varieties of goodness: the (un)predictability of modern consumption', in M. Harvey, A. McMeekin and A. Warde (eds), *Qualities of Food*. Manchester: Manchester University Press, pp. 38–60.
Gronow, J. and Warde, A. (eds) (2001) *Ordinary Consumption*. London: Routledge.

Guthman, J. (2002) 'Commodified meanings, meaningful commodities: re-thinking production–consumption links through the organic system of provision'. *Sociologia Ruralis*, 42(4): 295–311.
Guthman, J. (2011) *Weighing In: Obesity, Food Justice, and the Limits of Capitalism*. Berkeley, CA: University of California Press.
Guthman, J. and DuPuis, E. (2006) 'Embodying neoliberalism: economy, culture and the politics of fat'. *Society and Space* 24(3): 427–48.
Haidt, J. (2007) 'The new synthesis in moral psychology'. *Science* 316: 998–1002.
Haidt, J. (2012) *The Righteous Mind: Why Good People are Divided by Politics and Religion*. London: Allen Lane Press.
Haley, A. (2011) *Turning the Tables: Restaurants and the Rise of the American Middle Class, 1880–1920*. Chapel Hill, NC: University of North Carolina Press.
Halkier, B. (2009) 'Suitable cooking? Performances and positions in cooking practices among Danish women'. *Food Culture and Society* 12(3): 357–77.
Hardyment, C. (1995) *Slice of Life: The British Way of Eating Since 1945*. London: BBC Books.
Harvey, M., Quilley, S. and Beynon, H. (2002) *Exploring the Tomato: Transformations of Nature, Society and Economy*. Cheltenham: Edward Elgar.
Hodgson, G. (2006) 'What are institutions?' *Journal of Economic Issues* 40(1): 1–25.
Holm, L. (2013) 'Food consumption', in A. Murcott et al. (eds), *The Handbook of Food Research*. London: Bloomsbury, pp. 324–37.
Ilmonen, K. (2011) *The Social and Economic Theory of Consumption*. London: Palgrave.
Inglis, D. and Gimlin, D. (eds) (2010) *The Globalisation of Food*. Oxford: Berg.
Ingold, T. (2000) *The Perception of the Environment: Essays on Livelihood, Dwelling and Skill*. London: Routledge.
Jackson, S. and Scott, S. (2014) 'Sociology of the body and the relation between sociology and biology', in J. Holmwood and J. Scott (eds), *The Palgrave Handbook of Sociology in Britain*. London: Palgrave, pp. 563–87.
Jacobs, J. A. and Frickel, S. (2009) 'Interdisciplinarity: a critical assessment'. *Annual Review of Sociology* 35: 43–65.
James, W. (1981 [1890]) *The Principles of Psychology*. Cambridge, MA: Harvard University Press.
Johnston, J. and Baumann, S. (2010) *Foodies: Democracy and Distinction in the Gourmet Foodscape*. London: Routledge.
Jones, A. and Murphy, J. (2011) 'Theorising practice in economic geography: foundations, challenges and possibilities'. *Progress in Human Geography* 35(3): 366–92.
Julier, A. (2013) *Eating Together: Food, Friendship and Inequality*. Urbana, IL: University of Illinois Press.

Karpik, L. (2000) 'Le Guide Rouge Michelin'. *Sociologie du Travail* 42: 369–89.
Kaufman, J. (2004) 'Endogenous explanation in the sociology of culture'. *Annual Review of Sociology* 30: 335–57.
Kaufmann, J.-C. (2010 [2005]) *The Meaning of Cooking*. Cambridge: Polity.
Kilpinen, E. (2009) 'The habitual conception of action and social theory'. *Semiotica* 173(1/4): 99–128.
Kilpinen, E. (2012) 'Human beings as creatures of habit', in A. Warde and D. Southerton (eds), *The Habits of Consumption, COLLeGIUM: Studies across Disciplines in the Humanities and Social Sciences, vol. 12*. Helsinki: Helsinki Collegium for Advanced Studies, pp. 45–69.
Kjaernes, U. (ed.) (2001) *Eating Patterns: A Day in the Lives of Nordic Peoples*. Oslo: SIFO Report No.7.
Kjaernes, U., Harvey, M. and Warde, A. (2007) *Trust in Food: An Institutional and Comparative Analysis*. Basingstoke: Palgrave Macmillan.
Korsmeyer, C. (ed.) (2005) *The Taste Culture Reader: Experiencing Food and Drink*. Oxford: Berg.
Kristensen, S. and Holm, L. (2006) 'Modern meal patterns: tensions between bodily needs and the organization of time and space'. *Food & Foodways* 14: 151–73.
Laporte, C. and Poulain, J.-P. (2014) 'Restauration d'entreprise en France et au Royaume-Uni: synchronisation sociale alimentaire et obésité'. *Ethnologie Francaise* XLIV: 1, 861–72.
Latour, B. (2005) *Reassembling the Social: An Introduction to Actor-Network Theory*. Oxford: Oxford University Press.
Lave, J. (1988) *Cognition in Practice: Mind, Mathematics and Culture in Everyday Life*. Cambridge, MA: Cambridge University Press.
Lave, J. and Wenger, E. (1991) *Situated Learning: Legitimate Peripheral Participation*. Cambridge: Cambridge University Press.
Levenstein, H. (1988) *Revolution at the Table: The Transformation of the American Diet*. New York: Oxford University Press.
Lévi-Strauss, C. (1965) 'The Culinary Triangle'. *Partisan Review* 33: 586–95.
Lévi-Strauss, C. (1969 [1964]) *The Raw and the Cooked: Introduction to a Science of Mythology*. London: Jonathan Cape.
Lhuissier, A. (2012) 'Weight-loss practices among working-class women'. *Food, Culture & Society* 15(4): 645–66.
Lhuissier, A., Tichit, C., Caillavet, F. et al. (2013) 'Who still eats three meals a day? Findings from a quantitative survey in the Paris area'. *Appetite* 63: 59–69.
Lizardo, O. (2010) 'Is a "special psychology" of practice possible? From values and attitudes to embodied dispositions'. *Theory and Psychology* 19(8): 713–27.
Lizardo, O. (2012) 'Embodied culture as procedure: rethinking the link between personal and objective culture', in A. Warde and D. Southerton (eds), *The Habits of Consumption, COLLeGIUM: Studies across Disciplines in the Humanities and Social Sciences, vol. 12*. Helsinki: Helsinki Collegium for Advanced Studies, pp. 70–86.

Lizardo, O. and Strand, M. (2010) 'Skills, toolkits, contexts and institutions: clarifying the relationship between different approaches to cognition in cultural sociology'. *Poetics* 38: 204–27.
Logan, G. (1989) 'Automaticity and cognitive control', in J. Uleman and J. Bargh (eds), *Unintended Thought*. New York: Guildford Press, pp. 52–74.
Longhurst, B. (2007) *Cultural Change and Ordinary Life*. Milton Keynes: Open University Press.
Lund, T. B. and Gronow, J. (2014) 'Destructuration or continuity? The daily rhythm of eating in Denmark, Finland, Norway and Sweden in 1997 and 2012'. *Appetite* 82(1): 143–53.
Lupton, D. (1996) *Food, the Body and the Self*. London: Sage.
Lyon, D. and Back, L. (2012) 'Fishmongers in a global economy: craft and social relations on a London market'. *Sociological Research Online* 17(2): 1–11.
Marshall, D. (2005) 'Food as ritual, routine or convention'. *Consumption Markets & Culture* 8(1): 69–85.
Marshall, D. and Anderson, A. (2002) 'Proper meals in transition: young married couples on the nature of eating together'. *Appetite* 39(3): 193–206.
Martin, J. L. (2010) 'Life's a beach but you're an ant, and other unwelcome news for the sociology of culture'. *Poetics* 38: 228–43.
Martin, P. (2004) 'Gender as a social institution'. *Social Forces* 82(4): 1249–73.
Mauss, M. (1973 [1935]) 'Techniques of the body'. *Economy and Society* 2: 70–89.
McIntosh, A. (1996) *Sociologies of Food and Nutrition*. New York: Plenum Press.
Mellor, J., Blake, M. and Crane, L. (2010) ' "When I'm doing a dinner party I don't go for the Tesco cheeses": gendered class distinctions, friendship, and home entertaining'. *Food Culture & Society* 13(1): 115–34.
Mennell, S. (1985) *All Manners of Food: Eating and Taste in England and France from the Middle Ages to the Present*. Oxford: Blackwell.
Mennell, S. (2003) 'Eating in the public sphere in the nineteenth and twentieth centuries', in M. Jacobs and P. Scholliers (eds), *Eating Out in Europe: Picnics, Gourmet Dining and Snacks since the Late Eighteenth Century*. Oxford, Berg, pp. 245–60.
Mennell, S., Murcott, A. and van Otterloo, A. (1992) *The Sociology of Food: Eating, Diet and Culture*. London: Sage.
Miller, D. (1987) *Material Culture and Mass Consumption*. Oxford: Basil Blackwell.
Miller, D. (ed.) (1998) *Material Cultures: Why Some Things Matter*. London: UCL Press.
Miller, D. (2010) *Stuff*. Cambridge: Polity.
Mintz, S. (1985) *Sweetness and Power: The Place of Sugar in Modern History*. Harmondsworth: Penguin.
Mintz, S. (2013) 'Foreword', in Murcott et al. (eds), *The Handbook of Food Research*. London: Bloomsbury, pp. xxv–xxx.

Mintz, S. and Du Bois, C. (2002) 'The anthropology of food and eating'. *Annual Review of Anthropology* 31: 99–119.

Moehring, M. (2008) 'Transnational food migration and the internalization of food consumption: ethnic cuisine in West Germany', in A. Nuetzenadel and F. Trentmann (eds), *Food and Globalization: Consumption, Markets and Politics in the Modern World*. Oxford: Berg, pp. 129–52.

Murcott, A. (1982) 'On the social significance of the "cooked dinner" in South Wales'. *Social Science Information* 21: 677–95.

Murcott, A. (1983) ' "It's a pleasure to cook for him": food mealtimes and gender in some South Wales households', in E. Gamarnikov, D. Morgan, J. Purvis and D. Taylorson (eds), *The Public and the Private*. London: Heinemann.

Murcott, A. (1988) 'On the altered appetites of pregnancy: conceptions of food, body and person'. *Sociological Review* 36(4): 733–64.

Murcott, A. (2013) 'A burgeoning field: introduction to *The Handbook of Food Research*', in A. Murcott, W. Belasco and P. Jackson (eds), *The Handbook of Food Research*. London: Bloomsbury, pp. 1–25.

Murcott, A., Belasco, W. and Jackson, P. (eds) (2013) *The Handbook of Food Research*. London: Bloomsbury.

Naccarato, P. and Lebesco, K. (2012) *Culinary Capital*. London: Berg.

Neal, D., Wood, W. and Quinn, J. (2006) 'Habits – a repeated performance'. *Current Directions in Psychological Science* 15(4): 198–202.

Nestle, M. (2006) *What to Eat*. New York: Macmillan.

Nicolini, D. (2012) *Practice Theory, Work and Organization: An Introduction*. Oxford: Oxford University Press.

Noble, G. and Watkins, M. (2003) 'So, how did Bourdieu learn to play tennis? Habitus, consciousness and habituation'. *Cultural Studies* 17(3/4): 520–38.

Noe, A. (2009) *Out of Our Heads: Why You are Not Your Brain, and Other Lessons from the Biology of Consciousness*. New York: Hill and Wang.

Nuetzenadel, A. and Trentmann, F. (eds) (2008) *Food and Globalization: Consumption, Markets and Politics in the Modern World*. Oxford: Berg.

O'Doherty, Jensen K. and Holm, L. (1999) 'Preferences, quantities and concerns: socio-cultural perspectives on the gendered consumption of foods'. *European Journal of Clinical Nutrition* 53: 351–59.

OED (1989) *Oxford English Dictionary*, rev. edn. Oxford: Oxford University Press.

Offer, A. (2006) *The Challenge of Affluence: Self-Control and Well-being in the United States and Britain since 1950*. Oxford: Oxford University Press.

Ogden, J. (2013) 'Eating disorders and obesity: symptoms of a modern world', in A. Murcott et al. (eds), *The Handbook of Food Research*. London: Bloomsbury, pp. 455–70.

Ortner, S. (1984) 'Theory in anthropology since the sixties'. *Comparative Studies in Society and History* 26: 126–66.

Oulette, J. and Wood, W. (1998) 'Habit and intention in everyday life: the multiple processes by which past behaviour predicts future behaviour'. *Psychological Bulletin* 124(1): 54–74.

Panayi, P. (2008) *Spicing up Britain: London: The Multicultural History of British Food*. London: Reaktion Books.
Pennycook, A. (2010) *Language as a Local Practice*. London: Routledge.
Peterson, R. and Kern, R. M. (1996) 'Changing highbrow taste: from snob to omnivore'. *American Sociological Review* 61(5): 900–7.
Petrini, C. (2001) *Slow Food: The Case for Taste*. New York: Columbia University Press.
Poggio, B. (2006) 'Editorial: outline of a theory of gender practices'. *Gender, Work and Organization* 13(3): 225–33.
Postill, J. (2010) 'Introduction: theorising media and practices', in B. Brauchler and J. Postill (eds), *Theorising Media and Practice*. New York: Berghahn Books, pp. 1–32.
Poulain, J.-P. (2002a) *Sociologies de l'Alimentation: les mangeurs et l'espace social alimentaire*. Paris: PUF.
Poulain, J.-P. (2002b) 'The contemporary diet in France: "de-structuration" or from commensalism to "vagabond feeding"'. *Appetite* 39: 43–55.
Poulain, J.-P. (2009) *Sociologie de L'Obésité*. Paris: Presses Universitaires de France.
Poulain, J.-P. (2012) 'Sociologie de l'alimentation', in J.-P. Poulain (ed.), *Dictionnaire des Cultures Alimentaires*. Paris: PUF, pp. 1283–95.
Pritchard, B. (2013) 'Food chains', in A. Murcott, W. Belasco and P. Jackson (eds), *Handbook of Food Research*. London: Bloomsbury, pp. 167–76.
Rao, H. (1998) '*Caveat emptor*: the construction of nonprofit consumer watchdog organizations'. *American Journal of Sociology* 103(4): 912–61.
Reckwitz, A. (2002a) 'The status of the "material" in theories of culture: from "social structure" to "artifacts"'. *Journal for the Theory of Social Behaviour* 32(2): 195–211.
Reckwitz, A. (2002b) 'Toward a theory of social practices: a development in culturalist theorizing'. *European Journal of Social Theory* 5(2): 243–63.
Régnier, F., Lhuissier, A. and Gojard, S. (2006) *Sociologie de l'Allimentation*. Paris: La Découverte.
Rotenberg, R. (1981) 'The impact of industrialization on meal patterns in Vienna, Austria'. *Ecology of Food and Nutrition* 11: 25–35.
Rouse, J. (2006) 'Practice Theory', in S. Turner and M. Risjrod (eds), *Handbook of the Philosophy of Science, vol. 15: Philosophy of Anthropology and Sociology*. Dordrecht: Elsevier, pp. 500–40.
Rousseau, S. (2012) *Food Media: Celebrity Chefs and the Politics of Everyday Indifference*. London: Berg.
Rozen, E. (1983) *Ethnic Cuisine: The Flavour Principle Cookbook*. New York: Stephen Greene Press.
Rozin, P. and Fallon, A. (1987) 'A perspective on disgust'. *Psychological Review* 94(1): 23–41.
Sahlins, M. (1976) *Culture and Practical Reason*. Chicago, IL: University of Chicago Press.
Saint Pol, T. de (2006) 'Le dîner des français: un synchronisme alimentaire qui se maintient'. *Économie et Statistique* 400: 45–69.

Sassatelli, R. (2007) *Consumer Culture: History, Theory and Politics*. Oxford: Berg.
Sayer, A. (2005) *The Moral Significance of Class*. Cambridge: Cambridge University Press.
Schatzki, T. (1996) *Social Practices: A Wittgensteinian Approach to Human Activity and the Social*. Cambridge: Cambridge University Press.
Schatzki, T. (2001) 'Introduction: practice theory', in T. Schatzki, K. Knorr Cetina and E. von Savigny (eds), *The Practice Turn in Contemporary Theory*. London: Routledge, pp. 1–14.
Schatzki, T. (2002) *The Site of the Social: A Philosophical Account of the Constitution of Social Life and Change*. Pennsylvania: Penn State Press.
Schatzki, T. (2003) 'A new societist social ontology'. *Philosophy of the Social Sciences* 33(2): 174–202.
Schatzki, T. (2009) *The Timespace of Human Activity: On Performance, Society, and History as Indeterminate Teleological Events*. Lanham, MD: Lexington Books.
Schatzki, T., Knorr Cetina, K. and von Savigny, E. (eds) (2001) *The Practice Turn in Contemporary Theory*. London: Routledge.
Schau, H., Muniz, A. and Arnould, E. (2009) 'How brand community practices create value'. *Journal of Marketing* 73(5): 30–51.
Schudson, M. (1993 [1984]) *Advertising, the Uneasy Persuasion: Its Dubious Impact on American Society*. London: Routledge.
Shove, E. and Southerton, D. (2000) 'Defrosting the freezer: from novelty to convenience; a narrative of normalization'. *Journal of Material Culture* 5(3): 301–19.
Shove, E. and Spurling, N. (eds) (2013) *Sustainable Practices*. London: Routledge.
Shove, E., Pantzar, M. and Watson, M. (2012) *The Dynamics of Social Practice*. London: Sage.
Simmel, G. (1994 [1910]) 'The Sociology of the Meal', trans. M. Symons. *Food and Foodways* 5(4): 345–50.
Sobal, J., Bove, C. F. and Rauschenbach, B. S. (2002) 'Commensal careers at entry into marriage: establishing commensal units and managing commensal circles'. *Sociological Review* 50(3): 378–97.
Southerton, D. (2006) 'Analysing the temporal organization of daily life: social constraints, practices and their allocation'. *Sociology* 40(3): 435–54.
Southerton, D. (2013) 'Habits, routines and temporalities of consumption: from individual behaviours to the reproduction of everyday practices'. *Time & Society* 22(3): 335–55.
Southerton, D., Díaz-Méndez, C. and Warde, A. (2012) 'Behaviour change and the temporal ordering of eating practices: a UK–Spain comparison'. *International Journal of the Sociology of Agriculture and Food* 19(1): 19–36.
Spang, R. (2000) *The Invention of the Restaurant: Paris and Modern Gastronomic Culture*. Cambridge, MA: Harvard University Press.
Sudnow, D. (1978) *Ways of the Hand: The Organization of Improvised Conduct*. Cambridge, MA: MIT Press.

Sutton, D. (2001) *Remembrance of Repasts: An Anthropology of Food and Memory*. Oxford, Berg.
Sutton, D. (2010) 'Food and the senses'. *Annual Review of Anthropology* 39: 209–23.
Swidler, A. (1986) 'Culture in action: symbols and strategies'. *American Journal of Sociology* 51: 273–86.
Thaler, R. and Sunstein, C. (2009) *Nudge: Improving Decisions about Health, Wealth and Happiness*. Harmondsworth: Penguin.
Thompson, C. (1996) 'Caring consumers: gendered consumption meanings and the juggling lifestyle'. *Journal of Consumer Research* 22: 388–407.
Throsby, K. (2012) 'Obesity surgery and the management of excess: exploring the body multiple'. *Sociology of Health & Illness* 34(1): 1–15.
Tomlinson, M. and Warde, A. (1993) 'Social class and change in the eating habits of British households'. *British Food Journal* 95(1): 3–11.
Triandis, H. (1980) 'Values, attitudes, and interpersonal behavior', in H. Howe and M. Page (eds), *Nebraska Symposium on Motivation: Beliefs, Attitudes and Values, 1979, vol. 27*. Lincoln, NE: University of Nebraska Press, pp. 195–259.
Trubek, A. (2000) *Haute Cuisine: How the French Invented the Culinary Profession*. Philadelphia, PA: University of Pennsylvania Press.
Truninger, M. (2011) 'Cooking with Bimby in a moment of recruitment: exploring conventions and practice perspectives'. *Journal of Consumer Culture* 11(1): 11–37.
Truninger, M., Horta, A. and Teixeira, J. (eds) (2014) 'Children's food practices and school meals', special issue. *International Journal of Sociology of Agriculture and Food* 21(3).
Turner, B. (1982) 'The government of the body: medical regimens and the rationalisation of diet'. *British Journal of Sociology* 33(2): 254–69.
Unrah, D. (1979) 'Characteristics and types of participation in social worlds'. *Symbolic Interaction* 5: 123–39.
Van den Eeckhout, P. (2012) 'Restaurants in the nineteenth and twentieth centuries'. *Food & History* 10(1): 143–53.
Verplanken, B., Myrbakk, V. and Rudi, E. (2005) 'The measurement of habit', in T. Betsch and S. Haberstroh (eds), *The Routines of Decision Making*. Mahwah, NJ: Lawrence Erlbaum, pp. 231–47.
Wacquant, L. J. (2004) *Body and Soul: Notes of an Apprentice Boxer*. Oxford: Oxford University Press.
Wacquant, L. J. (2014) '*Homines in extremis*: what fighting scholars teach us about habitus'. *Body & Society* 20(2): 3–17.
Wansick, B. (2006) *Mindless Eating: Why We Eat More than We Think*. New York: Bantam Books.
Wansick, B. and Sobal, J. (2007) 'Mindless eating: the 200 daily food decisions we overlook'. *Environment and Behavior* 39(1): 106–23.
Warde, A. (1992) 'Notes on the relationship between production and consumption', in R. Burrows and C. Marsh (eds), *Consumption and Class: Divisions and Change*. London: Macmillan, pp. 15–31.
Warde, A. (1999) 'Convenient food: space and timing'. *British Food Journal* 101(7): 518–27.

Warde, A. (2000) 'Eating globally: cultural flows and the spread of ethnic restaurants', in D. Kalb, M. van der Land, R. Staring, B. van Steenbergen and N. Wilterdink (eds), *The Ends of Globalization: Bringing Society Back In*. Boulder, CO: Rowman & Littlefield, pp. 299–316.

Warde, A. (2003) 'Continuity and change in British restaurants, 1951–2001: evidence from the *Good Food Guide*', in M. Jacobs and P. Scholliers (eds), *Eating Out in Europe: Picnics, Gourmet Dining and Snacks since the Late Eighteenth Century*. Oxford, Berg, pp. 229–44.

Warde, A. (2004) 'La normalita del mangiare fuori' ('The normality of eating out'), *Rassegna Italiana di Sociologia* (special issue on 'Sociology of Food', ed. R Sassatelli) 45(4): 493–518.

Warde, A. (2005) 'Consumption and theories of practice'. *Journal of Consumer Culture* 5(2): 131–53.

Warde, A. (2009) 'Inventing British cuisine: representations of culinary identity in the *Good Food Guide*, 1951–2007'. *Food, Culture & Society* 12(2): 151–72.

Warde, A. (ed) (2010) *Consumption (Volumes I–IV)*. Benchmarks in Culture and Society Series. London: Sage.

Warde, A. (2012) 'Eating', in F. Trentmann (ed.), *Oxford Handbook on History of Consumption*. Oxford: Oxford University Press.

Warde, A. (2013) 'What sort of a practice is eating?', in E. Shove and N. Spurling (eds), *Sustainable Practices: Social Theory and Climate Change*. London: Routledge, pp. 17–30.

Warde, A. (2014) 'After taste: culture, consumption and theories of practice'. *Journal of Consumer Culture* 14(3): 279–303.

Warde, A. and Hetherington, K. (1994) 'English households and routine food practices: a research note'. *Sociological Review* 42(4): 758–78.

Warde, A. and Kirichenko, S. (2012) A comparative study of modern feasts: 'Eating: comparative perspectives'. Colloquium poster, Helsinki: Helsinki Collegium for Advanced Studies.

Warde, A. and Martens, L. (1998) 'Food choice: a sociological approach', in A. Murcott (ed.), *The Nation's Diet*. London: Longman, pp. 129–46.

Warde, A. and Martens, L. (2000) *Eating Out: Social Differentiation, Consumption and Pleasure*. Cambridge: Cambridge University Press.

Warde, A. and Southerton, D. (eds) (2012) 'The habits of consumption', *COLLeGIUM: Studies across Disciplines in the Humanities and Social Sciences, vol. 12*. Helsinki: Helsinki Collegium for Advanced Studies.

Warde, A., Cheng, S.-L., Olsen, W. and Southerton, D. (2007) 'Changes in the practice of eating: a comparative analysis'. *Acta Sociologica* 50(4): 365–85.

Warde, A., Olsen, W. and Martens, L. (1999) 'Consumption and the problem of variety: cultural omnivorousness, social distinction and dining out'. *Sociology* 33(1): 105–27.

Weber, M. (1978) *Economy and Society: An Outline of Interpretive Sociology, vol. 1*, ed. G. Roth and C. Wittich. Berkeley, CA: University of California Press.

Wenger, E. (1998) *Communities of Practice: Learning, Meaning and Identity*. Cambridge: Cambridge University Press.
Whitford, J. (2002) 'Pragmatism and the untenable dualism of means and ends: why rational choice theory does not deserve paradigmatic privilege'. *Theory & Society* 31: 325–63.
Wilhite, H. (2012) 'Towards a better accounting of the role of body, things and habits in consumption', in A. Warde and D. Southerton (eds), *The Habits of Consumption, COLLeGIUM: Studies across Disciplines in the Humanities and Social Sciences, vol. 12*. Helsinki: Helsinki Collegium for Advanced Studies, pp. 87–99.
Wilhite, H. (2014) 'The body in consumption: perspectives from India', in D. Southerton and A. Ulph (eds), *Sustainable Consumption: Multi-disciplinary Perspectives*. Oxford: Oxford University Press.
Wilk, R. (2004) 'Morals and metaphors: the meaning of consumption', in K. Eckstrom and H. Brembeck (eds), *Elusive Consumption*. London: Berg, pp. 11–26.
Wilk, R. (2006) *Home Cooking in the Global Village: Caribbean Food from Buccaneers to Ecotourists*. Oxford: Berg.
Wood, R. (1994) *The Sociology of the Meal*. Edinburgh: Edinburgh University Press.
Wouters, C. (1986) 'Formalization and informalization: changing tension balances in civilising processes'. *Theory Culture & Society* 3(2): 1–19.
Wouters, G. (2008) *Informalization: Manners and Emotions since 1890*. London: Sage.
Wu, D. and Chee-beng, T. (eds) (2001) *Changing Chinese Foodways in Asia*. Hong Kong: Chinese University Press.
Yates, L. and Warde, A. (2015) 'The evolving content of meals in Great Britain: results of a survey in 2012 in comparison with the 1950s'. *Appetite*, 84(1): 299–308.
Yates, L. and Warde, A. (forthcoming) 'Eating together and eating alone: meal arrangements in British households', *British Journal of Sociology*.
Zerubavel, E. (1981) *Hidden Rhythms: Schedules and Calendars in Social Life*. Berkeley, CA: University of California Press.

Index

Abbott, A. 23
Abend, G. 16
action
  and cognition 101, 112–13
  constrained 36, 125, 150
  decision-making models 103–5, 125–6
  and environment 101–10
  externalist account 111–12
  individual in collective context 123
  institutional settings of 31, 166
  intentional and habit 36, 108
  purposive 40, 173
  stimulus-response model 106
  unconscious (Weber) 106–7
  voluntaristic theory of 4, 10, 35, 143
  see also portfolio model of action; *praxis*
additives 20
advertising 88, 90, 103, 113, 135, 137, 142
aestheticization 27, 68–9, 139, 140–2

aesthetics 3, 15, 54, 55–6, 70, 71, 75, 76, 89, 93, 96, 145, 161, 163
affluence 24, 72, 74, 139–40, 162
agency 3, 5, 22, 28, 35, 42, 44–6, 50–1, 144, 168
  'distributed' 114
  and practice theories 11, 142–6, 152, 154–5, 165–6
  reflexive 125–6
  and structure 33–4, 38
  and weight gain 72
'agri-food studies' 13, 16, 25, 53
agriculture 13, 16, 98
allergies, food 72
animal welfare 20
animals, taboos on eating 54
anorexia nervosa 70, 71
anthropology 15, 24, 28, 29, 59
  praxis in 33
  structuralist 25–6, 55
anxieties about food 19–21, 28, 76, 80–2, 162, 171
Appadurai, A. 27, 67
appetite 71, 102
appreciation 22, 132

Association for the Study of Food and Society (ASFS) (US)   14
automaticity   100–1, 101–5, 106, 108, 112–13, 117, 123–4, 131, 138, 146, 156

Barthes, Roland   26, 65
behaviour
  acceptable   50, 91, 110, 118, 137, 149, 153, 155–6, 174
  change and external circumstances   133–4, 138–42, 166
  change and policy making   7, 20, 104, 115–19, 132–4
  change and practice theories   10–11, 149–57
  complaining   161
  dominant models of   103–4
  past and future performance   108
  role of environment in   111–15, 134–6, 147–8, 155–7
  social nature of   18
  unintentional consequences   38, 103, 165–6
behaviourism   102, 106, 107
Belasco, W.   15, 16
Berger, P.   95, 172
best practice   48, 92–3, 153
BMI measures   115–16
body   1, 3, 28, 29–30, 32
  and food   52
  habits of the   122, 130–1
  management   1, 15, 132–4
  and mind   101, 106, 147
  shape   15, 56, 116
  as a social construction   70
  techniques of the   69, 70, 73–4, 75–6, 131, 132, 146
  weight control   71–2, 93, 115–19, 133–4
  see also embodiment; incorporation; sociology of the body

Bourdieu, Pierre   8, 10, 16, 24, 25, 26–7, 32, 33, 39, 55–7, 58, 73–4, 76, 125, 126, 131
  Distinction   37, 55–7, 78
  habitus   30, 35–7, 56–7, 70, 107, 124
  Logic of Practice   35
  Outline of a Theory of Practice   35, 55
  on practice   35–7, 168
Boyle, J.   144
brain, automaticity in the   100–1, 105, 109–10, 131
brands   90, 136
breeding, new techniques   20
Brillat-Savarin, J.-A., *The Physiology of Taste*   89
budgeting   14, 19, 24, 27, 158
Burnett, J.   66

Camic, Charles   106, 149, 172
Campbell, C.   175
capitalist societies   19, 116, 136
Carolan, M.   13
catering industry   65, 86, 98, 158, 163
chain, commodity food   13, 25, 52, 62, 86
Chambliss, D.   131
chefs   75, 140, 142
  celebrity   97, 98, 135, 162
chemistry   29, 90, 116
chewing   74, 171
children
  'comfort food'   67
  eating patterns   145
  effect on parental eating habits   133–4
  presence at events   64
  and school meals   15, 90
  table manners   73, 91, 131
Chinese food   73, 141

choice 4–7, 142–6, 173
  of food varieties 20, 28, 64–9, 80–2, 102, 115–16
  ideology of consumer 94, 97, 158
Christensen, Bodil 171
Christiakis, N. 118
class structure 4
  eating regimes 61–2
  and food consumption 25, 26–7
  habitus 37
  and handling of food 73
  and meals 61
  and taste 26–7, 55–7, 162–4
codification 84–5, 94, 121
cognition
  and action 101, 112–13
  'dispersed' 114
cognitive science 100, 107, 112–13, 123–4, 131, 154, 156, 166
collective practices 6, 8, 36, 40–6, 48, 144–6, 149–50, 152, 166
Collins, H. 84
'comfort food' 67
commensality, rules of 59–64, 70, 93, 153
commodification 13, 27, 69, 139, 142
common sense 37, 93, 143, 166
communication
  commercial 23, 28, 93, 121
  consumption as 3, 35
  symbolic 27, 54, 83, 111, 134–5, 162–3, 174
'communities of practice' 47
competence 30, 40, 41–2, 125, 155
  levels of 147, 161–2
  practical over strategic reasoning 32, 35–6, 156
  repetition and the foundations of 10, 120–1, 122–48
  see also transmission of competence
competition 92–3, 136

complaints 161
compound practice 5, 10, 50, 86, 98–9, 134, 153, 165
  intermediation of 89–94, 147–8, 165–6
consensus 37, 48
consumer
  the active 144
  behaviour 12, 101, 109, 175
  choice 94, 97, 158
  expectations 161
  as mindless 101–4
  model of sovereign 4–5, 13–14
  watchdogs 87–8
consumerism 27, 28
consumption 2, 12, 47, 166
  and acquisition 14, 22
  changes in 173
  as communication in pursuit of self-identity 3, 35
  defined 6, 22
  'distributed' agency in habits of 114
  eating as a moment of consumption 3
  levels of 102–3
  multidisciplinary research 3–4, 8, 14–16, 21
  organization of 22–3
  as a practice 30–1
  processes of 14, 22–3
  and production 12–14, 18, 22, 24
  and provisioning 66–8
  see also relations of consumption; sociology of consumption; sustainable consumption
convenience foods 20, 73
conventions 3, 10, 18, 31, 50, 62, 68, 92, 96–7, 118, 120, 122, 129–30, 134, 137, 150, 152, 166
  cultural and aesthetic 141, 156, 163–4
  interventions and 174

linguistic 151–2
   and visual prompts 102
cookery 48, 49
   competitions 135
   learning 168, 174
cookery books 66, 86, 91–2, 135, 162
cooking 14, 55, 84, 91–2, 97, 163
Crossley, Nick 36, 70, 72, 106
cuisine 15, 26–7, 139
   case study of exotic 138–42
   flavour combinations in national and regional 74, 174–5
   identifying national 67, 82, 139, 141, 153
   taste for foreign 11, 138–42, 162, 164
'culinary revolution' 2
cultural analysis 4–5, 25–6, 27–8, 65, 70
cultural capital 26–7, 55–6, 82, 160–4
Cultural Capital and Social Exclusion (CCSE) 59, 77, 91, 159–60, 169
cultural frame of reference, food choice 57, 64–9, 150, 169
cultural intermediaries 5, 9–10, 11, 83–9, 94, 98, 147–8, 153, 155–7, 162–3
cultural studies 15, 28
'cultural turn' 2, 3–4, 8, 14, 23, 24, 27–8, 35, 44, 47
   criticism of 70
   developments after the 28–31
culture
   depth of 172
   popular 82
   as public property 10, 135, 153–5
   as a system of signs 54
   tool-kit theory 111–12, 113, 174
   see also sociology of culture
culture industries 49

custom 10, 122, 129–30
cutlery, use of 73

Darmon, Isabelle 133
Darmon, Muriel 71, 133
Davis, M. 75
DeLanda, M. 60
deliberation 6, 35–6, 100, 101, 108–9, 126, 142–6, 150, 166
   a critique of 101–5, 156
DePuis, E. 14
developmentalism 23, 25
Dewey, John 124, 173
diet
   balanced 93
   failure of 10, 116–17, 133–4, 146
   and health 90
   ideal content and structure 20
   medicalization of 144, 170
   of the poor 30
   regimes 61–2, 71–2, 82, 93–4, 153
   specialized 145, 166
   weight-loss 10, 71–2, 93, 104, 132, 136, 146
   western 54, 72, 90, 93
DiMaggio, Paul 112–13, 134, 136
disciplines
   food and eating 12–16, 53
   and theory 21
dishes 66–8, 158, 170–1
   foreign 66
   history and provenance of 92
   names of 66–8, 69, 103, 159
   portions getting larger 117
   selecting 143
dispersed practices 8, 40, 46, 168
dispositions 10, 36, 79, 104, 123, 124–5, 126, 130, 137, 146, 147–8, 150
   and gender 57

doing
  over thinking 32, 33, 84
  and sayings 39–40, 42
domestic science 132
Douglas, Mary 24, 26, 58, 60, 62, 64–5, 78, 170
dress codes 91, 160
drinking 116, 132
Durkheim, Emile 69

eating
  aestheticization of 27, 68–9, 139, 140–2
  aggregate patterns 24, 28, 61–2
  beyond satiation 102–3, 117
  bodily processes 69–76
  boundaries of 49–50
  changing patterns of 28, 70–1, 138–42, 159–60
  as a compound practice 86, 98–9
  conversations about 156
  coordination and regulation of 5, 76–8, 96–9
  defining 3, 8, 52, 169
  disorderly 80–2
  elementary forms 52–79, 150
  and exercise balance 115, 116
  healthy 71–2
  location of 170
  more quickly 72–3
  organizing 9, 27, 56–8, 80–99
  practical objectives 18–21
  as a process of consumption 3, 24, 69
  referents of term 48
  research for alternative framings 23–8
  as a scientific object 8, 52–4, 150
  sensory processes 9, 29, 69, 70, 74–5
  social role of 57–8, 59–64
  symbolic aspects of 23, 25
  textual representations of 9–10, 27, 83–6, 98, 102, 152
  and theory of practice 5–7, 18–23, 76–8
  time-use studies 128–9
  training 130–4
  triggers of 111, 113–14, 134–6
  see also sociology of eating
eating alone 60, 62, 64
eating disorders 69, 70, 166
eating out 15, 28, 60, 62, 68–9, 83, 89, 98, 138–42, 165, 166
  case study 11, 159–64
  consumer guides 87–8
  discomfort 76
  frequency of 157
  practice theory and 150–66
  reasons for 160
  restaurant experience 87
  spending on 158
  western 139–40
eating together 58, 59, 62–3
  see also meal(s)
economic geography 47
economics 12, 13, 22, 24, 53
  behavioural 10, 109, 131
Ehn, B. 127
Elias, Norbert 24, 53, 58, 153
  civilizing process 24, 73, 168
embodiment 29, 31, 56, 76–8, 130–1, 146, 149, 154–5, 156, 159, 166
Engel's law 24
entertaining, domestic 83, 165
enthusiasms 145, 153
environment
  and action 101–10, 147–8, 155, 173
  cues from 10, 112–15, 117–18, 120–1, 130, 134–6, 147–8, 149, 159, 164
  cultural 101, 154–5, 163

degradation 20
and habit 10, 104, 107, 109–10, 111–19, 120–1
obesogenic 104, 115–19, 173
responses to 136–42
epidemiology 115
ethical issues 6, 15, 144
ethnicity 15, 28, 82, 139
ethnomethodology 38
etiquette *see* manners
etiquette books 73, 86, 91, 94
events 60–1, 76–8, 158, 170
episodic 9, 60
hierarchy of eating 62
location 61, 62
timing 61–2
who is present 62–4
everyday life 3, 6, 43, 57, 79, 82, 114, 119, 126, 133–4, 145, 152, 154
exercise
and eating balance 115, 116, 174
regimes 72
exotica, case study 138–42
experience
and the command of procedures 123–6
past and future performance 125, 134, 137–8, 142, 143–4, 147–8, 149–51
expertise 109, 120, 136–8, 172
explanations 17, 40

fair trade 20
family meals 30, 59–60, 62, 91, 165, 169–70
idealization of 20, 26
fast food 15, 98, 117, 162
fasting 93
feasts 62, 93
feminism 26, 69
Ferguson, P. 89
fertilizers, chemical 20

field, concept of 36, 37, 38, 94
Fischler, Claude 24, 80–1
fish 73–4, 93
flavours 74, 93, 117, 143, 174
Fletcher, Horace 74, 171
food
anxieties about 19–21, 28, 72, 76, 80–2, 162, 171
appropriate to occasion 57, 63, 158–9
availability 13–14, 19, 22, 58, 72, 167
edible 54, 64
foreign 138–42
menus and dishes 64–9
presentation 65, 75, 91, 98, 117
research on 3–4, 16
role in social relations 28, 55
as a 'social question' 1, 21
symbolic meaning 27, 53, 55, 57, 63–5
texture of 74
see also sociology of food
food banks 168
food choice, cultural frame of reference 57, 64–9, 150, 169
food content 65
food industries 20, 49, 92, 135
food preferences 26–7, 30, 56–7, 74, 82
food preparation 47, 86, 92, 132, 142
food preservation 75
food processors 29
food quality 20
Food Standards Agency (FSA) 157
food storage 117–18
'food studies' 14–15, 27, 70, 80
food supply 19–20, 97
food system 13, 21, 25, 52, 81, 116
crises in 1, 8, 16, 18, 69
food writers, professional 12, 66, 69, 92, 171

'foodies' 89–90, 163, 165, 166
formalization 84, 98–9, 123, 160
Foucault, Michel 33
Fowler, J. 118
framings, alternative 23–8, 57, 64–9, 150, 169
France 55, 60, 73, 81, 89, 93, 97, 98, 118, 169
Frickel, S. 21
frozen foods 29
fruitarianism 144
functionalism 23
fusion foods 74

game theory 38
gastro-anomie 9, 72, 80–1, 99, 166, 169
gastronomy 74, 75, 81, 89–90, 98
gender
  and dispositions 57
  relations in eating together 62–3
gender studies 26, 47
geography 15, 47
Giard, L. 67, 159
Giddens, Anthony 8, 32, 33–5, 37, 39, 80, 107, 125, 174
  Central Problems in Social Theory 34
  Modernity and Self-Identity 35
  The Constitution of Society 34, 35
  Transformation of Intimacy 35
globalization 2, 13, 15
  cultural consequences of 27–8, 62, 69, 73, 139, 142, 167
Good Food Guide (GFG) 87–8, 163
'good practice' 46, 84
Goody, J. 24, 26
government/state regulation 81, 93, 97, 135, 152
  guidelines 82, 132
Gracia Arnaiz, Mabel 71
Grignon, C. 24
group norms 6, 18, 123, 162–4

gustemes (Lévi-Strauss) 57
Guthman, J. 14, 116

habit(s) 10, 35, 119–20, 122, 126, 173
  change of 143–4
  defining 106–8, 172
  embodied 118–19, 122, 146
  and environment 10, 104, 107, 109–10, 111–19, 120–1
  food 25, 28, 55, 56
  and habituation 105–10
  and intention 110
  new psychology of 107
  and self-actuation 110, 119–20
  strong and weak 156, 166, 173
  and technology 114
  use of term 103, 106
habituation 10, 100–21, 130–1, 136–8, 146, 149, 150, 156, 166
habitus (Bourdieu) 30, 35–7, 56–7, 70, 107, 124
Haidt, J. 124
Handbook of Food Research (Murcott, Belasco and Jackson) 16
health 12, 69, 70, 71, 136
  and diet 90, 93, 145
  and good taste 89
Hetherington, K. 173
Hillersdal, Linne 171
historical materialism 24–5
holism 38, 110
Holm, Lotte 30, 71
hospitality 30, 63, 91, 157
household
  culinary traditions 68
  expenditure on food 24
  meal arrangements 26
hunger, and instinct 172
hunter-gatherer societies 19
hygiene 20, 136

identity   4, 5, 15, 27–8, 35
  collective   113
  national culinary   28, 67–8, 163
  projects   143, 144
Ilmonen, K.   57, 58
improvisation   128, 131, 132, 150, 152, 164
incorporation   9, 64, 69–78, 89–90, 114, 147, 150
Indian food   67
individualism   12, 17, 31, 32, 38, 42, 45–6, 109, 168
individualization thesis   35
individuals
  between environment and habit   114–15
  as carriers of practices   44–6, 151
  initiative of   101, 172
  and interdependence   109
  personal schemata   112–13
  reflection and personal projects   142–6
industrialization   24
inequality
  gender   26
  social   19
informalization   60, 91, 97, 118, 153, 160, 169
instinct, and hunger   172
institutional analysis   166
institutionalization   95–6, 98–9, 152, 156–7, 163–4
institutions   112
  individualism and   38, 45–6
  practices have form of   50, 83–9, 92, 156–7
  social   156–7
instruction, and Practices   83–9, 155
integrative practices   8, 9, 40–2, 45–6, 48, 49–50, 84, 94, 99, 134
  cookery as an   91–2
  criteria for   41, 85

disputes within   153, 165–6
  and performances   97–8
intelligibility, mutual   32, 39–42, 83, 151–2, 161–4, 165–6
interdependence   109, 134
intermediation   9–10, 83–9, 92, 121, 141
  of a compound practice   89–94, 98–9, 147–8, 155–6, 165–6
  impact of   153
  see also cultural intermediaries

Jackson, S.   16, 70
Jacobs, J.A.   21
James, William   107–8, 172
Juliet, Alice   90, 91
  Eating Together   63

Kabyle, the   33, 55
Kant, Immanuel   106
kitchen equipment   29, 47
Knorr Cetina, K.   31, 32
  The Practice Turn in Contemporary Theory   37–8
know-how   36, 40–2, 76, 84–5, 137–8, 156, 172
knowledge   101
  frail   121
  shared and institutionalized   135, 147
  tacit   40, 46, 79
Kristensen, S.   71

labelling of food   72, 132
labour
  domestic division of   6, 14, 26, 173
  migrant   15
Laporte, C.   118
Lave, J.   47
learning   130–6, 137–8, 147, 149–51, 172
  of cookery   168, 174

learning (cont.)
  new tastes   10–11, 138–42
  and repetition   128, 149–50
  routines   128
leftovers   64
Lévi-Strauss, C.   24, 26, 57
lifestyles   3, 4, 27, 28, 35, 72, 143–6
linguistic turn   47
literature, on food   83–6, 88, 89, 94, 99, 135, 142
Lizardo, Omar   32–3, 174
Lofgren, O.   127
Luckmann, T.   95, 172
Lyotard, Jean-François   39

machines   29, 114
malnutrition   19
management learning   47
manners   3, 20, 30, 49, 53, 56, 73, 91, 93, 131, 159, 168, 169
manuals of practice   46, 48, 83–6, 89, 155, 171
marketing   12, 47, 164, 173
Martens, Lydia   175
Martin, J. L.   154–5
Marx, Karl   96
Marxism   22, 26, 33, 54
material culture   29, 31, 44, 70, 155
Mauss, Marcel   69, 131
meal(s)
  as an institution   24–5
  away from home   158–60
  concept of   53, 57–8, 59–60
  delivery   117
  destructuring of arrangements   20, 60
  dinner parties   91
  informalization   60, 91, 97, 118
  model of British   68
  for occasions   64–5, 160–1, 163
  patterns   59, 61–2, 118, 129
  provisioning and preparation of   26
  school   15, 90

sequence   61, 65
  and social class   56, 61, 91, 163–4
  terms for   61
  for travellers   157
  see also eating out; family meals
mealtimes   71, 118, 127, 128–9, 133, 143, 158, 165
meat
  differing status of   54
  red and masculinity   65
media   1, 23, 28, 30, 90, 121, 137, 153, 155
  anxieties about food in   19
  TV programmes   66, 69, 135, 142
media studies   47
medicine   12, 70, 90, 93, 116
memory   48, 113, 131, 166
Mennell, S.   23, 24, 26
  All Manners of Food   24
menu(s)   64–9, 65–6, 76
  conventional   67
  as device for restricting choice   68, 159
  personal   66, 67
  selection   9, 147, 160
methodological individualism   38, 168
Michelin Red Guide   87
migration   15, 28, 141–2, 144
Miller, Daniel   29
mind, and body   101, 106, 147
mindlessness   101–5, 108, 119, 172
Mintz, S.   25
  Sweetness and Power   24
Moehring, M.   67
molecular gastronomy   74, 75
moral panic   115
morality   56, 71, 91, 96, 105, 124, 133
motoring analogy   96, 171
mouth, dealing with food in the   73–4, 76
multinational corporations   21

Murcott, A. 16
Myrbakk, V. 107–8, 173

neo-classical economics 4, 31, 38
neo-liberal politics 115
neo-Marxism 24
neuro-science 10, 107, 109
new behavioural bent (NBB) 100, 106, 107, 109, 115
nexus 39–40, 42, 45, 97, 137, 147
Nicolini, D. 4
Noe, Alva 173
  Out of Our Heads 109–10, 114, 119
norms 6, 10, 18, 31, 43–6, 61, 83–9, 98, 100–1, 123, 137, 151, 154, 162
  and normality 41–2, 96, 119, 152
nutrition 12, 16, 24, 29, 49, 53, 54, 89, 90, 93, 153, 173
  education 86, 132
  science of 93, 115–16
  worries 20

obesity 166
  case study 10, 115–19
  causes 119
  dealt with by surgery 70, 171
  debate 104–5, 115–17
  and environment 104, 115–19, 173
  'epidemic' 15, 24, 29, 56, 69, 72, 102
  recovery from 71
  and social networks 118–19
objectivation 83–4, 86–7, 92, 94, 95, 98–9, 121, 152, 154, 172
objectivity 37
occasions and events 59–64, 76–8, 147, 150, 151, 158
  meals for 64–5, 86, 163, 170
omnivore's paradox 81
omnivorousness, and taste 82, 141

organizational behaviour 47
organizations, and integrative practices 95–6, 152
Ortner, Sherry 33, 35
Oulette, J. 108, 128

packaged products 72
Panayi, P. 67, 141
path-dependency models 108, 127, 150
performance(s)
  competent *see* competence
  of eating 53–4, 74, 76–8, 155, 159
  errors in 143–4
  orchestrated 127–9, 146–8, 150, 151, 159, 163–4, 166
  practice as 39, 40–2
  and Practices 42–6, 48, 50, 79, 83–9, 155, 172
  and *Praktik* 44
  standards of 83–9, 92, 137–8, 160–2
phenomenology 70, 102
physiology 3, 9, 69, 72, 130–1
picnics 158
policy making, and behaviour change 1, 7, 19–20, 115–19, 132–4
political economy 13–14, 16, 21–2, 24, 33, 52, 115
politics of food 1, 16, 20, 135
portfolio model of action 10, 51, 101, 107, 124, 126, 150, 154, 169
post-functionalism 4
post-humanism 4
post-modernism 38
post-structuralism 4, 38–9
Postill, J. 47
posture 73
Poulain, Jean-Pierre 20–1, 24, 69, 81, 89, 118

poverty 19, 30, 54
practical consciousness 34–5, 126, 128, 156
practical sense 10, 123–6, 130, 147, 156
practice 33–7
  as an entity 167
  as a nexus of elements 39–40, 97, 137, 147
  as performance 39, 40
  as a unit of analysis 38–42
  see also praxis
practice theories *see* theories of practice
practice theory
  applications 47–50, 149–66
  new in 1970s 33–7, 39
'practice turn, the' 32, 37–8, 47
Practices
  boundaries between discrete 7, 48–50, 134, 165–6
  compared with practice (*praxis*) 44
  conceptualized as entities 5, 42–6
  coordination and regulation of 5, 48, 94–8, 152–3
  and instruction 83–9
  interdependence of 134
  and performances 42–6, 48, 50, 79, 172
  set of possible responses 125
  sharing of 5, 42–6, 48, 94–8, 122, 149–50
  as site for understanding and intelligibility 39, 152, 159–64
  as units of analysis 38–42, 48–50
  use of term 167
  see also compound practice; dispersed practices; integrative practices
pragmatism 107, 110, 123, 125, 154, 173
Praktik, and performance 44

praxis 37–42, 44
  rediscovering in the 1970s 33–7
  see also action; practice
pregnant women, and food cravings 74
procedures 132, 146, 149, 156, 166
  changing 139–42
  embodied 154–5, 159
  experience and the command of 123–6, 148, 163–4
  triggering of skilled 136–8
production 54
  analyses of food 21–2, 52, 64
  and consumption 12–14, 16, 18, 22, 24
propositions 17
provisioning 8, 14, 26
  and acquisition 14, 22
  changes re domestic food 29
  class effects 27
  and consumption 66–8
  dominant regime 118
psychology 12, 16, 29, 31, 106, 120
  cognitive 112–13
  economic 109
  evolutionary 110
  experimental 10, 102
  social of habit 107, 109
purchase 6, 14, 20, 136

Rao, H. 87
rationality 105, 115, 150, 166
recipe books 48, 66, 69, 84, 88, 91–2, 97, 113
Reckwitz, Andreas 44, 47, 151
recreation 116, 157
recursiveness 34, 40, 136–8, 150, 173
reflection 125–6, 142–6, 154, 156
reflexivity, individual 35, 125, 145
refrigeration 29
regime theories 13, 61–2

Regulation School 24
relations of consumption 13–14, 29, 30, 76–8
religious authority 93, 145
repetition 6, 36, 103–4, 105–6, 108, 149
  concepts governing 126–30
  and the foundations of competence 10, 122–48, 156
  habits and 103–6, 108–10, 114, 119, 120–1, 130–1
  in learning 128, 149–50, 155
  in practice 146–8
representation 39–40
  symbolic and beliefs 55
reproduction of practices 10, 34, 40, 96, 127, 137–8, 149–51, 154–7
research institutes 21
restaurant 157, 164, 165
  choosing a 163–4
  handling food in a 73, 162
  menus 66, 69, 113, 136, 143
  opening times 158
  and portion size 117
  preferences 82
  sensory experiences 75, 138–42
  spread of foreign 138–42
restaurant guides 86–9, 98, 113, 162–3
retailers, power of 20
risk 20, 21, 35
rituals 25, 48, 50, 55, 116, 122
  meal organization 59–64, 160
role theory 95
Roman Catholic Church 93
Rotenberg, R. 61
routine 4, 6, 10, 35, 47, 59, 63–4, 112–13, 122, 149, 150, 175
  as an anchor 110, 118
  collective 127–9
  effects of disrupted 70–1

individual 127
  and path 127
  sequential 127–8
  temporal 10, 118, 119, 126–9, 156
routinization 35, 44, 62, 119, 128, 174
Rudi, E. 107–8, 173

Sahlins, Marshall 33, 54, 58
Schatzki, Theodore 4, 8, 31, 32, 38–44, 42–3, 44, 45, 48, 84, 85
  Social Practices 38–42
  The Practice Turn in Contemporary Theory 37–8
schemata 36, 112–13
scholasticism 168
schools
  meals 15, 90, 174
  teaching cookery 132
Scott, S. 70
self, presentation of *see* identity; lifestyles
selling techniques, manipulation by 20
semiotics 25, 65
sensory processes 9, 29, 69, 70, 74–5, 138–42
shopping 6, 14, 20, 136
Simmel, G. 25, 53, 58
Skinner, B. F. 106, 107
Slow Food movement 82, 90, 98
snacking 60, 170
Sobal, J. 104
social constructionism 53, 70
social differentiation 4, 125, 137, 161–4
  see also class structure
social ecology 109
social interactionism 70, 164
social movements 15, 20, 23, 28, 97, 145, 163

social networks   149
  and food pairing   74
  and obesity   118–19
social practices   34–5, 38–44, 47, 150–1
social relations
  and eating occasions   58, 76–8
  reproduction of   26–7
  role of food in   28, 30, 55
  see also relations of consumption
social sciences
  concept formation   52–3
  the pursuit of theory   8, 16–23
  standard models   6
social worlds   145
socialization   112, 173
society, as the field of practices   38
sociolinguistics   47
sociology
  defined   18, 111
  French   23–4
sociology of the body   24, 31, 70
sociology of consumption   1–7, 30–1, 47, 175
  reaction to economistic explanations   22
sociology of culture   10, 107, 123, 154, 156
sociology of eating   12–31, 52–79
  elementary concepts   58–78
sociology of food   101
  terms   65–9
Southerton, Dale   127, 171, 174
sport   131
standards   10, 42–6, 48–50, 63, 83–8, 121, 151, 165, 166
  aesthetic   163–4
  changes in   94, 140–2
  and complaints   161
  transmission of   137–8, 156–7
stomach, the 'reformed'   70–1
Strand, M.   174
structuralism   23, 25, 25–6

structuration theory   34, 37
structure
  and agency   33–4, 38
  duality of   34–5
stylization *see* lifestyles
Sudnow, D., *Ways of the Hand*   131
Sunstein, C.   100–1
supermarkets   62, 90, 97, 136, 142
sustainable consumption   47
Swidler, Ann   111–12, 136
symbolic interactionism   24, 38, 163–4
symbolic meaning   27, 53, 55, 57, 63–5
  culinary identity   67, 163
synaesthesia   70
systems, defined   34

table setting   117
taboos
  on eating animals   54
  religious   93
takeaway food   158, 162, 165
taste   5, 55–6, 58, 86, 93
  discourse of   88, 153
  discrimination through in France   37
  eclectic   82, 140–2
  formation of   30, 86–9
  good   55–6, 74
  good and good health   89
  hierarchy of   26–7, 162–3
  learning new   10–11, 138–42
  manipulation of memory and emotion   75
  and omnivorousness   82
  shift in   138–42
tasting   69, 70, 75
taxonomy   17
Taylor, Frederick   39
teach-yourself books   84, 85
'teleo-affective structures'   39–42, 43, 48

texts, on alimentary practices   9–10, 83–6, 98, 152
Thaler, R.   100–1
theories of practice   3–7, 8, 31, 149–57
  and agency   11, 142–6
  criticisms of   10–11, 138, 165–6
  eating out   149–66
  elements of   32–51
  repetition and   122–48, 136–8, 146–8
theory
  definition proposed   17
  as instrument of selective attention   18
  role in social sciences   8, 17–18
  uses of term in social sciences   16
theory of eating, obstacles to a   18–23
time-use studies   59, 128–9
tool-kit theory   111–12, 113, 174
tourism   141
trade, international   20
training   130–4, 155
transmission of competence   42, 83, 85, 120, 130–6, 137, 147–8, 155–7
Triandis, H.   107

understandings *see* intelligibility, mutual
unit acts   108–9, 120, 146

United States   14, 54, 63, 67, 91, 102, 107, 141–2
  consumerism   27
universalism   24
utensils   47, 73, 76, 142, 166
utilitarianism   38

value
  Marxist theory of   26
  monetary of food   20, 22
  symbolic of food   53, 57
veganism   82, 144
vegetarianism   82, 144–6
Verplanken, B.   107–8, 173
von Savigny, E.   31, 32
  The Practice Turn in Contemporary Theory   37–8

Wacquant, L. J.   131
Wansick, B.   102–5, 117, 132
  Mindless Eating   10
Warde, A.   71, 173
waste   47
water supply   116
Weber, M.   106–7
Wenger, E.   47
Whitford, J.   51, 126, 169, 173
Wilhite, H.   114
Wilk, R.   69, 175
wine appreciation   132
Wood, W.   108, 128

Zagat   87
Zerubavel, E.   127